Contents

Contributors

Barthelemy, M., Director, Agricultural Legislation, Directorate General VI, Commission of the European Communities, Rue de la Loi 200, 1040 Brussels

Egan, Dr. H., B SC, PH D, DIC, FRIC, FRSH, FIFST. Government Chemist, Laboratory of the Government Chemist, Cornwall House, Stamford Street, London SE1 9NQ

Elton, Dr. G. A. H., D SC, PH D, FRIC. Chief Scientific Adviser (Food), Ministry of Agriculture, Fisheries and Food, Great Westminster House, Horseferry Road, London SW1P 2AE

Evans, F. J., MBE, DPA, FITSA. County Consumer Protection Officer, Northamptonshire County Council, Wootton Hall Park, Northampton NN4 9BL

Giles, R. F., Under-Secretary, Ministry of Agriculture, Fisheries and Food, Great Westminster House, Horseferry Road, London SW1P 2AE

Goldman, P., CBE. Director, Consumers' Association, 14 Buckingham Street, London WC2N 6DS

Kermode, G. O., Chief, Joint FAO/WHO Food Standards Programme, Food and Agriculture Organization of the United Nations, Via della Terme di Caracalla, 00100 Rome

Lawrence, G. K., DSO, DFC. Chairman, Food and Drink Industries Council, J. Lyons and Co., Cadby Hall, London W14 0PA

Schmidt, Dr. A. M., Commissioner of Food and Drugs, United States Department of Health, Education and Welfare, Rockville, Maryland 20852, USA

Ward, Professor A. G., CBE, MA, F INST P, FIFST. Procter Professor of Food and Leather Science, University of Leeds, Leeds LS2 9JT

Weedon, Professor B. C. L., CBE, FRS. Department of Chemistry, Queen Mary College, University of London, Mile End Road, London E1 4NS

Yellowlees, Sir Henry, KCB, FRCP, FFCM. Chief Medical Officer, Department of Health and Social Security, Alexander Fleming House, Elephant and Castle, London SE1 6B1

Zuckerman, Lord, OM, KCB, FRS. Cabinet Office, Whitehall, London SW1A 2AS

iv

Symposium Organizing Committee

Chairman

Dr. G A H Elton   Chief Scientific Adviser (Food), Ministry of Agriculture, Fisheries and Food

Mr. R F Giles   Under-Secretary, Food Standards and Subsidies, Ministry of Agriculture, Fisheries and Food

Mr. L E E Jeanes   Chief Information Officer, Ministry of Agriculture, Fisheries and Food

Dr. H Egan   Government Chemist

Dr. F Fairweather   Senior Principal Medical Officer, Department of Health and Social Security

Secretary

Miss C P West   Food Standards Division, Ministry of Agriculture, Fisheries and Food

Symposium Organizing Committee

Introductory Address

The Rt Hon Frederick Peart MP
Minister of Agriculture, Fisheries and Food

We are today celebrating the centenary of effective food law in this country. This is an important date, not merely for those involved in the food industry in its widest sense and in the enforcement of the law but for all of us, because we are all consumers and therefore have, or should have, an interest in what we eat and drink and what goes into it. I remember back in 1945 I became Parliamentary Private Secretary to Tom Williams, the Minister of Agriculture, and I was asked why I had decided to take an interest in agriculture when I represented a largely industrial constituency. I replied simply to my questioner: 'Don't you eat?'

Now today we have no need to fear that the tea we drink will be rich in black lead nor that the bread we eat will contain alum. We run little risk of sickness and infection from consuming food. But in 1875 consumers received little protection under the law.

The Sale of Food and Drugs Act 1875 was the beginning of a new era. Manufacturers began to take ever increasing advantage of developing technology. Food was produced in larger-scale units. Greater attention was paid to hygiene and to the quality of ingredients. Effective measures could be taken to root out those who had taken unfair advantage of the absence of legislation. Consumers reaped the benefits of all these developments. They also began, slowly at first, to become increasingly vocal and influential in their own interests. We have come a very long way over the past 100 years.

Our basic Food and Drugs Acts now form only the basis of a larger structure of consumer protection. They are amplified by detailed regulations controlling the composition of most of our staple foods, the presence of additives and contaminants in them and their labelling. Consumers, some probably without ever being made aware of the protection they receive, can be sure of eating food which is not harmful and which is very unlikely to be adulterated or debased. The manufacturer knows that he will not be subjected to unfair competition because everyone is subject to the law. And the enforcement officer has the advantage of detailed guidelines to assist him in his work.

But in a gathering such as this we must not adopt an insular approach. The growth of food laws has been widespread, first in the industrialized countries of the world and latterly in the developing countries. As the food processing industries of the developing world take advantage of the techniques evolved elsewhere and as the international and national trade in processed food increases, it has been vital to develop international standards for foods. The United Kingdom played a leading role in the creation of the Joint FAO/WHO Food Standards Programme under the auspices of the United Nations.

The objectives have been to protect the health of consumers, to ensure fair practice in the food trade and to remove barriers to trade. The work of the Codex Alimentarius Commission is of advantage to all countries who wish to participate in international trade in food, but it is of particular value to those countries who are seeking to develop their own food laws for the first time. It is in all our interests to help them to do so.

As members of the European Economic Community we are also seeking to harmonize our food laws with the other Member States. This does not mean that we are seeking to impose a uniform diet on our people, to make them eat only a standard Euro-bread or Euro-jam. On the contrary, it should lead to a wider range of food products becoming available in our shops by removing technical barriers to trade. At the same time it opens up considerable export possibilities for our food manufacturers who, I believe, are among the most efficient and competitive in Europe.

I would like now to say just a few words about our national food supply and the way in which this relates to the world situation.

One hundred years ago the difference between the diet of the rich and the poor in this country was enormous. The former used to eat meals of a size we would today consider gluttonous; the latter had to make do with grossly inadequate fare in terms of both quantity and quality. Today we have succeeded in closing the gap to the extent that problems of obesity seem in this country to be more pressing than hunger. We are faced with a wide variety of foods from all over the world.

Considerable sums are regularly spent on buying foods specially formulated to help us control our intake of calories. But we must never forget that we are the fortunate ones.

In many parts of the world there is neither plenty nor choice. The gap between the availability of food in rich and poor countries is greater than ever it was between rich and poor in this country. In congratulating ourselves on our achievements as we celebrate this centenary we must, I believe, never overlook the darker side of the coin.

But what of the situation here over the coming years? There are those who predict that as world population grows, and as standards of living increase in other parts of the world, we will be faced with shortages of food and with a diminution of the choice of foods. We must hope that these prophecies will not be fulfilled and strive to ensure that they are not. An expanding domestic agricultural industry, new technology and new food sources have, I am sure, a big contribution to make to solving these problems. As regards legislation, we must above all ensure that we build on the legacy of the past. We set high standards for food; we enforce these standards fairly but forcibly where necessary and we all benefit from these labours.

We now have a sensible and consistent body of legislation which we shall continue to expand and adapt as necessary. But we must beware of legislation for its own sake. We must not make our laws so extensive, rigid or detailed that development of new techniques is inhibited. This would be in the interests of neither the consumer nor the manufacturer. Equally we should ensure that those who wish to go on using traditional methods and processes are not prevented by legislation from doing so, for in many cases, as with beer, they too satisfy an important consumer demand.

To conclude, may I say I am sure that, with the excellent array of speakers who are here to address you, the centenary celebrations will be both interesting and fruitful. I wish the centenary every success.

The Development of Food Legislation in the United Kingdom

R F Giles

Under-Secretary, Ministry of Agriculture, Fisheries and Food

Background and introduction

It is a sorry fact that as far back as history is recorded man's desire to obtain something for nothing wherever he can has led him to try to trick or defraud his fellows. As one of the basic staples of life, food has been particularly susceptible to exploitation. Indeed, one can almost regard Adam himself as the first dissatisfied consumer, since he was led by means of a misleading statement to eat an apple which was scarcely of the nature, substance or quality demanded! Measures for the protection of the consumer against the adulteration of food or other commercial or manufacturing malpractices are among the earliest examples of social legislation.

The earliest food legislation in the British Isles appears to be an Act passed in England in 1266 to protect the purchaser against short weight in bread and the sale of unsound meat. This Act was as ineffective as the various other statutes passed to deal with adulteration in specific foods or drugs between the thirteenth and nineteenth centuries. Throughout this period it was the duty of the Guilds to maintain the purity of the commodities with which their members dealt. It may be of interest to examine some of the practices with which they had to contend.

First of all there was pepper which, being highly valued and much in demand as a preservative of meat and other foods, was a prime target for adulteration. Gravel, leaves and twigs were common in pepper and, from about 1650 onwards, clove dust was often added as an adulterant. Other spices were also adulterated—mustard with wheatflour, pea flour, radish seeds and cayenne pepper. Sugar, which came into prominence in England in the sixteenth century, was often imperfectly refined. Exhausted tea leaves or other leaves were commonly added to tea which was then glazed with black lead. Coffee had a whole series of adulterants. Soon after it was introduced into England in the seventeenth century water, grass, butter and lard were used to extend coffee. When this was prohibited, burnt, scorched or roasted vegetable material such as acorns were substituted, and, when this in turn was banned, adulteration with chicory began. From the earliest times bread was subject

4

to the natural hazard of grit from the millstone entering the flour and this no doubt led to the practice of adding sand or ashes. Mashed potato for added bulk and alum for bleaching were also used. The most common adulterant for beer or milk has always been water, but it is interesting to note that originally beer was made from the fermentation of malt and that the introduction of hops as a flavouring in the fifteenth century was regarded as a gross adulterant.

The difficulties inherent in attempting to identify and prevent practices such as these before the development of reliable methods of analysing food can be easily recognized. Indeed, by the middle of the nineteenth century the abuses that were rife could only be described as appalling. The situation was greatly aggravated by the fact that in the previous 50 years the population had doubled and the industrial revolution had caused a massive shift from the country to the town. Thus, not only were there more people to be fed, but a growing proportion of them, who had previously produced their own food, was becoming dependent on others for its supply. With this growth in urban living came a change in eating habits to more sophisticated foods, such as white bread, previously a luxury of the well-to-do, which provided even greater opportunities for transgression.

The coming of the 1875 Act

Two factors helped to bring about a reform. First, the greater development of analytical chemistry in the late eighteenth and early nineteenth centuries, which increasingly permitted the accurate and scientific identification of the ingredients of foods. Secondly, the widespread publicity that began to be given to the subject of adulteration, not only in scientific journals but also in the press and in the popular literature of the day. Public pressure led to the setting up of a Select Committee on Adulteration of Food in 1855, and the revelations that it brought to light made it inevitable that legislation would be introduced. There was in the late 1850s some voluntary reform undertaken by the trade but the diet of the majority of the population continued to be adulterated. Unfortunately, there were wide differences of opinion as to how the position should be remedied, and the first Adulteration of Food and Drink Act, which was passed in 1860, reflects these conflicting views. It empowered but did not require various local authorities to appoint public analysts to examine samples of food and drink brought forward by public spirited private citizens who were prepared to pay a fee of up to 10s 6d. It made no provision for sampling and left the responsibility for food quality a local and purely optional one.

Not surprisingly, the Act appears to have been a complete failure. Only seven analysts were appointed, and only one of these, the Medical Officer of Health and Public Analyst for Dublin, brought proceedings before the magistrates and successfully obtained convictions. Despite its ineffectiveness the Act did however establish for the first time that consumer protection was the proper role of the State. An attempt to strengthen the law was made by the Adulteration of Food and Drink and Drugs Act 1872. This was more successful in that it made the appointment of public analysts mandatory, and provided that local authority inspectors should be empowered to procure samples of food, drink and drugs for analysis. It also required analysts to make quarterly reports to local authorities.

However, enforcement of the Act remained very patchy and after numerous petitions from the larger towns complaining about weaknesses, a Select Committee was set up in 1874 to study the 1872 Act and make recommendations. The result of these was the 1875 Sale of Food and Drugs Act.

This Act is the basis of our present law—with numerous amendments of course to cover the many changes in food technology which have taken place over the years. Here for the first time appears the provision that:

'No person shall sell to the prejudice of the purchaser any article of food or any thing which is not of the nature, substance or quality demanded by such purchaser.'

The Act had a great impact on the quality of basic food, the suppression of adulteration and the establishment of food purity. Section 3 imposed heavy penalties for adulteration of food, a fine for the first offence and for subsequent offences up to six months hard labour. You will note that this is one penalty which no longer exists in our modern food law. However, much still depended on enforcement and, as the law was still permissive, local authorities had to be persuaded to take enforcement action and appoint public analysts. Even where appointed the analysts varied greatly in their knowledge and skills. Indeed, the Local Government Board in its report for 1880-81 stated that some large towns had not appointed analysts and had offered as a reason no more than the 'general statement that as adulteration is not suspected to exist the Town Council deems it unnecessary to harass the local tradesmen'.

But to the average consumer the law had at last begun to have an effect on the purity of his food. Certainly by 1900 bread, flour, tea and sugar were as pure as could be wished. Adulteration of some other foods still existed but this tended to be more the relatively simple watering of milk and beer rather than the addition to many foods of adulterants which were harmful.

6

Further legislation

The 1875 Act remained in force until 1928, when it was repealed by the consolidating Food and Drugs (Adulteration) Act. This followed a decade when regulations dealing with composition and labelling of specific products began to appear. In 1925 the use of preservatives in food was prohibited except in certain foods where their presence had to be declared on the label.

The 1938 Food and Drugs Act combined food and drugs legislation and all the public health legislation relating to foodstuffs. Here we see many more familiar provisions of the present Act appear, penalties for false or mis-leading labels and advertisements, and the power to make regulations to control the composition and labelling of foods.

THE FOOD AND DRUGS ACT 1955

The 1938 Act stood throughout the war when Governmental control of food supply and advice on nutrition were greater than ever before. Many of the early compositional regulations were however made under the Defence (Sale of Food) Regulations 1943. Ten years after the war ended the present Act of 1955 came into being. This seeks to ensure that the consumer can buy safe wholesome food and is not misled about the character or quality of the food, and also to protect the honest trader from his less honest competitors. As from 1 January 1974 the 'drug' aspects were superseded by the Medicines Act 1968. Consequently those aspects are not being dealt with in this paper. Apart from the obvious developments in the food law over the last 100 years there have been others, less readily apparent but equally important. The 1875 Act applied to England, Wales, Scotland and the whole of Ireland. The position is now very different. England and Wales have the 1955 Act, the Scottish Act dates from 1956 and the Northern Irish Act from 1958, but all share the same philosophy: all are direct descendants of the first major Act and similar regulations are made under all three.

The terms of the main provisions of the Act are probably well known. Section 1 makes it an offence to sell for human consumption any food to which substances have been added or abstracted or which has been processed so as to render it injurious to health. Under Section 2 it is an offence to sell to the prejudice of the purchaser any food not of the nature, substance or quality demanded. This is reinforced by Section 6 which makes it an offence to use a description which falsely describes a food or which is calculated to mislead as to its nature, substance or quality. In addition, Section 8 makes it an offence to sell food which is unfit for human consumption. The Act also contains sections specifically relating to milk and dairies and to

7

slaughterhouses, knackers yards, markets and cold stores. I shall not be dealing with these issues in this paper.

Regulations—purpose and process

Today, although the Food and Drugs Act provides the basic legislation, much of what the government is seeking to do in fulfilling its policy on food standards is done by regulations made under the Act. Ministers have powers to make regulations 'in the interests of public health or otherwise for the protection of the public' covering the composition of food, including additives and contaminants: labelling including claims for benefits or qualities of foods: treatments or processes and hygiene. The Minister of Agriculture, Fisheries and Food takes the lead in making regulations dealing with composition and labelling, the Secretary of State for Social Services the lead where the subject matter is hygiene. In making any regulations under the Act Ministers are required to consult all interested parties.

In practice these two Ministers and those responsible for the same legislation in Scotland and Northern Ireland seek advice first from independent advisory committees and go on to a very wide series of consultations. Not everybody appreciates the way food regulations are made in the UK and the many chances given to anybody, including the 'average housewife', to contribute to the process.

THE ADVISORY COMMITTEE SYSTEM

There are two advisory committees, the Food Standards Committee which advises Ministers on their powers regarding the composition, labelling and advertisement of food, and the Food Additives and Contaminants Committee which advises Ministers on the need and safety in use of additives and the levels of contaminants that should be permitted in food. Members of the Committees are appointed in a personal capacity, as experts in their own fields, and not as representatives of particular interests.

When a topic is chosen for review and referred by Ministers to one of the Committees an announcement is made by press notice, and comments and evidence as appropriate are sought from interested parties. The Committees may conduct their reviews as they wish, seeking evidence from whomsoever they think best suited to provide information, and then report their recommendations to Ministers. The Report is published by HM Stationery Office and publication announced by press notice without commitment by Ministers to its recommendations. Comments are invited from anyone interested, manufacturers and distributors at home and abroad, trade and other organizations, consumers, enforcement authorities, scientific bodies and individuals. On the basis of the Report and the comments on it departments draw up proposals for regulations.

MAKING THE REGULATIONS

The proposals are widely distributed and once again comments are sought. Although the Committees often take oral evidence in compiling their reports, departments frequently have discussions at both comments stages with associations representing the trade, consumers and enforcement authorities both at the Ministry's and, perhaps more often, the association's request. On the basis of the proposals and comments received Ministers decide what should be done and regulations are drafted. Any draft regulation dealing with hygiene or labelling then goes to the Food Hygiene Advisory Council— a statutory body—for any comments they wish to make, and finally the regulation is laid before Parliament. Regulations made under the Food and Drugs Act 1955 are subject to a negative resolution procedure, and therefore unless a Member of Parliament prays against a regulation and initiates a debate a regulation becomes law without being debated. Regulations rarely come into force straight away; time must be given for the composition of foods to be altered if necessary, for labels to be used up and new lines run off to comply with new requirements and for food that has already been distributed to be sold.

This whole process may seem time consuming, complicated and laborious, and it is all of these. But it does ensure that everyone has his chance, indeed many chances, to have his say, that nothing is overlooked and that all possibilities are considered before the new law comes into force.

While this procedure is the same for all regulations it is of course true that there may well be significant differences in the room for manoeuvring between matters of composition and labelling and of food additives and contaminants which have been considered by experts to be injurious to health. In the latter case the process can be speeded up and very quick action taken in an emergency. Ministers may have different views from the Food Standards Committee on what information about a food the consumer expects to find on the label but where safety is concerned Ministers will accept the views of experts with little query.

ENFORCEMENT

Once the regulations are firmly part of United Kingdom law Ministers and Ministry officials can perhaps sit back and hope to admire the results of their labours. But the law must be enforced. I have made reference to the problems the Local Government Board had in cajoling local authorities to appoint public analysts and enforce the 1875 Act. One hundred years has changed the position. Ministers no longer cajole. Enforcement of the main provisions and the regulations is the statutory duty of the food and drugs authorities and this duty is fully carried out. These authorities—the counties, metropolitan counties and the London Boroughs—must appoint a public analyst, and he is still required to make quarterly returns to the authority and the authority to send them on to the Minister

The public analyst is of course far removed from his predecessor who analysed adulterated tea in 1875, both in his own skills and knowledge and in his laboratory and equipment. Similarly the food and drugs inspector must watch for misleading claims on labels and products not complying with compositional standards rather than for alum in bread. Environmental Health Officers appointed by the district councils enforce those parts of the Act dealing with hygiene in food processing establishments, restaurants and cafes as well as with unfit food caused, for example, by a failure on the part of someone to follow proper hygienic practices.

Between the two sets of officials the law is capably enforced. Much enforcement action is by warning, advice and assistance from the authorities, although of course there are still cases that end up in Court. At least manufacturers and retailers no longer face hard labour if it is found that the food being sold is adulterated.

The United Kingdom system of the law being written by central government and enforced by local government is beneficial to all. The law as written is enforced, not the law as the drafters thought it had been written. The drafters are therefore subject to the strict discipline of making sure that their intentions are properly expressed and indeed both they and the enforcement officers are subject to the final discipline that only the Courts can interpret the law. When an important case is being fought in Court it is not only those involved who watch the developments with interest, it is the Civil Servants to see if their understanding of the law is the same as that of the judges.

International developments

CODEX

The United Kingdom, although geographically an island nation, has never been insular in its approach to food standards. Food is exported from this country, and it is imported, and it seems sensible that food should comply with similar standards both of composition and labelling throughout the world. The United Kingdom has always played a full part in the work of the main international food standards organization, the Codex Alimentarius Commission, which is a joint body of two United Nations bodies—the Food and Agriculture Organization and the World Health Organization. It is obviously difficult to attempt to produce food laws which can apply to many different countries. Industrialized countries such as the United Kingdom have a long history of food law with the present law being the result of years of development. Some of the developing countries have as yet no food law and the standards of other countries may prove to be totally inapplicable. Yet national food laws such as compositional requirements can impose trade barriers, and as Codex develops we are seeing an attempt to lower trade barriers and to ensure that all food in international trade meets a certain agreed standard. Codex standards, working from a fresh start which is not dependent on any country's legislation, aim at setting substantive principles, and the acceptance procedure enables member countries to accept the whole standard or to maintain reservations to take account of national and constitutional procedures.

EUROPEAN ECONOMIC COMMUNITY

Another international development which makes a major impact on United Kingdom food law is the European Economic Community. Harmonization of member states' food laws is a necessary part of the overall aim of removing non-tariff barriers to trade within the Community. Progress is not as rapid as one might wish since no member state is willing to give up its own legislative principles and accept another member's, but compromises are made, progress is achieved and a number of United Kingdom regulations are now being made which put EEC directives into United Kingdom law. Even in the development of EEC directives consultation with interested parties takes place. The Commission, in formulating a directive, consults trade and consumer associations as well as government experts before putting the draft directive to the Council of Ministers. A Council Working Group, set up to discuss the directive, meets frequently in Brussels to argue it into its final form. The United Kingdom representatives consult trade, consumer and enforcement authority associations both by letter and at meetings in preparation for discussions in Brussels. Directives agreed by the Council of Ministers do not immediately become law in member states and only become so in the United Kingdom when a regulation implementing the directive is made under the Food and Drugs Act. Thus all regulations are in the same style and are based on the same principles.

Reasons for new regulations

The United Kingdom has always tried to ensure that food law keeps pace with technological developments in food processing and that development should not be held back by out-dated legislation. The Food Standards Committee aims to review all regulations after five years, but with the increasing number of regulations being made and their ever-growing complexity this time scale cannot always be met. However the reviews do all take place. With compositional regulations it is changing processes and the possibility of new products which cause both new reviews and original reviews. The oldest 'new' food—margarine—celebrated its centenary six years ago and so to the regulation makers is as well established on the market as butter— both have their own regulations. But there are more modern new foods.

Margarine was originally introduced as a replacement for butter. Today, as food prices rise, substitutes for the more expensive foods are developed and ways of making cheaper foods more acceptable and palatable are constantly being discovered. Large scale production of food brings down costs; canning and freezing of fruit and vegetables have eliminated seasonal scarcities and consequent price variations. Food processing industries have also grown by providing easily prepared whole meals for a larger sector of the population. Pieces of meat and fish which in the past had to be condemned as waste despite high nutritional value can now be made into readily acceptable foods. But perhaps one of the most interesting developments of recent years and the one that holds out most hope for feeding the increasing world population is that of novel protein products. Products currently in human use are mainly based on soya bean protein although protein from other sources, notably yeast protein grown on hydrocarbons, is now being used for animal feed. It is most unlikely that these products will ever replace roast sirloin of beef but they may eventually replace meat in some pies, to make products very similar nutritionally to such traditional products as shepherd's pie. Here we have an example of a Committee review taking into account new developments. The Food Standards Committee published its Report on Novel Protein Foods earlier this year. Consultations have started with the aim of producing regulations to implement some of the recommendations. These will seek to ensure that developments can continue, while ensuring that the health of consumers is protected and that they are informed of what they are eating.

ADDITIVES AND CONTAMINANTS

With regulations controlling additives and levels of contaminants in foods there are different reasons for reviews of the situation and consequent action. New additives—be they preservatives, colours, flavours, anti-oxidants, emulsifiers—may be developed which the food industry claim would be useful. The substances are looked at by the Food Additives and Contaminants Committee to see whether they are really needed and if so whether they will be safe in use. If approval is given, then new regulations are made and the additive is permitted to be used in food. Or, indeed, the opposite may happen. An additive which is permitted in food may, as a result of further research either here or abroad, appear to give cause for concern. The evidence is evaluated. If the concern is justified the additive will be removed from the regulations and its use in food prohibited. In addition, the Food Additives and Contaminants Committee review each class of additive at broadly five-year intervals and consider the need and safety in use of each additive as a class. Contaminants of food are also kept under review.

CONSUMERS AND LABELLING

With regulations dealing with labelling the reasons for reviews are different again. Perhaps one of the major developments of the last few years which has influenced food legislation is the growth of organized consumer interests and the increasing awareness of the average consumer of her rights and requirements. Food labelling has grown in step with those developments. The consumer is now provided with information on the label about what the food is, what is in it and who is responsible for it. Detailed rules on many aspects of labelling exist but we can never be sure that the consumer can take advantage of the rules. The consumer associations press, rightly, for information about the food to be given to the consumer so that she can find out all she wants to know about the food. But how many of us read labels or know what to look for if we do? In 1875 there were no consumer associations, and consumers were just beginning to appreciate that the food they bought was grossly adulterated. In 1975 there are consumer associations of varying size and influence, and hardly any intentional adulteration. Interest has turned elsewhere. The law now gives very good protection but to take full advantage of this the consumer must be educated to understand that protection and the law.

As new foods are developed and as more processed foods come on to the market it becomes increasingly important for everybody to know what is in the food. The last 100 years has seen a major improvement in food standards and the virtual elimination of food adulteration. During the next 100 years we must ensure not only that protection is offered to the consumer but that the consumer is aware of and knows how to take advantage of that protection.

Introductory remarks by Mr. Giles

Food is now purer and safer than it has ever been. However, new considerations constantly arise through technological developments, the use of new scientific and analytical techniques and the interpretation of results of this work. United Kingdom food law is already detailed but with developments in the harmonization of food laws within the European Economic Community legislation will become even more complex. It is essential for the United Kingdom Government to consult widely and this in itself will require more effort from industry, consumer organizations and enforcement officers. We must keep a reasonable balance and ensure that the law does not become so complex as to require legislative, scientific, enforcement and financial effort out of all proportion to the benefits to be derived from it. A legislative programme in itself is not enough. Education and advice to consumers is needed to enable them to take full advantage of what the law does for them.

Discussion

Mr. F J Lawton (Food Manufacturers' Federation): Mr. Chairman, the speaker and I have known each other for a number of years and I have probably worked just a little longer than he has in this vast field of food legislation. There is rather a lot of it, it has grown very much over the last twenty-five years since I have known it and, looking around these days, I find that there is an increasing tendency to say 'Why don't we try to avoid legislation and get into the area of agreements amongst ourselves, as it were', and by 'ourselves' I suppose one means the Government, consumers and the industry. I was interested to see in the *Sunday Times* yesterday an article dealing with Mr. Methven's* efforts to inaugurate codes of practice and his belief in that area. I have always had a great deal of belief that codes of practice can do a lot where legislation sometimes can fail.

I wonder whether perhaps the speaker would care to comment a bit further on this area of codes of practice. Legislation is expensive in time, in enforcement, and it is expensive for the actual manufacturer who has to comply with the legislation. Perhaps codes of practice would be a little cheaper and it is possible that, in this era when we are all trying to save money, we could save a little in this area.

Another aspect which may be of interest is, do people understand what it is all about? The speaker has already touched on this, but I wonder whether all of us ought not really to put more effort into educating the consumers as to what is being done for them. There is a very great neglect in this area. The consumer, on the whole, is encouraged to be dissatisfied—

*Mr. Methven was then Director of Fair Trading.

14

I am sorry to say this, but I think it is true—by the media, by a lot of people saying 'This is wrong, that is wrong. Why isn't this done? Why isn't that done?' I think that perhaps we should spend a little more time telling the consumer all that is done, and perhaps that will be one of the results of this Symposium. We should try, in other words, to have sometimes on the television not critical but informative programmes.

That brings me to my last point which is, does the speaker think that it might be more advantageous to spend more money on educating the consumer both to understand food and in the nutritional field rather than in more legislation?

Lastly, may I say that I am very glad indeed to hear him say that he was always interested in a balance in legislation. If I may pay him a tribute, I think that all of us who know him know that when the Ministry has been engaged in legislation it has preserved that balance.

Mr. R F Giles: The first point was, I believe, on codes of practice. I see a great advantage in a code of practice because I feel it is better if people do something voluntarily and do not try to get round what is required by legislation.

There are two slight problems in this field. One is that, although we could have a code of practice in relation to the food manufactured in this country, we do import a great deal of our food and it would be very difficult to impose a code of practice throughout the world. However, this is not an impossible situation. In the United Kingdom the Courts interpret the law. In interpreting the general requirements of the Act and the horizontal regulations they will take note of the most authoritative information that is available, and a code of practice would be authoritative. If you sold some food which was not of the nature, quality and substance demanded by the code of practice there is a possibility of the Court backing up any prosecution made in this field.

The other snag with a code of practice is that, ignoring the point I made about the possibility of the Court enforcing it through the general provisions, anyone who wants to drive a coach and horses through a code of practice can make it a nonsense, and one then has to turn to legislation. In fact, in the *Sunday Times* article that has already been quoted there was reference to the 'whip of legislation' that Mr. Methven holds in one or perhaps both hands.

The second point was education, and this is something about which I personally feel very strongly. I think it is most important that we should get across to consumers not only what is being done for them but how they can take advantage of it. We have made a film, but of course this does not reach very many people, and we produce a few leaflets, but what we should like to do is to persuade supermarkets—this is very much in the future—to have at their check-out points a little stack of leaflets that will give consumers the help and advice they need.

One of the most important channels of education and advice is direct contact with the consumer through what the manufacturer puts on the label.

Should we spend more money on education and less on legislation? I accept that in the end the cost has to be met by the consumer either as purchaser or taxpayer but I should be pleased if we could devote more resources to education. It is never the right time to spend money on information and it is always the first thing to be cut in periods of economic hardship but I certainly take your point.

And thank you very much for the kind comment about trying to get a fair balance.

The Chairman: I am sure that there are others present who would like to pursue these particular points. It has often been stated that legislation is expensive.

May I ask a question? Is there any yardstick by which one can measure the diminishing returns from further expenditure on legislation in this field? At the beginning, no doubt, the results were enormous; are the results measurable today? Do we know that the health of the population on the one hand, or their protection from disaster on the other, is commensurate with the increasing efforts which are being put into this field?

Mr. R F Giles: The Chief Medical Officer of Health will fortunately be able to back me up, but from all the information we receive the health of the population is improving because the protection is there. We die from diseases that we did not die from in the past, because we live longer so that these diseases can attack us. If we died first we should be all right. This is one of the problems that one has about carcinogens and animal experiments. You can do experiments in mice and rats and decide that, if you eat something, you may die of cancer when you are 150 to 200. How much of a problem is this?

Diminishing returns? Fortunately in this country we have very law-abiding and co-operative food manufacturers and we have seen no sign of diminishing returns in the sense that we are still getting improvements in our food and in the standard of our food. I think that if we made a law which was nonsense people would just take no notice of it and then we would begin to know that we were entering this area of diminishing returns. At the moment, however, thanks to the inherent good sense of the food industry and not only to our efforts, I am quite sure that we are not getting a falling off in the effectiveness of the food law.

Mr. B J R Havelock (ICI Ltd): One of the things that has concerned me a little in recent years—I am fairly newly involved in this field—is the lack of incentive, or the increasing lack of incentive, to development. The law seems to become more and more detailed and restrictive and less general. The original Act said that if you did not harm people that was all right; nowadays you have to get products on a list before you may use them. Perhaps I could underline that with what seems to me a slightly old-womanish approach. When we were on holiday recently we had a delicious seafood cocktail which my wife very much enjoyed. In fractured English afterwards we discovered that it included sliced squid, and I am quite sure that if my wife had known that she would never have enjoyed it.

Mr. R F Giles: I think it is fair to say that to the uninitiated the vast body of law we have is very daunting, but we do try our very best to prevent it inhibiting development. I agree that the cost of testing a new additive is very high indeed and this may mean that you will not get so many new additives which would give you longer life, or new flavours, or better colour. You have to make sure that the additive you use is more pure than the food you put it in. However, I am sure that Professor Weedon, who is Chairman of the Food Additives and Contaminants Committee, will explain that his Committee are far from wanting to inhibit new developments.

In fact, we feel that this country and the United States are probably as liberal as any countries in the world in encouraging new food technology. Indeed, I think it is essential that other countries will have to follow suit if we start running short of food and have to produce new foods. There are of course novel proteins and other things in the pipeline which, if the need arises, can be used.

So far as the squid is concerned, it is a matter of judgment. Most people like to know what they are eating and we think that, on balance, there is an advantage in telling them.

Dr. J H Hamence (Public Analyst, Dr. Bernard Dyer and Partners): My Lord Chairman, I should like to take up this point that Mr. Lawton raised on codes of practice. Before doing that, I would like to go back just a little more than 100 years—101 years—and look at the reason for the passing of this Act. We are often told that the Act of 1860 and the following one of 1872 were a washout. I said that on this platform some 12 years ago; I was wrong. The second Act was a most vigorous Act. Many public analysts were appointed, many foods were examined and there were many prosecutions. It was that mass of prosecutions which led to the Select Committee which recommended the new Act of 1975. The Select Committee heard of an enormous dispute between the manufacturers and the public analysts. Neither of them could agree on standards for the simplest of articles. The big disputation was about Prussian blue, a legitimate additive to green tea to improve its colour. The public analysts said 'No' and, as a result, that particular variety of tea nearly went off the market. There were awful squabbles and, when this new Act was introduced, the first thing that the Society of Public Analysts—which was formed almost simultaneously—had to do was to sort out reasonable standards.

For years and years there were bitter squabbles as to what was a fair standard for this food or the other. Now, Ladies and Gentlemen, that was for simple food—milk, bread, very simple things—but there were disputations that went on and on. That is the difficulty that you have, I think, if you have no central body to make your law. The public analysts for many years implored the Government to set up committees. Government Committees were set up and they said, in 1900, that there should be central authorities to decide on the toxicology of different things.

It is with all those facts in mind that we look at codes of practice. Would we, with our multifarious foodstuffs, with the many different substances, ever get agreement if we left it to a code of practice? Have we not really got to have a central authority, particularly on the toxicity angle, to decide? I would suggest this, that action on cyclamates, as our speaker said, was decided in a few hours. Now if this had been subjected to a code of practice I would suggset, with great respect, that we should still be arguing about it today.

Mr. R F Giles: I agree that it is very difficult to have codes of practice for additives and contaminants and this is the field where, as I said in my paper, we are going to propose legislation which in the end will include all additives on permitted lists. However, I feel that there is scope for codes of practice on the composition of foods; we have standards for bread and for butter. I am quite sure that with good sense the food industry and the enforcement officers could make progress. They have been working, as Dr. Hamence knows, for this for a very long time in the Local Authorities' Joint Advisory Committee. It seems to me that it is rather taking a hammer to crack a nut to have legislation for some of the commodities which, although important, do not enter widely into or form a staple part of the diet.

Dr. L E Coles (County Analyst, Mid-Glamorgan County Council): In considering codes of practice and obtaining comments on impending legislation, and having regard to the advanced technology of the food industry and its expertise, do you think that the representatives of the enforcement authorities are a fair match for the trade when negotiating with them?

Mr. R F Giles: Yes! I think you will find that there are officers on local authorities—one of them will be talking to you later today—who have made a study of how to do this sort of thing. They talk to me, sometimes at length and always with a very great deal of sense. I should have thought that a modern, top-tier authority not only has the people to argue a case but also has the scientific back-up, either through its scientific branch or through its public analysts, to be able to match the food trade. By and large I have not regarded the food trade as always trying to pull wool over our eyes. They know that we and enforcement authorities have scientific advisers and that we can get independent scientific advice. I think it is extremely rare for any scientist working for the food industry deliberately to try to mislead you on a scientific fact. If it is a matter of opinion, everyone holds his own. I think that it is a pretty even match.

Mr. J W Colquhoun (Products Director, Rowntree Mackintosh Ltd): As one who has spent many happy hours with Mr. Giles and his legions, I am concerned that industry is losing the opportunity to discuss with its legislators the various implications of what they are trying to do. By and large my particular sector of the food industry is happy with our relationship with the Ministry but we feel that much of the legislation which is now descending upon our heads is far more bureaucratic and lacks the benefit of the discussions which we have enjoyed in this country. I wonder if Mr. Giles could indicate to us if there is any possible remedy to allow the voice of food manufacturers to be more loudly heard, or at least more loudly expressed, in Europe?

Mr. R F Giles: I hope that you will continue to talk to us both on general philosophy and on detailed points.

On the EEC proposals, as I said in my talk, we feel that the consultation we have with the food industry on the individual directives is in almost permanent session. We have a word with the manufacturers and consumers, we go out to Brussels, we come back and report and there is another meeting in a month's time. This may make you feel that the legislation is worse than it really is because it takes two, four or, in the case of chocolate, twelve years to get a directive through the machine, and a very great deal of time is spent in consultation.

As to a voice in Europe, we feel very strongly in MAFF that we must know before we go to Brussels what the United Kingdom wants. This does not necessarily mean what the United Kingdom food industry wants; it is equally important to know what the United Kingdom consumer wants. We also consult the enforcement officers. We then argue the case for the United Kingdom in Brussels.

However, it is equally important that the food industry, and I know that they are aware of this, should join in the international discussions of the industry in Europe. I am not trying to get subscriptions for the European trade organizations, but industry must get involved in discussions in Europe and make sure that they put forward the United Kingdom view, or at least a rational view that is acceptable to the United Kingdom industry.

Finally, there is that fine old-fashioned system where you take a Commission official out to lunch.

Dr. A A Leach (Technical Secretary, The Brewers' Society): This is perhaps more by way of an appeal rather than a question. The Government's policy for supporting research has meant that the support for BIBRA, the British Industrial Biological Research Association, has become somewhat more piecemeal. This means that the second laboratory they have built with the assistance of the Ministry is not functioning properly. I feel it is a great pity that the Government is not supporting this research in order that the basic techniques of toxicology can be improved. I would appeal to the Ministry to find some other way of keeping this body functioning as it was, and very successfully.

Mr. R F Giles: I think I have to declare an interest on this question because I am on the Council of BIBRA.

BIBRA is a first class toxicological institution and, with their increased laboratory space from the latest building programme, they have facilities possibly unrivalled in this country and a lot of other countries as well. Government support for BIBRA is just as much, in cash terms, as it was. The only difference is that, instead of making a pound-for-pound type of grant, it now commissions basic research at BIBRA to the same amount of money as it used to grant. I think that what has really hit the organization is inflation, and who has it not hit? In these circumstances I think that it will take some little time, but I am confident that the new BIBRA laboratory will be fully in operation and the Research Association, as it develops, will have more work available than it can cope with. It is difficult to fill a large new laboratory with new scientists overnight, especially in the toxicological field where we are very short of scientists, and BIBRA would not want to take on staff unless it could see a firm future for the specialists it proposed to employ. However, I am quite convinced that, if you ask me a question on the RA in three or four years' time, it will be phrased somewhat differently.

Dr. G F Wilmink (Cabinet Adviser, Ministry of Agriculture and Fisheries, The Netherlands): If you will allow me as a foreigner to put a small question in connexion with the development of the Food and Drugs Act in the United Kingdom, I should like to ask what the Government's intention has been in the development of food law. I think the first point is very clear indeed, that it is to protect the health of the consumer, and I can see that it is developing in the direction of making a positive list of additives and so on and establishing criteria for hygiene to protect the consumer from food poisoning. That is clear and those are your horizontal regulations. However, in your vertical regulations on the products is it the intention to guarantee the consumer a minimum quality of the product as described, or is the development of food law in the United Kingdom also going in the direction of guaranteeing different qualities, so that you get a mixing up of requirements from minimum requirements at minimum levels to protect the consumer, but also to protect the trade and the producers in the levels of qualities in the different products?

Mr. R F Giles: You are quite right, Dr. Wilmink, that basically the law is to protect the health of the consumer, especially on the additives and contaminants front.

So far as our vertical regulations are concerned, we have aimed at ensuring minimum quality for the basic foods, of which bread is an example. On the other foods we have been aiming in our philosophy to give the consumer the widest possible choice, but the consumer must be told what he or she is getting. This is why we feel it is so essential to have food labelled properly. We are faced with the argument that many housewives would prefer the price to be kept down rather than to be given more information, but I think that manufacturers could achieve a great deal in their labelling without increasing prices. If you put a lot of information on the label, it may make it look untidy and even uninviting but a first class designer can meet this challenge.

Perhaps I can conclude by repeating that we want the widest possible choice for consumers but, manufacturers, please give the housewife all the information you can.

Advising on Food Standards in the United Kingdom

1. The Changing Role of the Food Standards Committee

A G Ward
Chairman, Food Standards Committee

Introduction

The present terms of reference of the Food Standards Committee are: 'To advise the Minister of Agriculture, Fisheries and Food, the Secretary of State for Social Services, the Secretary of State for Scotland and the Secretary of State for Northern Ireland on the composition, description, labelling and advertising of food with particular reference to the exercise of powers conferred on Ministers by Sections 4, 5 and 7 of the Food and Drugs Act 1955 and the corresponding provisions in enactments relating to Scotland and Northern Ireland.' Although these formal phrases accurately represent the tasks the Committee is called on to undertake, which are illustrated by examples in later sections, it by no means exhausts further functions which the Committee itself aims to fulfil, which are outlined on page 23.

Founded in 1947, the Committee now has an extensive history, in the course of which it has undergone change and evolution. Some of the earlier history may be unfamiliar to those who encounter the Committee's work currently and so it is briefly recorded in Section 3. This is followed by an account of how the Committee carries out its work today and the effects which membership of the European Economic Community, the growth of the consumer movement and increasing pace of technological change in the food industry are having on the Committee's mode of operation. Finally, a few speculative thoughts are included concerning future developments.

It must at the outset be stressed that the Committee is an independent body, whose reports do not require to be accepted by government before publication. Its members are, however, appointed by Ministers and its secretariat is provided by the Ministry of Agriculture, Fisheries and Food. An independent Committee of this type to advise Ministers on aspects of food law is almost unknown outside the United Kingdom, although rather similar committees have recently been created in Australia and New Zealand. The advantages and disadvantages which result from independent status and from the procedure which is followed to preserve it will be apparent in succeeding sections.

The functions undertaken by the Food Standards Committee

The sale of food involves an immense variety of transactions ranging from the sale of raw foods in shops to the supply of complete meals by a caterer. It includes the sale of drinks, other than water, and even (Food and Drugs Act 1955, Section 135 (2)) the supply of meals in institutions, such as welfare homes, schools and hospitals, where no payment for the meal is made. Enforcement by local authorities has a vital part to play in securing conformity with the provisions of the Food and Drugs Act and of the regulations made under its powers but compliance with these laws is greatly aided if, by and large, those affected by them regard their provisions as reasonable. In this way, their observance is secured mainly by voluntary conformity rather than by the fear of prosecution. The reviews which the Food Standards Committee are asked to carry out into whether regulations are needed in a given area and, if so, the form they should take, provide extensive opportunities for the submission of evidence and for the expression of views, both in writing and orally. The Committee, in almost every case, issues its considered conclusions, together with the arguments on which they are based, in a published report, for all to read and to comment on to Ministers. All this takes place before any attempt is made by the government to reach final views and to prepare draft regulations. The debate between the Committee, the food industry, consumers, organizations representing the enforcement side and others (including officials of the appropriate Ministries) aids the search for the most generally acceptable solutions and is one of the main means of ensuring consent by the participants to the regulations which may and frequently do eventually stem from the Committee's reports.

In the 28 years of the Committee's existence, extensive technological progress has taken place in the food industry, stimulated by its own researches and technical expertise and aided also by government funded research in food science, nutrition and food technology. The resulting increased complexity of food processing creates obligations on all concerned to inform consumers of changes which affect their foods. The Committee seeks to render its own reports as informative as possible concerning the foods themselves, the manufacturing processes involved in their production and changes in manufacture when they arise. Some readers of the reports will have only a modest background in science, so the reports are drafted to be intelligible to a wide readership among consumers and also among both technical and non-technical staff in industry, in local authorities, in government departments and abroad.

Since joining the EEC the participation of the UK government in the preparation of directives related to food composition and labelling has involved the Committee in formulating, when requested by Ministers, critical assessments of draft directives from a viewpoint which attempts to reconcile the varied views of all those in the UK (manufacturers, consumers, etc) likely to be affected. In advising on such matters, the Committee also has to keep in mind the need to maintain the uniformity and harmony of UK food legislation as a whole. The Committee's discussions, in which officials take a full part, and the reports which are prepared have served to assist those UK officials carrying out negotiations in the EEC by clarifying some of the issues involved as well as providing them with evidence concerning the whole spectrum of relevant UK opinion.

The Committee is encouraged to attempt its sometimes complex tasks, involving apparently conflicting views, by one basic principle. This is that, in the long term, there can be no fundamental divergence of interest between the consumer and the industries which supply him with his food. The food manufacturing industry must satisfy the desires, preferences and nutritional needs of the consumer. Even where it is difficult for these to be clearly expressed, they make an impact on the manufacturer. The consumer is able to exercise the purchaser's right to buy or not to buy particular food products. The retailer's interest, again in the long run, is served by enabling the consumer to be aware of what he is purchasing and by creating conditions during storage and sale which reduce deterioration of the food he is selling to the minimum. The caterer is even more directly limited in his actions by the need to provide immediate satisfaction to his customers, except in those institutions where residents have no alternative sources of food. In seeking regulatory solutions for particular problems, the Committee always assumes that a solution or solutions, which will in time prove generally acceptable, exists and so it applies its collective ingenuity to seeking such a solution.

The Committee has always, as is clear above, accepted that its deliberations and recommendations have, as a primary important objective, to ensure that the interests of the consumer are adequately safeguarded concerning the character and composition of foods for sale as well as by their appropriate labelling and advertising. A further objective, which is entirely concordant with this, is to protect manufacturers, retailers and caterers who are aiming properly to serve the public with food of the appropriate composition and description from unfair competition from those whose products are less adequate in some respect. This applies whether any defect arises from ignorance and incompetence or from a deliberate debasement of standards. Abuses by one firm bring, all too often, discredit on a whole industry and the Committee has been assisted in many of its tasks by the responsible and non-partisan viewpoints submitted to it on many occasions by various sectors of the food industry.

Not only are the food industry, the distributive and catering industries almost completely dependent today on science and technology for their continued operation, but they are increasingly having to make modifications as a result of changes imposed on them by external conditions. Variations in the supply position of raw foods, accompanied by drastic changes in relative price levels, rising energy costs and the potential developments created throughout the world by food science itself, all make restrictive food legislation, which might seek to standardize existing products, and exclude others, undesirable. Too close restriction would not only needlessly hamper the manufacturer but would also affect the consumer's choice. So the Committee, in framing recommendations, attempts to ensure that food legislation is sufficiently flexible to allow for future technological change. It is not always easy to reconcile the need for precision in legislation with providing the possibility of change. The principal weakness of the UK system for bringing food regulations into being, which affects the areas dealt with both by the Food Standards Committee and by the Food Additives and Contaminants Committee, is the time scale the whole sequence of operations to create a new regulation takes. Since regulations are normally considered for revision only at lengthy intervals, every care has to be exercised to frame them so as not to make impossible impending changes which might be advantageous both to industry and to the consumer. The speed with which modifications can be made in food legislation is one area in which the contrasting but certainly very comprehensive Canadian system of food law is regarded by some as demonstrating an advantage over UK practice. In emergency, the UK system can operate quickly but at the cost of omitting consultative stages which in the ordinary way perhaps constitute its greatest advantage. Industry itself cannot always foresee all developments likely to arise in a period of five to ten years between two reviews—and occasionally the need for commercial security may preclude disclosure of changes known to be likely to arise. Criticisms by industry of the time which reviews take, of delays in implementing conclusions and the lengthy interval before the same subject is likely again to be reviewed, are very understandable. If, however, the merits of the UK system are to be retained, then all that can reasonably be attempted is to improve in detail the mode of operation of the consultation system, and in particular to ensure that the dialogue between industry, consumers and others and the Committee is even freer and franker than in the past. To the extent that the Committee and Government are well informed of the real problems in food legislation which have to be solved, so the tasks are expedited. Indeed the solutions proposed may then be such that the need for later representations is minimized.

The origins and development of the Food Standards Committee

Just before and in the early period of the Second World War the main control of food composition and labelling was exercised in succession by the Food and Drugs Acts of 1928 and 1938. Even under the earlier Acts it was found that additional precision needed to be given to the intentions of certain sections of the Acts by the introduction of a small number of regulations. These regulations were made under the special powers conferred on Ministers by the Acts. Examples in the 1920s were the Public Health (Preservatives, etc. in Food) Regulations 1925 and the Public Health (Condensed Milk) Regulations 1923 (amended 1927). A Departmental Committee on the Composition and Description of Food was set up in 1931 jointly by the Minister of Health and the Secretary of State for Scotland to examine whether 'the law relating to the composition and description of articles of food should be altered so as to enable definitions or standards to be prescribed, or declarations of composition to be required . . .'. Its Report, Cmnd 4564, was published in 1938. In addition to recommending amendment of the law to enable regulations to be made, the Committee considered the views of the Society of Public Analysts concerning the procedure for consultation and for reconciling different views about the provisions to be included in standards. The Report quoted from the Society's submission as follows:

'the Society is strongly of the opinion that the work should be given to a *permanent body that should have no other duties*. Its view is that a Statutory Advisory Committee should be formed by the Minister of Health, consisting of representatives of the Ministry, public analysts, manufacturers and consumers. . . . The Committee would make recommendations to the Minister of Health. It would deal with food standards and definitions, labelling and description of foods, processes of analysis and similar questions, and it should on request state definitely, with regard to any ingredient of a food, the interpretation of the term "injurious to health" '.

The Departmental Committee did not accept the Society of Public Analysts' submission, although it was widely supported by other bodies. It clearly regarded the proposal as reflecting on the competence of the Foods Department in the Ministry of Health. The succeeding paragraphs of the present paper will show, however, how, over the years, the need for such a body has resulted in a close approximation to the above proposals, which were drafted in the early 1930s by the Society of Public Analysts, in the present operation of the Food Standards Committee.

With the outbreak of the Second World War in 1939 a much higher degree of control was required for foodstuffs generally, to cope with wartime conditions and with the consequences of food rationing, raw material shortages and the possibility of deceptive substitute foods being introduced. Protection was secured through the Defence (Sale of Food) Regulations 1943 and orders made under these regulations by the Minister of Food acting, where appropriate, in association with other Ministers.

To advise on the provisions to be included in these orders, an Interdepartmental Committee was set up in 1942 'to advise the Ministry of Food, upon request, in regard to the standards that would be appropriate for foods for which the Ministry may decide to provide standards of quality'. Represented on the Committee were the Ministry of Food, the Ministry of Health, the Department of Health for Scotland and the Laboratory of the Government Chemist. The Society of Public Analysts appointed public analysts as members of the Committee to assist it in its work. This Interdepartmental Committee laid the basis, under wartime conditions, from which the whole future machinery for consultation and formulation of regulations has stemmed. Traces of its procedure can still be seen in the continued participation of a representative of the Government Chemist, currently the Government Chemist himself, and of a public analyst in the work of the Food Standards Committee.

In 1947, after the conclusion of the war, it was decided to continue the existence of a consultative body to review the need for food regulations but to replace the Interdepartmental Committee by a 'Food Standards Committee' with a measure of independence. The FSC was set up to 'advise the Ministers of Food and Health and the Secretary of State for Scotland as to the provision to be made concerning the composition of foods (other than liquid milk) and the labelling and marking of any foods for which provision is made, by:

(a) Statutory Orders under the Defence (Sale of Food) Regulations; or

(b) Regulations (other than Milk or Dairy Regulations) under the Food and Drugs Acts and corresponding enactments relating to Scotland;

for preventing danger to health, loss of nutritional value or otherwise protecting purchasers'.

The Committee was kept on a fairly tight rein by the Ministry by the assumption of the chairmanship by the Chief Scientific Adviser of the Ministry of Food. A wider viewpoint was secured by an extension of membership to include nominees from the Medical Research Council, the Food Manufacturers' Federation, the Co-operative Union and by the participation of the Government of Northern Ireland in the work of the Committee.

The minutes of the first meeting (4th March 1948) list as the topics discussed, the terms of reference, procedure, tomato ketchup and curry powder—a modest start to a long career! It is interesting to note that the review of tomato ketchup was initiated following proposals for a standard from the food industry. The Committee accepted that a compositional standard for tomato ketchup would indeed protect both the consumer and the industry from inferior products. The Committee's recommendations resulted in The Food Standards (Tomato Ketchup) Order 1949, made under the Defence (Sale of Food) Regulations 1943. This and other orders made under Defence Regulations were continued by Section 136 of the Food and Drugs Act 1955. Many of the early orders which followed the Committee's first reviews or were already in force when the Committee was formed were reconsidered in the late 1960s. The Committee's Report on the pre-1955 Compositional Orders includes some details of the origins of these Orders, some of which (curry powder, mustard, gelatine) barely justify their seniority in legislation!

The history of the Committee has been characterized by a steady growth in the volume of its work and in its complexity. By January 1951 it was found necessary to form a sub-Committee (the Preservatives sub-Committee), which continued to report through the main Food Standards Committee until 1964. Before this date the sub-Committee had been given a new name, the Food Additives and Contaminants sub-Committee, with suitably extended terms of reference. It was itself advised by its own Pharmacology Panel and, when appropriate, by a Ministry of Health Standing Panel on Carcinogenic Hazards in Food Additives and Food Contaminants. Finally, in 1964, the independent operation of the sub-Committee, which had existed in fact for a number of years, was recognized by its reconstitution as the Food Additives and Contaminants Committee, as a sister body to the Food Standards Committee. Joint or parallel reviews by the two Committees in some areas (eg, Bread and Flour, Beer, Infant Foods) are often necessary and frequent references of topics and consultation between the two committees take place.

The fusion of the Ministries of Food and Agriculture and Fisheries in the early 1950s did not affect the operation of the Food Standards Committee. With the departure in 1959 of the first Chairman of the Committee, Sir Norman Wright, Chief Scientific Adviser (Food) in the combined Ministry, the present constitution of the Committee was adopted, made up of an independent Chairman and nine members, three drawn from the food trade, three with appropriate scientific expertise and three members with special concern for consumer views. This change still further underlined the basic independence of the Committee's work from the actual law-making role of the Ministries. No members are appointed to act as, nor do they see themselves as, representatives of particular organizations, but they contribute as individuals, as is appropriate in view of their personal appointment by Ministers.

Major reviews, including meat products, bread and flour, and labelling, claims and misleading descriptions, in the early 1960s formed the basis of important new and revised regulations in the immediately following period. In the 1970s, partly as a result of renewed consumer interest in foods, such wide ranging subjects as the date marking of food and novel protein foods have been reported on by the Committee, as well as several more conventional commodity reviews (Bread and Flour, Soft Drinks, Yogurt). Among references to the Committee of subjects under negotiation in the EEC was a brief but thorough review of the draft Directive on Cocoa and Chocolate. This was the first time that an EEC draft directive was referred for comment to the Committee.

The current programme includes beer, infant foods, meat products, water in food and the labelling of food, all major subjects. In view of this extensive programme the Committee has been compelled to set up Working Sub-groups from its membership to remove discussion of detailed specialized points and of drafting from the main Committee's agenda. However, the main principles of each review, the final text of each Report, and any major matters revealed by Sub-group discussions, are discussed in full Committee and remain the collective responsibility of the entire Committee.

The full Committee now meets 11 times each year and the 250th meeting took place on 16th September 1975. Some 64 reports have been issued, if we exclude those prior to 1964 dealing solely with food additives, to which the main Committee made little contribution. It can perhaps be claimed that the Reports as a whole constitute a unique documentation on food legislation, which reflects not only the quality and quantity of the work of the Committee, its assessors and its secretariat, but also that of the many organizations and individuals who have contributed submissions to it over the years.

The mode of operation of the Food Standards Committee

In the following paragraphs an attempt will be made to give due weight both to the formal aspects of the Committee's work and to less formal matters which facilitate its operation.

MEMBERSHIP

The most striking aspect of the membership of the Committee is the continuity provided by the lengthy terms of service of many members. Of the founder members two, C A Adams and A Glover, served from 1948 to 1963 and R W Sutton served from 1948 to 1967. Colin Dence, a former President of the Food Manufacturers' Federation, served from 1955 to 1972. Three of the present members have had more than 10 years' service. As a consequence of the experience of working together for a number of reviews, the Committee can draw on a fund of common approaches built up over the years, in addition to the individual and differing viewpoints of its members. On issues for which there may superficially appear to be a 'manufacturers' viewpoint' or a 'consumers' viewpoint' or an 'enforcement approach', it by no means follows that the views expressed in committee by various members will reflect their own origins be they industry or elsewhere. The common conviction that an effective solution exists for each problem and has only to be sought sufficiently diligently has as its corollary the fact that any member may provide the first glimpse of that solution. Difficulties or anomalies it may create then become exposed and discussion enables them to be overcome.

The recent formation of *ad hoc* Sub-groups of the Committee, from among the membership, with their own chairmen, each lasting only for a particular review, has placed further emphasis on the need for a common basic view-point and approach among members of the Committee. This the Sub-groups apply in their detailed work.

It has been suggested from time to time that the membership of the Committee should be increased, partly to cope with the increased work, but also to make wider representation possible. A large Committee would however face greater difficulties in retaining a unified approach and in finding solutions which are acceptable to all its members. It is probable that 10 members (including the Chairman) is near the optimum.

THE SECRETARIAT AND THE PARTICIPATING MINISTRIES

In the Committee's early days, with the Chief Scientific Adviser (later, Chief Scientific Adviser (Food) in the Ministry of Agriculture, Fisheries and Food) as Chairman, the two secretaries of the Committee (administrative and scientific) had a key part to play under his close guidance in ensuring that the views of the Committee and of the Ministries did not diverge so far as to create major difficulties. The greater independence of the Committee today means that this responsibility no longer rests on the secretaries. It is however still true that for the views of the Committee and Ministries to diverge so far as to be irreconcilable would not aid the formulation of constructive legislation and would make the work of both much more difficult. In practice, officials aid the Committee by a full and free expression of their own views. Equally their views become modified in response to the arguments within the Committee. In this way, without need for any formal arrangements, the Committee's final views as expressed in its Reports are in all normal circumstances acceptable to the Ministries concerned as a basis for the further stages of consultation with industry and the public.

It is not, perhaps, widely understood that the representations which are invited by Ministers, following the publication of a Report, are not normally seen by any member of the Committee. The purpose of the representations is to aid in the drafting of Regulations, or in reaching some related decision. This part of the process is not within the competence of the Committee. It is open to Ministers to refer some specific query to the Committee, making available the representations on that query, but this occurs only rarely. Exceptionally, as happened early in 1975, when the Meat Product Regulations were referred to the Committee for review immediately after publication of the Committee's Report on Novel Protein Foods, relevant representations on one report are made available to the Committee to assist it in the further review.

Until the last few years, the drafting of Reports, the management of Committee business, the maintenance of contact with the various interested organizations and all other matters to do with the work of the Committee fell to the administrative secretary aided, where scientific and technical points arose, by the scientific secretary. Such outstanding secretaries as J H V Davies and L G Hanson had much more than a formal role to play in the work of the Committee. The increased intensity and complexity of the Committee's work have required new administrative arrangements to cope with each new review. These have been particularly valuable in maintaining continuity in the recent period, when there have been frequent changes of administrative secretary. A small team of officials, usually of two to four persons, is made up to assist in each review, drawn normally from Food Standards Division of MAFF.

These officials may have responsibility for legislation for the particular commodities or subject of review, including acting as negotiators in the EEC. The group is usually supported by the most appropriate member of the Food Science Division of the Ministry. Such a team will be responsible for all those duties connected with a review previously discharged by the two secretaries, except that formal matters may still pass through the administrative secretary. The team only attends the meetings of the Committee for the particular review with which it is concerned. This leaves to the administrative secretary the general running of the Committee. The scientific secretary ensures that the Committee receives all the aid that is available from within the Ministry's Food Science Division and from other sources within the Scientific Civil Service.

The devolving of each review to a team of officials matches the new Committee procedure, leaving the detail of each review to a Sub-group of its members. Although experience of the complete system as at present constituted is limited, the new arrangements have every appearance of aiding and speeding the Committee's work.

Although the primary task of servicing the Committee's work falls to the Ministry of Agriculture, Fisheries and Food, the attendance at all meetings of an official of the Department of Health and Social Security, aided when necessary by specialist medical staff of that department, assists in ensuring that DHSS views are known to the Committee and that its resources of knowledge can be fully utilized. In recent years the Scottish Home and Health Department have played an increasing part in the work of the Committee. The Secretary of State for Northern Ireland is entitled to be represented at meetings but contact is usually limited to that available through the Committe papers.

ASSESSORS

The Committee is often conscious of its own limited knowledge of a particular industry or group of commodities or of some aspect of food science or nutrition. Despite the increasing aid which the Ministry's Food Science Division and DHSS have been able to give, the need for specialist advice outside this framework frequently arises. In these circumstances assessors are appointed to give technical and scientific advice and to assist the Committee at all stages of a review, including the preparation of the Report. The Committee alone is responsible for the views and recommendations expressed in the Report but the assessors have a duty to ensure that these views are based on full and accurate information. They also assist in making the informative and educational aspects of the Report a true reflection of current knowledge of the subject under review. In practice, as would be expected from the standing and reputation of those appointed as assessors, the assessors make their own views freely known to the Committee and aid and contribute to the debate. Such distinguished scientists are Professor J B M Coppock, Dr. T Moran, Dr. G A H Elton, Dr. D W E Axford (the two Bread and Flour Reviews), Professor E L Crossley (Cream), J C Dakin (Jam and other Preserves), Dr. B A Wharton (Infant Foods), Dr. A MacLeod, Dr. C E Dalgleish (Beer), Professor M Ingram, Professor E F Williams (Meat Products) have acted as assessors for reviews at different periods in the last 15 years.

ADVICE FROM OTHER OFFICIAL COMMITTEES

Reference has already been made to joint working with the Food Additives and Contaminants Committee. There is also a continuing link with such committees as the Committee on the Medical Aspects of Food Policy, DHSS and the Committee on Medical Aspects of Chemicals in Food and the Environment, DHSS mainly through officials, but occasionally through over-lapping membership. Particular problems on which the Food Standards Committee seeks advice (e.g., nutritional aspects of the bread and flour and infant food reviews; the nutritional and toxicological aspects of the novel protein food review) may well be reviewed by a standing sub-Committee of one of these bodies or by a Working Party. The advantage of such action is to make known to the Committee the agreed views of a number of experts on specific questions. Incorporation of the conclusions into the framework of the Committee's recommendations, may, however, occasionally present problems. The Committee's reviews have necessarily to take into account many factors other than the specific questions which have required specialist comment. Where difficulty arises, discussions between the members of the two Committees, aided by officials who have taken part in the review from the beginning, will normally enable satisfactory solutions to be achieved.

REVIEW PROCEDURE

As has already been made clear, the choice of subjects for review by the Committee is a matter solely for Ministers, who have many considerations in mind when making their selection—public interest, timeliness, the need to look again at a major area, EEC developments, the attempt over the years to review the need for legislation for the major classes of foods. Terms of reference for a review, often with supporting information from within the Ministries, are placed before the Committee as the first step in the review. Occasionally, as with the review of novel protein foods, members of the Committee had themselves expressed informally their opinion that in the near future regulations would be required for these foods. The review was, however, initiated only because the Ministers concerned had reached the same conclusion.

The next steps in a review involve the issue of a press release inviting representations, which may, often following a brief Committee discussion, list topics of especial importance within the area of the review, to which the Committee would like attention to be directed. Meanwhile a decision is made whether assessors will be needed and background papers are prepared, including any legislative provisions on the subject elsewhere (especially in

Europe, the Commonwealth and the USA) and the current position in the EEC and in the Codex Alimentarius Commission Committees. Advice will also be sought about any relevant specialized aspects of the review (nutrition, additives, etc.) from other official bodies.

Although representations will in the main stem from Manufacturers Associations, the Local Authority Associations and Consumer bodies, organizations such as the Association of Public Analysts, the Association of Public Health Inspectors, the British Nutrition Foundation and the Institute of Food Science and Technology provide wide ranging views and comments. From its inception the Committee has leaned heavily on public analysts and their association to provide analytical data and, in many instances, special samplings and analyses, giving surveys of current practice. It is open to any member of the public to make a submission of his personal viewpoint and a number of these are received. Although in a specialized commodity review (e.g., cream, jams and preserves) perhaps only 20 to 30 representations would be received, more general topics arouse a much wider circle of response. One hundred and ninety-three submissions were received for the review of the date marking of food.

A special responsibility falls to manufacturers to provide the Committee with the fullest background information in their submissions. The Committee has its own members drawn from the food industry, its assessors have close contact and experience of industrial problems and members with knowledge of food science and technology also appreciate the real difficulties some legislative approaches might create for manufacturers. Committee members whose personal background is as consumers, who have close day-to-day contact with other consumers, are well able to judge submissions based on industry's authentic evaluation of the area, backed by facts and figures. This is not always possible with those submissions which set out to 'make a case' and so are one-sided.

Limited time restricts opportunities for the Committee to receive delegations, who may wish to present their viewpoint in person. It is customary to invite certain key organizations in any review to present their views orally to the Committee. As with written submissions, the Committee benefits most when it feels confident that it has listened to and understands the real problems being presented. Perhaps, additionally, these discussions are valuable when delegations show a recognition that there are other views than their own which have to be reconciled by the Committee. Once a year, the Committee holds its meeting away from MAFF, London. Three purposes are served by this meeting, which normally extends over two days. First, the opportunity is taken to visit factories or research establishments involved with foodstuffs forming one of the Committee's current reviews. Discussions with technical and other staff assist both Committee and its officials in appreciating the nature of processes employed and the limitations these may create. Secondly, it makes it possible for the Committee to visit Scotland and Northern Ireland, whose Ministers it serves equally with the Ministers in London. Finally, opportunity arises for members to discuss, under less urgent pressure of time and in an informal atmosphere, their various interests and viewpoints. Such discussions aid the steady development of a common approach to food legislation among members.

It would be tedious to follow through the many stages of discussion of submissions and draft reports in main Committee and in the Sub-groups, the final outcome of which is the printed report. Critics of the time taken by the Committee in preparing its reports are often also the critics of some minor discrepancy which may creep through in the final report, despite the care exercised by both the Committee and officials. But the outcome of a review is a public document for all who wish to read and to contribute their comments. This is the purpose behind the entire Committee procedure. Usually reports, although read in detail by industry, enforcement authorities, consumer associations and some others, do not make headlines in the press. Only such reports as those on date marking and on novel protein foods make an immediate impact in this way.

It has been a continuing concern of the Committee that the consumer is so little informed about measures for the control of the food available for sale, about the safeguards provided and about the information which the food label is required to give. The UK contrasts in this respect adversely with the Canadian Government, which has recognized the need to make its food regulations widely known and has taken effective action. The Committee has welcomed the initiative taken by MAFF in commissioning the entertaining and instructive film 'Alice in Labelland'. The reception the film has had and its widespread showing should encourage further similar actions.

The Committee, the EEC and the Codex Alimentarius Commission

The EEC procedure for the preparation of directives concerned with the composition, labelling and advertising of food contrasts in many ways with UK practice. The directives are not framed in the context of reliance on the firm foundation of a general EEC food law, as is provided in the UK by the Food and Drugs Act 1955. The Commission does not attempt the complex task of unifying the entire food laws and regulations of the nine member countries, but has the limited aim of removing obstacles to intermember trade in foodstuffs. UK officials negotiating particular directives are able to secure extensive advice from UK industry and, where appropriate, from consumer bodies. Equally, federation of EEC manufacturers' associations and, increasingly, the corresponding consumer bodies can present their overall view on the form a directive should take to the Commission. In none of these procedures is there adequate opportunity for the type of exploratory discussion, debate and research into the need for, and the most appropriate form of, food legislation which it is the duty of the Food Standards Committee to provide in the UK. So the Committee's major reviews, because of the way they are carried out, may have relevance for and influence in subsequent EEC negotiations. This has already been evident in connection with EEC interest in the Report on Novel Protein Foods.

The Food Standards Committee has given close attention to draft directives related to its reviews of the same areas. The Committee's reports may include discussion of particular issues raised by a draft directive. UK officials can, where appropriate, draw for their EEC work on the information given in submissions, Committee papers and reports and on the arguments which are put forward during a review. The Committee may also be asked to express a view on some particular query arising—although it is reluctant to do so on topics isolated from its main work at any particular time.

In case of need, the Committee is able to undertake a brief intensive review of a subject, specifically to assist and inform UK negotiators involved in EEC negotiations. A normal Committee review of cocoa and chocolate was indeed overdue, when the need for a balanced statement of the UK view of the implications of the EEC draft directive on cocoa and chocolate was required to assist in resolving problems which had arisen in negotiations. The Committee was able to receive sufficient information from industry and consumer bodies to express firm views concerning the need to retain, in the interests both of the UK consumer and the manufacturers, the types of chocolate long manufactured and eaten in the UK, which differed compositionally from types with similar names, also long established in other EEC countries. The Committee's report was of some assistance in securing a directive recognizing this position. The directive should shortly be implemented by means of a UK regulation.

While the Committee has always taken note of the drafts and deliberations of the committee of the Codex Alimentarius Commission in its reviews, the optional character of Codex Standards has not created the same element of urgency as EEC directives. However, some care will be needed in future, since Codex Standards may be considered for adoption by the EEC on behalf of the whole nine countries, rather than country by country. This may result in an increased need for the Committee to comment on Codex drafts at stages where changes could still be negotiated, to avoid later difficulties with an EEC directive.

Conclusion

The Food Standards Committee can be regarded as an example of British ability to create institutions to reconcile apparently opposed viewpoints and to provide pragmatic solutions which often prove practical and acceptable. It is the Committee's especial concern to increase the confidence of consumer and manufacturer alike, in the integrity of its approach and its readiness always to pay attention to comment and criticism. Although for a brief period its future role seemed less clear after the UK entered the EEC, it would now appear that this entry has reinforced its basic purpose of providing extensive reviews within its terms of reference, while entry has also added to the volume of its work. No doubt the Committee will continue to adapt to changed circumstances, despite the added pressures the various changes have imposed on its members.

In conclusion, I would like to acknowledge my debt, both in chairing the Committee for nearly 11 years and in writing this paper, to the members of the Committee for their knowledge, skill and patience during the various reviews, to the Committee's officials for their loyal aid and cheerful willingness to see cherished ideas first criticized and then sometimes finally accepted and not least to all those who have submitted their views to the Committee, for their help in its work and for their general confidence that the Committee can achieve a valuable outcome to the reviews to which they have contributed.

Appendix

Reports of the Food Standards Committee

	Date of publication	
Soya in Sausage	1942	
Soya in Sausage (Supplementary)	1942	
Coffee Essence	1942	
Self Raising Flour	1942	
Soft Drinks	1943	
Baking Powder and Golden Raising Powder	1943	
Mustard	1943	No
Shredded Suet	1943	longer
Vinegar	1943	available
Dripping and Tallow	1943	
Coffee Essences	1944	
Custard Powder	1945	
Salad Cream and Mayonnaise	1945	
Self Raising Flour	1945	
Fluorine	1946	
*Tomato Ketchup	1948	
*Curry Powder	1948	
*Processed Cheese	1949	
*Iodized Salt	1950	
*Edible Gelatine	1950	
*Fish Paste	1950	
Ice Cream	Not published	
*Cream	1950	
Ice Cream (Supplementary)	Not published	
*Fish Cakes	1951	
*Coffee Mixtures	1951	
Soft Drinks	Not published	
Edible Gelatine (Supplementary)	Not published	
*Synthetic Cream	1951	
*Artificial Cream	1951	
Fish Cakes (Supplementary)	Not published	

38

	Date of publication
*Saccharin and other sweetening tablets	1952
*Shredded Suet and Block Salt	1952
Coffee Mixtures (Supplementary)	Not published
Jam and Marmalade	1952
*Vitaminisation of Margarine	1954
†Sausages	1956 (No longer available)
†Processed Cheese and Cheese Spread	1956 (No longer available)
Ice Cream Standard	1957 (No longer available)
†Soft Drinks	1959 (No longer available)
Starch Syrup in Table Jellies	Not published
*Milk Bread	1959
†Bread and Flour	1960
†Hard, Soft and Cream Cheese	1962 (No longer available)
†Dried Milk	1962
†Canned Meat	1962
†Meat Pie	1963
†Food Labelling	1964
†Fish and Meat Pastes	1965
†Claims and Misleading Descriptions	1966
†Cream	1967
†Soups	1968
†Jams and Other Preserves	1969
†Condensed Milk	1969
†Pre-1955 Compositional Orders (Baking Powder and Golden Raising Powder, Edible Gelatine, Mustard, Curry Powder, Tomato Ketchup, Fish Cakes and Suet)	1970
†Offals in Meat Products	1972
*(Interim) Date-Marking of Food	1971
†Vinegars	1971
†Date-Marking of Food	1972
*Condensed Milk (Supplementary)	1973
†Bread and Flour (Second Report)	1974
†Novel Proteins	1975

	Date of publication
†Soft Drinks—Part I, Fruit Juices and Nectars	1975
†Yogurt	1975

*Printed and published by Her Majesty's Stationery Office. All these reports are priced.
†Available in duplicated form free from MAFF.

Introductory remarks by Professor Ward

In 1965, when I first became closely acquainted, as Chairman, with the work of the Food Standards Committee, we were engaged on one minor review, while a working group was preparing a draft report on claims and misleading descriptions. Today there are, at various stages, six major reviews in progress which include such significant topics as infant foods and food labelling, not to mention beer! We have a formidable task, which it is only possible to undertake through the aid given by our officials, assessors and colleagues in the food industry and elsewhere.

Three points from my paper merit underlining, because of their significance in the UK approach to the preparation of new or modified food laws, with which is associated the complex consultative process used to bring food regulations into being. The first point is that, although the subjects for review are laid down by Ministers, the Food Standards Committee carries out its reviews as an independent body, whose members draw on experience from industry, from nutrition and food science, from enforcement and from organizations of consumers. Common ground is reached by consideration of submissions and by discussions in which officials serving the Committee play a full part. So Reports, on publication, have the assent of all the Committee and also, in general, of the officials who have taken part.

Representations on Reports rarely commend acceptable conclusions and usually highlight points to which objection is taken. Lack of a balanced picture in these representations may lead to changes, at draft regulations stage, which in reality represent only a minority view. The safeguard against this is to make each representation on a Report (and indeed also on draft regulations) a balanced critique aimed at preserving acceptable provisions although, perhaps, opposing others. It is worth while also to add that submissions to the Committee itself achieve more readily their objectives if they state the full facts, together with the real difficulties and firmly held convictions of those submitting them. A 'made up' argument can discredit an entire submission, for the Committee is very experienced in detecting such cases.

The inevitably slow process of legislation—further complicated by EEC procedures—makes it essential to provide in legislation for future change.

This forms my second point and I would encourage the food industry to make clear its views on expected future changes in products or processes which the Committee should take into account. Often recommendations could be framed so as to accommodate a new process or new raw material if its impending introduction was known. Even where the future is difficult to foresee, the Committee aims to avoid unnecessary restriction. The use of informative labelling may obviate a need for compositional barriers to innovation and allow wider choice to the consumer.

Thirdly, the Committee is very conscious of the limited extent to which the ordinary consumer—perhaps in contrast to the consumerist—is aware of the work of the Committee and of the Ministries in safeguarding the quality, safety and nutritional value of foods. Only rarely, as with date-marking, do reports of the Committee feature in the press, on radio or on television. The Reports are now framed to inform the enquiring consumer about the foods being discussed, their raw materials and production processes, their place in the diet and those aspects of them worth regulating or recording on labels. They may well also inform some in industry, in enforcement or elsewhere about factors which are significant in proposing or opposing features which might be in new or changed legislation. The Committee can achieve little more on its own in informing the public—further steps are the responsibility of the industry, government and the consumer organizations.

The open publication of Reports, which are the product of an independent review by the Committee of some of the many problems arising in particular food legislation, are an invaluable step in securing protection for both consumers and honest and conscientious manufacturers and distributors and also in ensuring the continuation of the general assent and observance which our food laws receive.

41

Advising on Food Standards in the United Kingdom

2. Food Additives and Contaminants and the Role of the FACC

B C L Weedon

Chairman, Food Additives and Contaminants Committee

Introduction

The Food Additives and Contaminants Committee (FACC) was set up as a body in its own right towards the end of 1964, under the chairmanship of Professor R A Morton. Until that time Ministers had turned to the Food Standards Committee (FSC) for advice on additives and contaminants as well as on a variety of other topics. However, by 1964 it had become clear that the FSC was becoming fully occupied with food composition and labelling matters. Meanwhile, the UK food industry, which has always been in the forefront of developments in the field, was continuing to make rapid advances in technology, including the use of food additives, and consumer awareness and interest were increasing. In view of this mounting activity it had become obvious that a separate body was needed to devote its undivided attention and resources to the task of advising UK Ministers on food additives and contaminants. The Committee was, therefore, established and now has as its terms of reference:

'To advise the Minister of Agriculture, Fisheries and Food, the Secretary of State for Social Services, the Secretary of State for Scotland, and, as respects Northern Ireland, the Head of the Department of Health and Social Services, on matters referred to them by Ministers in relation to food contaminants, additives and similar substances which are, or may be, present in food or used in its preparation, with particular reference to the exercise of powers conferred on Ministers by Sections 4, 5 and 7 of the Food and Drugs Act 1955 and corresponding provisions in enactments relating to Scotland and Northern Ireland.'

So far as the scope of these terms of reference is concerned, it seems reasonable to assume that most people interested in the Committee's activities, and many 'laymen', would understand what is meant by the word 'contaminants'. It is probably unnecessary, therefore, to go further at this stage than to explain that the Committee normally deals with those chemical contaminants such as lead and arsenic that are not, as are pesticides and products used in veterinary medicine or animal husbandry, covered by other bodies. It does not deal with problems relating to the presence in food of foreign matter such as matchsticks, insects or rodent fragments. To circumscribe what is meant by the term 'additives' is more difficult. Attempts have been made in various circles, including international ones, to define the term, but it is extremely difficult to produce an ideal definition suitable for incorporation into UK legislation. Indeed, legislators in the UK have managed to avoid producing a definition of 'additive' and none is contained in current UK food additive regulations: instead, the regulations define the particular classes of additive being controlled (preservatives, anti-oxidants etc.). Thus, if a substance is capable of performing the functions of, for example, a preservative, it is subject to the provisions of the Preservative Regulations, unless it comes within any of the specified exemptions in these regulations. One of the difficulties is, of course, to decide where a food ends and an additive begins. Perhaps, in this respect, the problem is not eased by the fact that the definition of 'food' in the Food and Drugs Acts, under which the UK food additive regulations are made, embraces additives, since it includes 'articles and substances used as ingredients in the preparation of food'. But Section 4 of the 1955 Act, under which Ministers are empowered to make regulations, including those which flow from my Committee's recommendations, requires Ministers to have regard to the desirability of restricting, so far as practicable, the use of substances of *no nutritional value* as foods or as ingredients of foods. Although it would not be correct to say that food additives are invariably non-nutritional, and indeed the FACC is studying modified starches which, of course, have calorific value, food additives might be regarded in very general terms as substances which are added to food for purposes other than nutritional ones. It must, however, be stressed that this is only a rough and ready guide. The Committee's function regarding additives, as I see it, is to ensure that any substance which is not natural to a food, but which is added to food, is properly evaluated so that the interests of consumers and manufacturers are safeguarded; and it seems to me that those few words 'a substance which is not natural to a food, but which is added to it' represent in essence what is generally understood by 'an additive'.

Added chemicals in food

To be able to understand the control of food additives and contaminants, their development and use in food should be discussed. It is generally appreciated that many of our foods may contain 'chemicals' which were not intended by nature. As already indicated, 'chemicals', in this context refer in general to non-nutritive substances, and not the natural chemical constituents of the foods themselves. Both for sound economic reasons, and to meet the ever growing needs of an expanding world population, a great deal of effort is devoted to increasing food supplies and to avoiding wastage of sound foods. The use of food additives has an important role to play in this campaign. But, of course, this also means that fertilizers are now used on a far larger scale than ever before to grow more crops, and chemicals are widely employed to protect stocks of food from microbial spoilage, insect infestation, and rodent destruction. It has to be recognized that such uses may lead to the adventitious presence of 'added' chemicals in the final product.

In the developed countries substantial amounts of food are now pre-packed before sale, either for easy handling, general cleanliness, and attractive display, or to meet the demand for convenient ready prepared and frozen foods. Abrasion of the packing materials, or migration of chemicals from them, is another possible source of foreign substances to which considerable thought has been given recently. It is necessary only to recall the variety of chemicals used in the manufacture of plastics to realize the scope of this problem. These and related matters are to an increasing extent being highlighted as methods of analysis for the contaminants become ever more refined and sensitive. In some cases (and these are not restricted to constituents of food packaging) substances can be detected at levels as low as parts per thousand million. Such cases inevitably raise the question of the significance to human health of the very low levels of the substances detected.

The need for food additives

There is nothing new in the deliberate addition of chemicals to good food. Thousands of years ago the Chinese used ethylene and propylene produced by the combustion of kerosene to ripen bananas and peas, and pickling in salt, and fermentation processes resulting in the production of lactic acid, alcohol or acetic acid, are methods of food preservation that date from ancient times. But, of course, the world has changed considerably since those days and the reasons for using food additives today are many and varied. It may be helpful if I give some examples of current usage in the UK. Curing ham with brines containing nitrites and nitrates is a long-established process. The nitrites are at present considered to fulfil an essential role in the curing process, giving the ham a pleasing pink colour, which has been attributed to the conversion of myoglobin and haemoglobin into nitroso-derivatives. Of overriding importance, however, is the fact that they also prevent the development of *Clostridium botulinum*. If not checked, the growth of this micro-organism could result in the formation of toxins which are almost invariably fatal to the consumer.

Preservatives are now added to many foodstuffs to safeguard them from microbiological spoilage during transportation and storage. Antioxidants are widely used in oils and fats. Who would not rather eat a biscuit made with a shortening fat containing a small amount of butylated hydroxyanisole, or some other well tested antioxidant, than have to put up with a rancid flavour? And who would deny the need properly to ensure that sound food is not wasted? However, there is no case for the indiscriminate use of preservatives and antioxidants, and where possible it is far better to encourage the use of refrigeration and good handling techniques.

Artificial sweeteners are another form of additive in common use. In a society that is becoming increasingly weight conscious many people want a sweetening agent that will not add calories to their diet. Saccharin has long been used for this purpose—it is also cheaper than sugar and is suitable for use as a sweetener in a number of processed foods. For a time cyclamates were allowed in this country too but their use was prohibited as a precaution after tests in America cast doubts on its safety. The debate as to whether cyclamates are safe for use in food is, of course, still continuing—but that is another story! The fact is that the only artificial sweetener currently permitted in the UK is saccharin which is being kept under continuous review both here and in other parts of the world.

The appearance and taste of a foodstuff play a large part in determining its acceptability by the public. A nutritionally inert cellulose ether may therefore be added as an emulsifier to a bottled mayonnaise to prevent the constituents separating into layers on standing. Artificial colouring may also be used, for example to ensure that tinned peas look green and not a greyish brown, or to restore some of the colour to jam lost as a result of sulphiting and bleaching the pulp. Flavourings and flavour modifiers are also widely used in a whole range of processed foods.

It is said that, on the whole, the British public prefers a white loaf to wholemeal. Today much of the flour produced in the UK is treated with chlorine dioxide as a maturing and bleaching agent. Additional whiteness is achieved, if necessary, by bleaching with, for example, benzoyl peroxide. To improve the texture of the final product, much of our flour is also treated with improving agents—the commonest are based on ascorbic acid with either potassium bromate or potassium persulphate.

Reference must also be made to the differences, sometimes no doubt confusing to the discerning consumer, that exist between one country or region and another in the use of additives. It is sometimes said that there are more additives in food in the UK than in other countries—especially the other Member States of the EEC. This has by no means been shown to be correct, though it is true that additives are frequently used in different foods. These differences owe much to the different national traditions, dietary patterns and manufacturing techniques. Jam is a case in point. Bread and jam were for years the basis of the traditional British tea (although, with increasing affluence and the availability of an ever-increasing range of food the year round, this tradition appears to be declining) and the demand for jam as a cheap, ever-available, family food was high. The customary fruit ingredients (strawberries, raspberries etc.) have a short season and the UK jam industry therefore developed techniques for the non-seasonal production of this food, based on the use of sulphited pulp which could be economically stored. Production all the year round, based on fresh or frozen fruit, would be difficult, if not impossible, and would certainly be more expensive. On the Continent, however, traditions are different as far as jam consumption is concerned and their traditional manufacturing techniques differ accordingly.

Changing technology

In the food industry, as elsewhere, technology is making rapid advances. Food additives have an important part to play in this and I can perhaps illustrate their impact in the important sectors of the food and drink industry. In bread-making, for instance, traditional methods have to a large extent been replaced by mechanical dough development processes such as the Chorleywood Bread Process. Recently, increased interest has been shown in new improvers, e.g., azodicarbonimide, and some bakers have indicated that they would like to adopt entirely new processes of chemically assisted dough development, for example, that involving L-cysteine, which would avoid the need for expensive mechanical equipment and provide a very rapid method of producing batches of bread to meet a sudden demand. The FACC gave very careful consideration to representations concerning the use of these substances during its Review of Additives in Bread and Flour, and Ministers have accepted my Committee's recommendation as in the Committee's Report, published in 1974 with the Food Standards Committee's Second Report on Bread and Flour, that these improving agents should be permitted. Another area where there have been marked changes is brewing. Traditionally beer was produced locally for consumption within a few days. Today, brewing is largely centralized and beer must withstand transportation and storage. Though pasteurization is commonly used this is not entirely suitable for large batches and can lead to off-flavours. The use of additives is therefore advocated in some quarters. The FACC is currently evaluating all the additives which are used in beer and we hope to report on this subject next year.

Although the benefits of additives may not always be immediately apparent to or understood by the general public, most experts accept that some additives are technologically necessary in a modern food industry. It is also a fact that changes in society, such as the tendency for more wives to go out to work, are reflected in an ever-increasing range of convenience foods, the production of many of which involves the use of additives. We are becoming much more accustomed to having available throughout the year foods which used to be available only to a privileged few at a high price or were obtainable by most people only seasonally. These factors must not be forgotten. On the other hand, it is equally important not to forget that, although the amounts of additives used are usually very small, they are likely to be consumed over long periods and, cumulatively, they may become significant. This is obviously a situation which calls for careful surveillance and control.

The role of the FACC

Before explaining how the FACC operates it may be useful, by way of background, to return to the provisions of the Food and Drugs Act 1955. Section 1 of the 1955 Act makes it an offence to sell for human consumption any food to which substances have been added or which has been processed in such a way as to render it injurious to health; and Section 4 requires Ministers to have regard to the desirability of restricting, so far as practicable, the use of substances of no nutritional value. In the broadest terms, I see the FACC's main function in the context of these two provisions; that is to say, the Committee is responsible for evaluating substances in relation to safety and need.

It is an important feature of the legislative framework that the general provisions of the Acts can be, and have been, supplemented by regulations. These generally contain a 'permitted list' of additives which is likely to be of help to enforcement authorities and the Courts in interpreting the provisions of the Act as regards hazards to health. In practice, these regulations are based on the recommendations contained in FACC reports, subject to any representations received following publication of the reports. The Committee is consequently very conscious of the fact, when framing its recommendations, that these may well be given effect in the law of the land. My experience suggests that responsible food manufacturers generally welcome the making of food additives regulations, since, by doing so, the Ministers are, in effect, defining areas wherein the trade may operate without running foul of the general provisions laid down by Section 1.

Although the general philosophy under which we operate is set out in a published paper 'Memorandum on Procedure for Submissions on Food Additives and on Methods of Toxicity Testing', the factors to be considered in the evaluation of the acceptability of food additives and contaminants are complex, numerous and varied, not least because of the rapid strides in technology made by the food industry in the UK. It is therefore important that the Committee should be able to command the proper expertise to cope with all the problems that arise. Members do, in fact, bring to the Committee a wide range of expertise. All members are appointed by Ministers as individuals and not as representatives of any sectional interest—and it should be borne in mind that they and their families are all consumers and, as such, are by no means immune from the consequences of the advice they give to Ministers! At the risk of appearing over-defensive, this fact should be stressed because it is sometimes suggested that in food safety matters the consumer's voice is drowned by the noise of industry! This cannot be accepted. Apart from their common role as consumers, individual members are highly qualified to offer advice on one or more of a variety of relevant subjects which include food technology, chemical analysis, enforcement problems, biochemistry, organic chemistry and, to a certain extent, medical matters, although on these matters the FACC turns for advice to the DHSS Toxicity sub-Committee and the Committee on Medical Aspects of Chemicals in Food and the Environment and other expert bodies under the aegis of DHSS. In addition, some members have considerable direct experience of the many and varied problems in the food manufacturing and chemical industries, which are, of course, affected by the recommendations of the Committee.

So far as contaminants are concerned, the aim of the FACC is to encourage good agriculture, manufacturing and handling techniques so as to eliminate contamination of food as far as possible, or to reduce to a minimum the quantities that are unavoidable by setting limits as low as practicable. Legal limits have been set for the amounts of arsenic and lead that may be present in food generally. The Committee has recently completed a review of the Lead in Food Regulations and the report should be published fairly soon.

With additives, the aim is to produce statutory permitted lists of all classes of additives and thus erect a protective fence which, when completed, will mean that no additive which is not on one of the permitted lists may be added to food. At present, statutory permitted lists exist for antioxidants, artificial sweeteners, colouring matters, emulsifiers and stabilizers, preservatives and solvents, and for some 13 other classes of additives grouped together as miscellaneous additives. In addition, there are legislative controls on the use of mineral hydrocarbons for food purposes and on the use of additives in certain commodities, such as bleaching and improving agents in flour. There are two significant gaps in the fence: flavourings, of which it has been estimated that over 2000 are in use, and a further miscellaneous group of substances used as ingredients in the preparation of food, including, for example, enzymes and flavour modifiers. The Committee has completed its report on flavourings which is now with the printers, and is currently reviewing the remaining miscellaneous group.

It is not the intention that permitted lists should be handed down like the tablets of stone from Mount Sinai; it is proposed to carry out a complete review of each class of additives at intervals of about five years. Once a topic has been chosen for review and referred by Ministers to the FACC, comments and evidence are invited from all interested parties. The Committee has no facilities for toxicological testing and therefore relies on critical examinations of the reports of work carried out principally by the Research Associations and industrial and academic laboratories both at home and abroad.

For each additive the FACC has to be satisfied that there is a definite technological need that could not be met equally well by the use of an alternative, currently permitted substance, or by the employment of different production techniques which would obviate the need for additives; that the use of the additive does not constitute a hazard to health; and that satisfactory specifications for defining the purity standards of the substance for food use are available. Before arriving at a conclusion the FACC carefully weighs all the representations received and, if necessary, will seek advice from one of the Research Associations or invite representatives from industry to present further information. Particularly careful consideration must be given to the question of safety. The FACC seeks advice on the safety-in-use of food additives and on the implications for health of the presence of contaminants in food from the medical experts on the various committees and sub-committees of the DHSS. When sent to the Minister, the FACC's report normally includes the report of the Toxicity sub-Committee or other DHSS sub-Committees with reference to the biological tests which have been taken into consideration. Recommendations are made for each additive requested in the industrial submissions, a specification is given for each substance which is recommended for approval, and, where appropriate, limits are proposed on the amount that may be added to food. All these points are dealt with in the Committee's reports, which are normally published by Her Majesty's Stationery Office without commitment to Ministers. The issue of the reports is widely publicized by press notice and representations are invited on the recommendations contained in them. The door is not, therefore, firmly shut on anyone who failed to bring his problems to the Committee's attention during the review. Indeed, the process contains a further safeguard, because representations are subsequently invited on the detailed proposals for regulations arising from the Committee's reports. The representations received at all stages of this procedure are very carefully considered by the Committee, who are quite prepared, if the situation warrants such action, to modify their initial recommendations. It can be seen, therefore, that there is considerable consultation, at each stage, with all interested parties. It means that there is almost invariably a time lag between the announcement of a review of a particular class of additive, or the submission of an application to allow a 'new' additive, and the introduction of any consequential regulations. But the consultation arrangements are an integral part of the procedure and I would not wish to see any short cuts taken.

The use of many additives dates from a period when toxicological testing was neither required nor routine. If, in the view of the FACC and the TSC, there are inadequate toxicological data, the Committee's report will identify the areas in which further work is needed and may stress that, unless the work is carried out within a reasonable period, the Committee would find it hard to recommend continued use of the substance in question. The recent action to withdraw permission to use the colour Orange RN illustrates the consequences of further work not being undertaken.

Even long established practices must be included in any review and critically reassessed in the light of new information and advances in biological testing. For example, the use of nitrites and nitrates in the production of some foods, and the implications that this practice has for the formation of nitrosamines, are the subject of a comprehensive programme of research recommended by the Committee and financed to a considerable extent by the Government.

When an entirely new additive is proposed, adequate toxicological testing is required before its use is authorized. The FACC can sometimes help industry by giving a provisional decision at an early stage on the need for a proposed new additive. The biological tests necessary to clear the new additive may well run into many thousands of pounds and it will be a waste of money and facilities to carry out this work if the additive is to be turned down in any case on the ground of inadequate need.

From time to time, consideration may have to be given to an individual additive outside the general review of the relevant class. This may result from the necessity to assess at once new toxicological information on one of the currently permitted additives. In very exceptional circumstances, when a great deal of public concern has been aroused, as in the case of cyclamates, it has proved possible for advice to be provided to Ministers in time to enable them to announce their decision within 48 hours of the new toxicological data being received in London. In such a case, fortunately rare, the advisers are not seeking to prove to everyone's satisfaction that a particular substance is safe or not. They are advising Ministers on the execution of their statutory duties under the conditions prevailing at the time. In doing so they must use their judgment in evaluating all the information available to them, both published and unpublished. If a genuine doubt exists that cannot be resolved quickly, they will naturally regard the safety of the public as the overriding consideration. It should be stressed that at all times members of the FACC act as independent experts and are certainly never subject to manipulation by politicians or commercial interests. Ministers are not obliged to wait for their advice, and they can accept or reject it as they see fit.

Relationship with other Committees

The FACC takes advice from other bodies in their reviews. As has been mentioned, the Toxicity sub-Committee provides advice on safety-in-use, and advice may also be sought from MAFF's Working Party on the Monitoring of Foodstuffs for Heavy Metals which has produced extremely valuable reports on lead, mercury and cadmium in food. But the FACC also gives advice, as will be clear from Professor Ward's paper and from the reference to the review of additives in bread and flour. Indeed the FACC works very closely with the Food Standards Committee on some reviews. Other examples are the reviews of beer and infant foods where the FACC offers advice on the acceptability of certain substances.

International bodies

Since the UK's accession to the EEC the FACC has been called upon to provide advice on the implications for UK consumers of proposals in EEC draft legislation. This is a task which may become increasingly important. The EEC has recently established its own Scientific Committee for Food, of which Dr. P Elias of DHSS and I were both founder members. The main purpose of this Committee is to make recommendations to the EEC Commission on the toxicology of food additives and contaminants, in order to assist the Commission and ultimately the Member States in the drawing up of EEC legislation designed to harmonize provisions on food additives and contaminants throughout the EEC. It will be appreciated, however, that the establishment of the EEC Scientific Committee for Food, an important development in itself, does not in any way diminish the need for Ministers to have independent advice on factors relating to our own national situations and the particular needs of consumers and industries within the UK.

Another international body of importance is the Joint FAO/WHO Expert Committee on Food Additives. This body, which comprises recognized international experts in various scientific and medical fields, normally meets once a year to evaluate the latest information on food additives and to assess their safety-in-use. The reports produced by the Joint Expert Committee and the data which it draws together during its work provide valuable guidelines for national committees such as the FACC, although it is of course for the national committees to interpret the significance of the data produced in the context of all the relevant national factors, such as dietary patterns and intakes of particular foods.

Recent and current reviews and future problems

When the present review of flavourings and the remaining classes of additives used as ingredients in the preparation of foods is complete we should be some way towards closing the gap in the 'additives regulation fence'. The way will then be clearer ahead for the transfer of all statutory classes of permitted additives to an all embracing 'Additives in Food Regulations', an innovation which should make matters easier for all those with interest in additives legislation.

I have already mentioned some of the subjects on which the Committee is currently working. These include reviews of additives in infant foods and in beer, a review of modified starches, a review of solvents in food and a review of arsenic in food. Work has recently been completed on our reviews of flavourings, the Mineral Hydrocarbons in Food Regulations and the Lead in Food Regulations. One of the more difficult tasks currently facing the Committee is the review of the Colouring Matter in Food Regulations. Among the questions that the FACC have to examine is whether to recommend restrictions on the use of colours, in place of the almost total freedom to use colours in any food which exists at present. The toxicological data which have emerged in recent times suggest that there may be a need to restrict the intake of some colours. This in turn would call for a very careful evaluation of the 'need' for colours in particular foods, a subject which provokes considerable differences of opinion. All told, it is proving to be a difficult exercise, but one which must be faced. Although the final outcome must not be pre-judged, it seems possible that a very different situation will emerge on food colours in the future in the light of all the new data which have emerged since the last full review.

There will undoubtedly be many other problems in the future requiring the attention of the FACC. However, I am confident that they will all be resolved, knowing as I do the hard work which the members of the Committee, and the officials who serve it, willingly undertake in the public interest.

Appendix
Reports on Food Additives and Contaminants

a. By the Food Standards Committee

	Date of publication
Arsenic	1950
Arsenic (Supplementary)	1951
Lead	1951
Copper	1951
†Tin in Canned Food	1952
Fluorine	1953
Antioxidants	1953
†Zinc	1954
*Antioxidants (Revised Report)	1954
Antimony and Cadmium	Not published
*Lead (Revised Report)	1954
*Colouring Matters	1955
*Arsenic (Revised Report)	1955
*Colouring Matters (Supplementary)	1955
*Copper (Revised Report)	1956
*Emulsifying and Stabilizing Agents	1956
*Fluorine (Revised Report)	1957
*Preservatives in Food	1959
Preservatives in Food (Supplementary)	Not published
Citrus Red	Not published
*Mineral Oil in Food	1962
Limits for Arsenic + Lead in Yeast + Yeast Products	Not published
Antioxidants	1963
*Colouring Matters	1964
*Flavouring Agents	1965

b. By the Food Additives and Contaminants Committee

†Antioxidants (Supplementary)	1965
*Solvents	1966

*Printed and published by Her Majesty's Stationery Office.
†Available from MAFF.

Discussion

Mr. T V N Fortescue (Secretary General, Food and Drink Industries Council): My Lord Chairman, no one could remain entirely undaunted by the prospect of following two such distinguished Professors on the hallowed ground of the Royal Institution. I should like to say that the two speeches we have just heard were certainly of the nature, substance and quality demanded.

I am once again reminded of the extraordinary good fortune that we have in this country, and I think in the whole Continent of Europe, in having such eminent and dedicated men to chair the committees which look after all our work. It is an arduous task, it is a task which I think nobody envies, and they always shoulder it with the utmost goodwill and the utmost industry.

Speakers this morning have all, I think, paid tribute to the part which the food industry plays in these matters and they have told us that the food industry has been co-operative in the extreme. It has, of course, not always been so. I am reminded irresistibly of the recent changes brought about by the Appeal Court in the British law on rape. Under this new ruling, which has been questioned in legislative circles, a man accused of rape is able to prove his innocence if he states that he believed in all honesty that the lady concerned, when she said no, really meant yes. I am sure that throughout our history the food industry has often said no to proposals brought in by our legislators on food safety matters, but those legislators, with the utmost good sense, have always concluded that we really meant yes. And that is indeed the case.

We now have the position that an offence is very rarely committed.

I should like to draw your attention, Sir, to the anomaly that in this room we have many representatives of the food industry to celebrate— I emphasize the word—a century of control. Control is not the sort of thing that industrialists really like, and the fact that we are here in considerable numbers and listening with such attention surely means that the controls have been sensible and they have been acceptable.

However, there is one aspect of this situation which I think is worthy of remark. That is that, both in Whitehall and in Brussels—our new masters— there are powerful elements which look after the fortunes of agriculture, and there are equally powerful elements which look after the fortunes of consumers, but the food industry, which accounts for 70 per cent of food sales to consumers, is squeezed in the middle and has no strong voice to speak for it. We know that in this country we have a Ministry of Agriculture, Fisheries and Food, and that is the case I believe in Germany but in no other country in the Community.

We are faced on the one hand by rising costs of our raw materials and imports and, on the other hand, with price controls on behalf of the consumers. I should like to suggest that perhaps the time has come after 100 years for the emphasis of the food legislators to shift a little from controls and inhibitions towards care for the benefit and encouragement of the food industry. We are not complaining about the controls, as I say, especially when they are in the hands of such men as Professors Ward and Weedon, but we also need a little encouragement if the people are to continue to be fed. I should like to think that there are people in Whitehall and Brussels who are thinking along those lines.

Finally, tributes have been paid by everyone this morning to the good sense, co-operation and responsibility of the food industry and I am proud to think that that should be so. We do have in our possession, however, a paper from the Director of the Consumer Association which raises a lot of the old hares about the wickedness of the food manufacturer. This will be discussed tomorrow and I am sure that many comments will be made. However, I would just point out that always, throughout our history, there have been people who have taken pride, honestly, in saying to consumers— we used to call them 'customers', but they are now 'consumers'—that what they like is bad for them and that they should stop eating it because, although it does not do them any harm, it is immoral. Perhaps pre-eminent among them in our history were the Puritans of the seventeenth century, and I would draw your attention, Sir, to what Oliver Cromwell said to his own back-benchers. Oliver Cromwell, of course, was a master of the polemic style in the English language, and he said to his Puritans, 'I beseech you Gentlemen, in the bowels of Christ, think it possible that you may be mistaken.'

Thank you.

Mr. K J Gardner (Product Services Manager, Mars Ltd): My Lord Chairman, Professor Ward stated that he sometimes had difficulty in finding out what the real consumer feels about foods which his Committee are considering. In industry we do not have this difficulty; they just stop buying our stuff if we get it wrong. To save us from getting it wrong we use market research. I wonder if Professor Ward has thought of trying that for his purposes?

Professor A G Ward: We have on occasions had access to consumer research reports from industry in the areas with which we have been dealing. These reports are directed at specific purposes and do not always answer the sort of questions that the Committee would wish to ask. Such answers could only be obtained from a comparable survey actually directed to the specific ends. In the past there have never been financial resources available for this purpose and I hardly think that the present moment is the one at which to ask for them.

Professor J B M Coppock (Spillers Ltd): Could I make a comment about the EEC legislation from the industry's point of view? I think that most of us have thoroughly enjoyed for many years the consultative process which Mr. Giles mentioned this morning and which Professor Ward and Professor Weedon have underlined. In industry we have been very fortunate, I believe, in being able to consult, first of all, with either the Food Standards Committee or the Food Additives and Contaminants Committee. They then issue a report and ask for comment, which is freely given even if it is not always constructive, as Professor Ward has hinted. At least we tell them what we do not like. Those reports are then considered by the Ministry and they emerge either in the form of draft regulations or in more formal regulations, but again we have the opportunity to comment, and quite often we have a second opportunity to comment on a re-draft of the final regulations. This is all good.

When we get into the EEC process of law we are in a greater dilemma. As was said by Mr. Giles, we have to go through our trade associations and our trade association contacts and we then find, when they can no longer argue for us, that the only people who are able to argue for us are Government officials.

The question I want to ask is this: Professor Weedon has indirectly mentioned some of the problems we have with colours, for example—some of the people in France do not believe that we need brown colours for kippers;

they cannot understand why we eat kippers—and many other things of the same sort are not understood in western Europe and the EEC countries which are fully understood here. Do the two Chairmen think that in due course they might find a new part of their fulfilment in finding out, as they now do, from British manufacturers and the British public what they enjoy, and letting that be the basis of information which may be given to the officials who are going to the EEC to fight our case?

I think myself that there is a greater need for these two Committees than ever before, because they can act as a line of communication officially to the EEC which, so far as I can see, no other country has available to it. I should like to know whether the two Chairmen regard themselves and their Committees as ultimately being able to fulfil this function.

Professor A G Ward: The answer is that this is already current practice to some extent. If I could refer to a Directive which was quoted before, the Cocoa and Chocolate Directive, in order that our officials negotiating in a rather tricky situation in relation to this Directive could indicate what was the common viewpoint between industry and the consumer in this country, a very rapid review was carried out by the Food Standards Committee. It produced a report which could not, on this occasion, be published although it was made available to the main trade and consumer associations that had been interested in the problem. This report, as I understand it and as I was informed, served as a useful strengthening for the viewpoint common to both British consumer and manufacturing organizations.

It is now the practice of the Ministry, when particularly tricky areas in relation to negotiations for a directive are under way, to refer certain points to the Committee, and the Committee has been willing to do its best to provide answers, which reflect the range of knowledge and experience of the Committee.

The danger, from the Committee's point of view, is in the time scale, because the Committee's normal procedure involving very full consultation is a protracted process. For the Committee to be expected in a very short period to produce authoritative views on some of the complex issues involved is a difficult matter, but certainly the concept which I think Professor Coppock has in mind exists at least in embryo and is developing in the relationship between officials and the Committee. It is part of the changing function certainly of the Food Standards Committee and, I suspect, also for the Food Additives Committee.

Professor B C L Weedon: Mr. Chairman, may I add a few words to what Professor Ward has said in reply to Professor Coppock?

I think that in this country we are particularly fortunate because we have a well-established system of reviewing various areas and issuing reports from the Food Standards Committee and the Food Additives and Contaminants Committee. These reports carry a great deal of weight, as has been suggested by other speakers, in many parts of the world. It does mean that, with the review we try to have, the people who go to Brussels to discuss these matters with their counterparts in Europe are pretty well briefed as to what the situation is, what the demands are back home, what the needs of British industry are, and what are the preferences of the British consumer. That is not true in every case, of course. Some of the reviews are out of date where they have not been subject to the normal five-year review process, but by and large our people do go pretty well informed. Inevitably some questions do come up and then they are referred to the Committee, in the way that Professor Ward has described, and sometimes the Committee will make direct contact with industry.

Professor Coppock also referred to the question of colours, and there is a special situation here. When this country and the other new members joined the Community there was a special derogation from the Treaty of Rome permitting this and the other new member countries to continue using certain colours until a specific date, and to continue banning other colours until a specific date. These dates are rapidly getting closer, in fact the first of them falls due this December. Therefore, one of the urgent duties of the Scientific Committee for Food, for example, was to review the situation pertaining to colours in food and to arrive at some conclusion before this December. As you all know, the Scientific Committee for Food in Brussels has recently issued a report making its proposals for a revision of the Colours Directive. It is no coincidence that, 12 months ago, it was announced that there would be a review of the Colours in Food Regulations in this country, and this exercise went into operation straightaway and was of enormous value to those of us who were engaged in the discussions in Brussels.

In that sort of way it is sometimes possible to update the information. However, the question of colours having been raised, I think I should emphasize one aspect of the recent discussions in Brussels. It was necessary in Brussels to review the provisions of the Directive. This lists the compounds, the colours, which are acceptable for use in food. It does not list, with one or two very specific exceptions, the commodities in which they may be used. So Professor Coppock's question, for example, of whether kippers should be gold, or whether jam should be red or not, was not raised in the report. The report from Brussels specifically says that they are considering at this stage the safety of the compounds involved rather than the way in which they would be used. The latter question is a matter which at this time is left principally to national legislation although I suspect that, in due course, there may be proposals for Commodity Directives in Brussels in which it will be raised again. However, before that happens I very much hope that we shall have collected from industry and consumers in this country a great deal more information which will again guide the United Kingdom representatives when the topic is discussed in Brussels.

Miss M Corbridge (National Dairy Council): Hearing the discussion this morning, I am reminded to some extent of a meeting I attended in Northern Ireland not so long ago, where one of the consumer representatives in Brussels was talking about the way in which we refer to the consumer and not the customer. Mr. Fortescue has said that we no longer talk about the customer but about the consumer. I think that on this occasion we are, perhaps rightly, giving the food industry and the Ministry of Agriculture a pat on the back this morning because of the excellent legislation that has been produced and carried through in order to protect the consumer, but I wonder to what extent the customer is aware of this. Looking around this hall this morning I think there is no doubt at all that everyone is a consumer, but I doubt very much whether more than a handful are actual customers. By 'customers' I mean housewives. I think it is desperately important that all we are saying this morning should get across to the customer, to the housewife, and this is where education plays an important role. I should like to see the customers knowing a little more about the work of these committees.

Professor A G Ward: Very briefly, I did not in the few minutes I had to talk about the topics perhaps do full justice to the very strong views held within the Food Standards Committee on this issue. From time to time we include in reports, and in other comments, requests for action to inform the public on the provisions of the food laws. Although it is true that the food manufacturing industry is on the whole fairly well informed on legislative matters, it is not only the customer that needs this information. There is another sector of the food industry, that is the catering industry, where I suspect that the majority of practitioners in this industry know very little about their obligations under food law. They are equally as responsible for the food they sell as the food manufacturer. So there is more than one area here, but I would agree entirely with the need for information to be widely disseminated.

Professor B C L Weedon: I think that one of the consequences of being Chairman of one of these Committees is that, increasingly, one is being asked to give talks which are semi-public. For example, I talk fairly soon now to teachers of domestic science in Bournemouth. In ways such as this we can contribute to the process of spreading information.

60

However, there is another change that is coming in the near future. Increasingly in the reports we are drafting we are tending to add appendices so as to explain the background to some of the more technical points that have been discussed in the report itself. I hope that this, too, will help to promote a more informed discussion by various public bodies and members of the general public.

Mr. D J W Mills (County Councillor, South Yorkshire County Council): We have heard a lot about the communication art being most essential, which it is, and the first speaker this morning referred to the fact that the label is the most important communicator in the piece. Does the Committee really spend enough time on considering the terminology used on these labels? I am certain that the average housewife, if she could be persuaded to spend the time to read it, would be as wise when she had finished as when she started.

Professor A G Ward: This is, of course, a difficult question. The Food Standards Committee has currently under review the whole food labelling area and is considering submissions from various quarters. The problem is that there are certain items which the housewife or the purchaser sees, or at least can readily see, on the label. There is other information which has to be there to inform those who really seek it. It may be argued that the list of ingredients is almost never looked at by the purchaser, but there are some purchasers who wish to see in detail what is conveyed there and the exact terms in which it is conveyed. If you reduce the exactness of the terms you may defeat the object for that particular group of the population. However, it is in the main items, such as the appropriate designation on the label and perhaps a declaration of the content of key constituents, that there is an opportunity to give greater information in a clear way which the purchaser is able to appreciate.

Food Safety: A Century of Progress

Chief Medical Officer, Department of Health and Social Security

From early in the nineteenth century the role of the Local Authorities in securing a safe food supply began to expand; in those days the emphasis was on the prevention of adulteration of food and on the detection of organoleptically unacceptable food. The science of bacteriology did not then exist and food poisoning was considered to be due to ptomaines formed in decomposing food. At that time however the conditions that we now describe as bacterial food poisoning were probably of little importance in comparison with the morbidity and mortality from diseases such as tuberculosis, typhoid fever, dysentery and cholera, which were spread both by polluted food and water and by personal contact in the squalid and overcrowded living conditions prevalent in towns and cities at that time. In 1849 the death rate in the City of London was 28 per thousand of the population and it was estimated that over 20 per cent of the deaths were due to such diseases. It is difficult to say which factor played the greatest part in their propagation. In 1867 Pasteur's work began to lay the foundations of bacteriology; none the less belief in the theory of ptomaine poisoning did not eventually die until the early part of the twentieth century.

The Sale of Food and Drugs Act 1875 is concerned with the adulteration of food and its contamination with foreign substances. There was no realization at that time of the need to protect food against the risk of microscopic bacterial contamination, and, though powers to inspect food and to seize unsound food were given to the Medical Officer of Health or the Sanitary Officer of the Local Authority by the Public Health Act of the same year, unsoundness was only recognized as visible gross contamination or decomposition. After 1875 there was certainly a reduction in the incidence of infectious disease, but I do not think that one can claim that the provisions of the Sale of Food and Drugs Act, or the provisions relating to food in the Public Health Act, played anywhere as great a part in this success as did other measures stemming from the Public Health Act, such as improvement of sewers, housing and the water supply.

In 1884 Johne investigated an outbreak of food poisoning in Lauterbach, in which three people died after eating meat from a cow that had itself died from enteritis. He isolated an organism pathogenic to mice. In 1885 Salmon

62

and Theobald Smith discovered an organism in pigs, *Salmonella choleraesuis*, but did not connect this with disease in man. In Jena in 1888 Gaertner isolated the organism now known as *Salmonella enteritidis* from the spleen of a patient who had died in an outbreak of food poisoning that affected 58 people. They had eaten meat from a cow slaughtered because of persistent diarrhoea, and the organism was also isolated from the flesh and blood vessels of the cow. In 1890 Ballard compiled for the Local Government Board an important summary of what was then known about food poisoning, in which he stressed the role of infecting organisms, and Savage in the Reports of the Medical Officer to the Local Government Board from 1906 to 1910 emphasized the importance of the salmonella group of organisms. In 1894 Denys recognized staphylococcal food poisoning and in 1895 Van Ermingen described *Clostridium botulinum*.

By the time of the Great War of 1914–1918, contamination with bacteria was well established as the cause of food poisoning, and food manufacturers, particularly canners, were following procedures deliberately designed to achieve and maintain good standards of hygiene and safety. In the whole of the war, though immense quantities of preserved food were consumed by the troops, only one outbreak of food poisoning was recorded. It occurred in 1918 in a base in France and involved over 1000 cases; a carrier of *Salmonella typhimurium* may well have caused the trouble. In 1921 the Ministry of Health issued several advisory memoranda to Medical Officers of Health on the investigation of food poisoning outbreaks and around that time numerous detailed bacteriological studies were published. Local Authority control of food safety generally continued to be exercised under powers given by the 1875 and later Public Health Acts. There were, however, Orders made under the Milk and Dairies (Amendment) Act 1922 which was directed at the prevention of milk-borne tuberculosis, by empowering Local Authorities to issue licences to milk producers to sell milk designated as certified, pasteurized, tuberculin tested etc. and laying down the conditions under which these licences could be granted. These Orders provided the first example of a direct application of specific bacteriology to food legislation. Other Orders relate to the sanitation of dairies and equipment used in the handling, conveyance and distribution of milk.

The Food and Drugs Act 1938 was largely a consolidating Act, drawing together fragments from numerous previous Acts, but it did serve to bring measures for control of food hygiene within the ambit of food rather than public health legislation. It also made food poisoning notifiable for the first time in the country as a whole (in the County of London food poisoning had been notifiable since 1936 under the Public Health (London) Act of that year). By the close of the nineteenth century most of the diseases which are now classed as infectious had been made notifiable either under the Public Health Act of 1875 or under later legislation.

Under the powers of the Food and Drugs Act 1938 and various Emergency Powers Acts from 1939 to 1954, a large number of Regulations were made dealing with chemical contamination of food and a rather smaller number relating to bacterial contamination. A number of these were made to deal with specific problems, such as an ice cream-borne typhoid outbreak in Aberystwyth in 1946, which led to the Ice Cream (Heat Treatment etc.) Regulations 1947. These laid down strict procedures for the manufacture of ice cream, following which it has been among the safest of our foodstuffs. Section 15 of the 1938 Act did however give Local Authorities general powers to make Byelaws concerning sanitary conditions of food on sale for human consumption. Since 1955 we have had the very comprehensive Food and Drugs Act, which continues to work well. One of its many notable features is the powers that it gives the Minister of Agriculture, Fisheries and Food and the Secretary of State for Social Services to make Regulations about food hygiene. These powers have been used to make Regulations that govern the hygienic standards in slaughterhouses, in docks, in markets, mobile shops, stalls and food delivery vehicles, and in food premises generally. Milk hygiene is catered for separately under special powers relating to milk and dairies. Also the powers of the Act to regulate processing and treatment of food have been used to deal with specific problems, for example the Liquid Egg Pasteurization Regulations 1963, which were prompted by the occurrence of paratyphoid in association with liquid egg.

Food Hygiene Regulations are usually couched in general terms that can be applied to a multiplicity of trades and circumstances. They do not attempt to enforce numerical microbiological standards. Specific problems in areas of high risk such as liquid egg, ice cream manufacture, the milk and dairy industry, have been dealt with as they arose. Strict requirements are imposed for handling and processing of such foodstuffs, and to check routinely that proper procedures have been followed, simple biological tests are used, such as the Alpha Amylase Test for liquid egg and the Phosphatase Test for milk.

Quantitative or qualitative microbiological tests are undoubtedly of great value as a check on the effectiveness of hygienic methods, as an aid to quality control, in the examination of suspect food and in the investigation of outbreaks of food poisoning. However in this country microbiological standards have not been incorporated in legislation because it has been felt that on the whole it is not feasible to impose statutory maximum permitted levels for microbial contaminants of food, as has been done for chemical contaminants such as lead or arsenic. None the less, in some countries there is a growing interest in the use of guidelines for the microbiological quality of food and much work has been done in the World Health Organization and other international organizations. We, in association with others in the EEC and the Codex Alimentarius, are examining the need for and the applicability of such criteria for certain foods.

In 1939 there were reports of 83 incidents of food poisoning in England and Wales involving 94 people. Following the start of the Second World War the number of reports rose rapidly, reaching a peak in 1955 when 8961 outbreaks were reported involving about 20 000 people. Although the recorded figures can only be based on those cases that are recognized and reported, probably considerably fewer than the true total, none the less a change of this magnitude would seem likely to reflect a true increase, particularly since it was associated with a radical change in our eating habits since the start of the war; far more meals are eaten which have not been prepared in the home, e.g., at a restaurant or from a 'take away' establishment, and both housewives and caterers make much greater use of completely or partially pre-cooked 'convenience' foods. There is need for the maintenance of high standards of hygiene in all food premises but particularly in catering establishments, where the customer is especially vulnerable.

The policy in this country has always been that the onus to provide sound food lies with the manufacturer or trader. Microbiological control has not been seen to be practicable in every shop, store and vehicle involved in the food trade and the emphasis has been placed on education in proper hygienic principles, enforced where necessary by law. The years following the passing of the 1955 Food and Drugs Act and the introduction of the 1955 Food Hygiene Regulations saw the number of reported incidents of food poisoning decline to 3184 involving 7907 people in 1964. However, since that time there has been a slight increase. We do not feel that this is due to the failure of our principles of food hygiene legislation, but that it points to a need for stricter enforcement, which is difficult at the present time owing to the limited numbers of Environmental Health Officers. While many local authorities play an important part in the training of these officers there is still a significant proportion that do not take students. It is clearly important that all local authorities that are able should take part in the training of Environmental Health Officers in order to increase their numbers.

Our policy of placing the emphasis on the maintenance of standards of food hygiene rather than on microbiological controls means that, first and foremost, we must look to education in food hygiene, training of food handlers and their employers so that the standards will be maintained even though the workers are not immediately under the eye of the Environmental Health Officer, and education of the whole public so that on the one hand they will themselves observe hygienic practices and on the other they will be aware

65

of lapses in food hygiene in others and will be encouraged to bring these to the notice of the local Department of Environmental Health.

When considering the aspect of food safety concerned with the presence of chemicals in food, be these intentional additives or unintentional contaminants, we may note equally important progress over the past 100 years. Modern society, with its large urban communities, faces the need to provide adequate supplies of food, to ensure their availability and safety and so meet increasingly sophisticated consumer demands. This necessitates depots carrying sufficient stocks and arrangements to preserve food with minimum loss during importation, transportation and storage. As an increasing section of the population obtains greater opportunities for leisure, the demands are rising for new dietary concepts, for more manufactured convenience foods and for less slavery behind the kitchen stove. These social pressures have resulted in an unparalleled rise in the use of food additives, both intentional and unintentional, to meet the modern technological demands on food production and the consumer pressure for diversification, convenience of preparation, improved quality, better appearance and novel textures and tastes. This brings in its wake an expanding problem related to nutritional aspects and the safety of large populations potentially at risk from mishaps or malpractices. Hence controls are in the interest of public health and ultimately protect the consumer. However, they can only become fully effective if supplemented by responsible attitudes in the food industry and by education of the public in the proper use of food.

Historically, fresh and natural foodstuffs have always been assumed to be pure, sound and health giving. Today we know this to be wrong on occasions. Yet chemicals have been added to food in one way or another for thousands of years. Food additives are therefore not new and must have caused man to evolve some adaptive mechanisms to these substances. The use of fire to smoke meat for preservation, fermentation and pickling in salt, honey, wine and spices for similar purposes and the Chinese practice of using ethylene to ripen bananas and peas originated some thousand years ago. The real problem is therefore not so much when but how chemicals are used, bearing in mind that, in principle, no chemicals are ever harmless, but there are harmless ways of using them.

Since the earliest days of history ill health caused by food poisoning has always carried a special psychological connotation, because food has been the obvious and most easily accessible vehicle for the conveyance of deliberate poisonous 'additives'. Therefore the legislator has always taken an interest in it. The early statutory control was directed not at protecting the public but at the prevention of revenue evasion. Concern was mainly with preventing fraud by the producer or seller of food. Short weight, particularly in bread, watering of milk or beer, and dilution of spices and other expensive materials such as sugar with litharge and flour with alum were all covered in early laws. Before the realization that changes in quality could be effected in the course of preparation for sale, contamination of food and drink with arsenic and lead was commonplace.

Gradually governmental attitude changed as public attention was caught by a prolonged campaign largely carried on in medical journals such as the *Lancet* during the early 1850s, which revealed widespread food adulteration in Britain. With the developing formulation of standards to ensure that the public should receive clean supplies of water and food, modern British food standards legislation took its origin in 1860 from the Adulteration of Foods Act. This first pure food legislation established that the State had a duty to protect the consumer. It also empowered local authorities to appoint Public Analysts to examine samples of food and drink on complaint by private citizens. The Act had little success due to trade opposition but was greatly strengthened in the form of the Adulteration of Food, Drink and Drugs Act of 1872 which introduced controls over bread, margarine, milk, butter and other dairy products—all designed to ensure that the consumer was not being defrauded in the matter of content and purity. It also became an offence to sell a mixture containing ingredients added for bulk or weight unless the composition was declared. Within three years 150 of 225 districts authorized to appoint analysts had done so and over 1500 convictions had been obtained. The Sale of Food and Drugs Act followed in 1875 and essentially formed the basis of modern legislation on food composition. It was to remain in force for over 60 years. The Act provided that no one should sell, to the prejudice of the purchaser, any article of food or any drug which was not of the nature, substance or quality of the article demanded. Any adulteration injurious to health could be punished by a heavy fine and by imprisonment for a second offence.

As a consequence of the activities of public analysts in developing tests of and standards for food purity and the realization that consumers were being cheated rather than poisoned several important statutory standards for foodstuffs were promulgated. Standards for spirits appeared in 1879, for margarine in 1887, for milk in 1907 and butter in 1902, while from 1919 onwards several committees continued to consider the subject of food standards.

The decline in food adulteration from its peak in the 1850s can be gauged from the quarterly returns of public analysts to the Local Government Board and it is a satisfactory measure of the success of the 1875 Act. Adulteration of food samples throughout the country fell from nearly 20 per cent in 1877 to less than 9 per cent by 1900 and had levelled out at about 6 per cent by 1937.

At first the improvement had been partly due to voluntary efforts by conscientious producers and traders—and by more sophisticated methods of deception by the unscrupulous. However, the powers under the 1875 Act together with the improvement in production techniques and the disappearing 'need' for adulteration were highly effective in eliminating these nefarious practices.

Only much later and not until the Food and Drugs Act 1938 were Ministers empowered to promulgate regulations for the composition and labelling of food. This would have been an important step forward but the Act was suspended on the outbreak of war. Wartime Defence Regulations were concerned largely with rationing and price control, and what compositional standards were enacted covered foods of comparatively minor importance, such as mustard and fishcakes, and obviously had little relevance to peace time food conditions. The most important regulation which survived until 1973 was the Labelling of Food Order 1953.

Today the Food and Drugs Act of 1955 has superseded all previous measures. The two basic principles, protection of health and the prevention of consumer exploitation, are embodied in Sections 1 and 2 of the Act. Briefly Section 1 prohibits the sale of food which is injurious to health and Section 2 makes it an offence to sell food not of the nature, substance or quality demanded. In addition, Section 8 prohibits the sale of food which is unfit for human consumption e.g., microbiologically unsound or grossly contaminated with a poisonous chemical.

Similar legislation exists for Scotland and Northern Ireland. The Act thus gives general protection to the public, but Ministers have also used their powers to make specific regulations controlling the composition of certain individual foodstuffs e.g., bread, cheese; giving permission for the use of various food additives e.g., preservatives, colours, emulsifiers; and applying limits to the amount of specified contaminants e.g., lead, arsenic which may be present in food. The role of food regulations in the field of food safety is clearly to ensure that only those foodstuffs reach the individual consumer which will not be injurious to his health. However, they cannot prevent abuse of food by society or protect food perverts or food faddists against possible deleterious effects of their individual habits. Difficulties have come about with changes, particularly over the past 30 years, in food technology and agricultural practice. It has become a recognized technique to introduce deliberate food additives such as preservatives, colouring matters, emulsifiers, antioxidants, flavouring substances and so on to food, albeit in relatively small quantities. Secondly, in consequence of the application of pesticide chemicals to crops during growth and post-harvest storage, or the use of various compounds in animal husbandry and veterinary practice, residues of these unintentional additives or contaminants, again usually in minute amounts, tend to persist in the final foodstuffs. Even when the compounds concerned are possessed of some intrinsic toxicity, as a particular pesticide may be, it is not easy to sustain the allegation that the minute percentage present in that one consignment will 'render it injurious to health'. If in fact there is any hazard on these accounts it would probably come about only by consumption throughout life of a foodstuff contaminated in this way. Furthermore, with careful labelling and modern sales methods it is by no means simple to prove that the food product was other than that 'demanded by the purchaser'. Consequently, there has been an urge to introduce specific legislation to deal with problems of this kind.

Under the 1955 Act a large series of Regulations and Orders has now been introduced. Not all of these are concerned with additives or contaminants, but examples of such legislation are the Mineral Hydrocarbons in Food Regulations 1966, the Meat (Treatment) Regulations 1964, the Bread and Flour Regulations 1963 as amended in 1972, the Antioxidant in Food Regulations 1966 superseded by those made in 1974, the Emulsifiers and Stabilizers in Food Regulations 1962, the Colouring Matter in Food Regulations 1973, the Miscellaneous Additives in Food Regulations 1974, and Lead in Food Regulations 1961, the Arsenic in Food Regulations 1959 and others.

In principle, for each of the various classes a positive list of permitted additives has been scheduled and, so far as possible, quality specifications or standards for those substances have also been prescribed. Thus the only antioxidants approved in this manner are octyl, dodecyl and propylgallate, butylated hydroxyanisole, butylated hydroxytoluene, ethoxyquin, l-ascorbic acid and its salts, tocopherols and ascorbyl palmitate; all others are prohibited.

Independent expert advice about the composition of food and the acceptability of the various food additives is given to Ministers by a number of Committees, e.g., the Food Standards Committee, the Food Additives and Contaminants Committee, the Committee on Medical Aspects of Food Policy, and the Committee on Medical Aspects of Chemicals in Food and the Environment and various sub-committees, including the Toxicity sub-Committee, the Carcinogenesis sub-Committee and the Mutagenesis sub-Committee. The membership of these bodies includes both departmental and independent nominees, representing academic, health, analytical and food technology interests. In reaching decisions Ministers take account of the advice given by these Committees and comments received from the industries concerned and any interested parties.

The situation differs, however, for unintentional contaminants. Many potentially toxic agents which could enter food occur in the environment.

Pesticides, drugs, cosmetics, household chemicals, industrial chemicals, radio-isotopes, atmospheric and water pollutants are all potential hazards to man in modern society. Chemical contamination of food has recently attracted attention particularly in the more industrialized countries and some pollution of the environment, and hence of the raw materials of food, will occur inevitably as a result of expanding industrial activities. Examples of possible contaminants include heavy metals, polycyclic aromatic hydrocarbons, polychlorinated biphenyls and phthalate plasticizers.

In so far as pesticides protect foodstuffs from damage and spoilage they have become indispensable to modern agriculture. Furthermore, not all of them leave residues in the crops. For example, weed-killers applied to the land before the plants emerge bring about no contamination at all. But clearly, as pesticides are designed to be inimical to certain forms of life, e.g., insects, fungi, moulds and so on, they are intrinsically toxic, to a greater or lesser extent. Accordingly, where there is a likelihood that residues will occur, the amount must be detected analytically and the toxicity assessed. In the UK there is no statutory control over pesticides—except for a few of them—which may offer a hazard to those using them. Instead, there is a voluntary notification scheme, agreed upon between Departments and the pesticide industry. Each submission comprises a full statement on nature, usage and toxicity. These data are first considered by a Scientific sub-Committee, which reports in turn to the Advisory Committee on Pesticides and other Toxic Chemicals. The conditions of use after agreement with industry are endorsed by both agricultural and health departments and an appropriate 'recommendation sheet' incorporating all these conditions is published. It is assumed that users will abide by these instructions in order that any residues will be such as to constitute no risk to consumers.

Veterinary medicines, preparations and pesticides used on animals e.g., warble fly dressings, intramammary preparations for mastitis in cows, may also leave residues in the flesh, eggs or milk. For these statutory control now exists by licensing under the Medicines Act 1968. Licences prescribe the conditions of use, the size of residues to be permitted, among other things, and are issued only after efficacy and safety of each substance have been evaluated by the statutory body, the Veterinary Products Committee, which advises the Licensing Authority.

The most serious acute risks to health from food usually arise from biological contamination. Food animals may themselves be diseased or be carriers of infections. Micro-organisms may create toxic or infective hazards. Toxic metabolites of moulds, e.g., aflatoxin, have received increasing attention in recent years. To assess whether or not a substantial hazard exists from chemical contamination of food requires certain basic information which includes data on the probable daily intake of the contaminant from food and other sources by the average consumer; the food particularly at risk; the population groups who may be at risk because of special eating habits; and the toxicological profile of the contaminant. Fortunately examples of serious accidents due to food contamination with chemicals are very rare. In 1900 in the north of England there was a widespread outbreak of disease connected with beer drinking. It was estimated that about 6000 people were affected with 70 deaths. The cause was traced back to contamination with arsenic of sulphuric acid which had been used to prepare the sugar sold to brewers. A more recent example is the Epping Jaundice of 1965 with 84 people taken ill after eating a special wholemeal bread made from flour contaminated during transport with 4,4'-diaminodiphenyl methane, an industrial chemical.

In deciding on what action, if any, is needed to meet a possible hazard from food contamination, it is necessary to assess the probable degree of risk involved and to assess the degree of acceptability of the risk. Although it may be difficult to quantify these parameters, it is necessary to place the risk under consideration into perspective in relation to the risks which accompany every human activity. On the other hand, the deliberate food additives are not generally speaking intrinsically toxic. In single doses, at any rate, enormous quantities would have to be ingested to do any harm. Uncertainty prevails however about the consequences of ingesting even tiny quantities throughout life. Obviously such insidious possibilities are not easily checked by direct human observation and even epidemiological surveys would not be useful as a preventive measure. Accordingly tests are carried out in animals. Commonly rats and mice, sometimes dogs, and occasionally other species are fed at levels far in excess of those likely to be put into human food, both for short periods and also over their life-span. Any changes are noted in growth, body function, reproduction and, notably, tumour incidence as a measure of carcinogenic potential. In some cases special investigations are needed to elucidate the metabolism and to exclude the possibility of mutagenic potential. In extrapolating the results to man it is usually accepted that if a substance has no effects, when administered to animals over their life-span, at a level of at least 100 times the maximum amount likely to be added to food, then it is reasonably safe (Memorandum on Procedure for Submissions on Food Additives and on Methods of Toxicity Testing, HMSO 1965). No absolute assurance can of course be given from this sort of study unless supplemented by careful study of the effects, or lack of them, of ingestion by persons of all ages over long periods. While it is comparatively easy to eliminate additives which may produce deleterious effects in the short-term, it is unlikely that it will ever be possible to state

71

with certainty that a particular additive or foodstuff will never produce any ill effects, however slight, if ingested regularly over a period of many years. Occasionally, evidence of possible harmful effects of a traditional food additive is forthcoming and for such instances machinery exists to alter, when appropriate, legislation rapidly to take such evidence into account. Thus the use of the flour treatment agent agene (nitrogen trichloride) introduced in 1923 was abandoned in 1946 when it had been shown that dogs fed agenized flour developed central nervous system disturbances. Following the discovery of the metabolic conversion of the artificial sweetener cyclamate into cyclo hexylamine, a moderately toxic chemical, cyclamic acid and its salts were deleted from the list of permitted artificial sweeteners in 1969. Brominated vegetable oils, which are substances used as clouding agents for soft drinks, were prohibited as ingredients in soft drinks in 1970 when it was shown that their consumption over long periods led to accumulation of bromine in human fatty tissues. In the same year the colouring matter Ponceau MX was removed from the permitted list having been shown to cause toxic effects in long-term studies in rats and mice, while this year another food colour, orange RN, will be deleted from the permitted list because of its hepatoxic potential demonstrated in laboratory animals.

Increasing awareness of the importance of toxicological considerations in the relation between human health and factors existing in the natural environment has led to a more searching and critical assessment of the true health value of naturally occurring foodstuffs. It was gradually being realized that certain components of natural foodstuffs might be far from harmless to man. Thus food constituents and natural contaminants may form hazards which are as important as those arising from intentional food additives, whether by their presence alone or because of the results of their mutual interaction. Reviewing the present situation leads to the conclusion that too much or too little food is more harmful than all the additives, intentional or unintentional, likely to be found in food. It is also obvious that intelligent appraisal of all available toxicological and technological data is the only way to arrive at a scientifically valid decision on the safety-in-use of a food additive. There is very good evidence that infections conveyed to man by foodstuffs are a greater hazard than all food additives when properly used. On the whole our food regulations, despite all their imperfections, are effective in safeguarding the health of the population against hazards from additives and contaminants as long as there exists also a concomitant attitude of social responsibility on the part of the food manufacturing and food distributing industry.

Turning to another aspect of my subject, the past century has seen the rise of the science of nutrition, i.e., the study of food in relation to growth and development and to health throughout the life span, and of disease caused by too little or too much or the wrong kind of food. By the end of the nineteenth century much was known of the chemistry of carbohydrates, proteins and fats, something was known of their part in the physiology of digestion, but very little or nothing was known of their nutritional importance. Similarly much of the significance of mineral salts in nutrition was a mystery and vitamins had not been discovered. The idea prevailed that fats and carbohydrates, in equivalent caloric quantities, were interchangeable in metabolism. It was not until 1929 that Burr and Burr, working with rats, first showed the importance of certain fatty acids which were essential in the diet for health and survival.

The earliest animal experiment which clearly showed that proteins differed in biological value was made by Lawes and Gilbert at Rothamsted in 1854. These workers showed that, with *ad libitum* feeding, pigs fed on barley meal retained more of their food protein for conversion into body protein than when fed on lentil meal.

More than a century ago the isolation of individual amino-acid from proteins began with glycine (Braconnot 1820) and continued into the 1930s when Rose (1935) isolated threonine. It was in 1912 that Van Slyke and Meyer first demonstrated the rise in amino-acid nitrogen in the blood during protein absorption, but the recognition of the importance of eight essential amino-acids (nine in the case of infants) without which the body cannot manufacture its protein, was left to the work of Rose and others in this century.

Hopkins (1906), in a notable lecture which received much publicity, gave the necessary stimulus for the discovery of vitamins when he said 'No animal can live on a mixture of proteins, carbohydrates and fats, and even when the necessary inorganic material is carefully supplied, the animal still cannot flourish'. This recalled the work of Lind in the eighteenth century, who cured scurvy by the use of citrus fruits, and the work of Eijkman (1896), who realized that beri-beri was a deficiency disease due to eating rice from which the husk had been removed. As a result the early part of this century was the heyday of vitamin research. By the 1920s Mellanby and others had elucidated the parts played by the fat-soluble vitamin D, calcium and phosphates in the development of healthy bone and in the cure of rickets—the English disease which became so prevalent at the time of the industrial revolution when life in cities, with crowded narrow streets and a dark pall of 'smog', cut off the sunlight with which the body can make for itself a sufficient supply of this vitamin.

At the same time, the unhealthy condition of many men who were recruits for the army in the First World War opened the eyes of the authorities to the poor nutritional status of a large proportion of the population. Between the Wars dietary surveys were made—notably under the guidance of the late Lord Boyd Orr at the Rowett Research Institute. In the 1930s, for example, 555 children aged 2–13 years, mostly in poor circumstances, were fed for one year an amount and kind of food calculated to make good the deficiencies previously indicated by a dietary survey. The children who received the supplements at all ages and in all expenditure groups gained ¼ to 1 cm in height more than controls during the year of investigation.

With the onset of the Second World War and the difficulty in maintaining the import of food supplies to this country, all the relatively new knowledge of nutrition was put to good use in the development of what proved to be a most efficient and beneficial rationing system. The Government decided that the health of the younger generation must especially be safeguarded, and early in 1940 the so-called 'Welfare Foods Scheme' was introduced. This scheme ensured cheap milk to all pregnant and lactating women, cheap dried milk powder (National Dried Milk) for infants who were not breast fed, together with a supply of cod liver oil and concentrated orange juice as a source of vitamin A, D and C for all pregnant and lactating women and for children up to the age of five years. In addition cheap or free school meals became available in all schools. There was an enormous effect on the health of our children. Surveys showed that rickets and scurvy had virtually disappeared and the increased height of schoolchildren was an index of growth.

Virtually the Welfare Foods Scheme has continued to date. The supply of a daily one pint of milk to pregnant and lactating women is now free to all with large families (three or more under five years including the foetus), and to all who are in need, independent of family size. The spectrum of those in need has been increased. Cod liver oil, the taste of which was disliked by mothers though not by babies, and concentrated orange juice, which was misused undiluted on dummies and in 'dinkie feeders', thus putting newly erupted teeth at risk of rampant caries, have been replaced by vitamin drops available free or at cost price. The school meal system is still the largest catering concern in the country.

Threats to our shipping in the early 1940s reduced grain imports so making it imperative for home grown wheat to be used to the maximum to ensure the bread supply. Thus the extraction rate for milling was compulsorily raised from the 70 per cent which ensured a white flour to 85 per cent and even to 90 per cent in May 1946. This resulted in a National loaf, which was darker in colour but not as dark as wholemeal bread. The control of the extraction rate of flour was not lifted until August 1953 and by this time an inter-departmental conference between the Ministry of Health, Department of Health for Scotland, Ministry of Agriculture and Fisheries, Ministry of

Food, Medical Research Council and the Flour and Baking Industry had reported (1945) to the effect that 'A return to white flour which was commonly in use before the war would be thoroughly bad for the nation's health' (page 9). However, it was alleged by the millers that the public preferred white flour and the scientists finally agreed that an extraction rate of less than 80 per cent should be permitted, but to the resulting white flour the vitamins thiamin and nicotinic acid and the mineral iron should be added in specified amounts to bring their concentration to that present in an 80 per cent extraction flour. Other nutrients which are lost in milling were known to be obtained in more than adequate amounts for other foods. The most recent Report on Bread and Flour (Ministry of Agriculture, Fisheries and Food 1974) suggests that nicotinic acid need no longer be added since recent research proves that this vitamin can easily be derived in the body from the amino-acid tryptophane, amply present in flour.

Flour continues to be fortified with calcium carbonate, originally added compulsorily early in the Second World War because it was thought to be advantageous to increase the calcium content of the diet as a whole at a time when dairy products were possibly in short supply. The report quoted above still supports the addition of calcium carbonate, although for quite another reason related to the known fact that mortality from coronary heart disease is higher in soft water areas than in hard water areas and the hardness of water is due to the presence of calcium salts. Hence it is just possible that to stop the fortification of flour with calcium might have an effect on the prevalence of coronary heart disease.

Rationing ended between the years 1952 and 1954 and the success of the rationing system could be inferred from the improved nutritional status of the population compared with before the war. As might be expected, the end of the system brought changes in the diet. These changes are monitored by the National Food Survey made throughout the year (except for the week in which Christmas falls) by the Ministry of Agriculture, Fisheries and Food. Housewives are asked to keep a record of all food bought for domestic consumption and of all meals eaten by the family. The survey was started in 1940 among the poorer, larger urban families but was extended after the War to include all households in Great Britain. Although the response rate is not high, it is consistently about 55–60 per cent. Thus in spite of certain limitations, such as that no account is taken of meals outside the home, or of ice-cream or soft drinks, the survey is of use in following trends in dietary changes.

These trends show that the total energy value of the average household diet is remarkably constant at about 3000 kcal/head/day. The protein content is also very constant and provides about 11 per cent of the total energy. There has been a steady rise in the amount of fat foods (dairy products etc.), and a concomitant fall in carbohydrate foods. Dietary fat provides about 42 per cent of the total energy. The nature of the carbohydrate foods has changed. Far less of the starch-containing foods (cereals etc.) are eaten and more sugar foods (cakes, biscuits, pastries and confectionery). The average daily amount of sugar has risen over the past century from about 35 g/head in 1860 to 120 g/head in 1970.

This taste for refined sugar is nutritionally disadvantageous for two reasons. In the first place refined sugar (sucrose) is a source only of energy and does not supply the nutrients i.e., mineral salts, some protein, a little fat and vitamins, which are found in the naturally occurring starchy foods. Secondly, satiety is reached with the starchy foods long before it is with chocolate or biscuits etc. Hence the energy intake tends to exceed output with resulting storage of the excess as fat in adipose tissue. This eventually leads to obesity, i.e., over-nutrition, which is perhaps the commonest form of malnutrition of our day. Obesity is associated with a higher mortality from diabetes mellitus, coronary heart disease and has other disadvantages.

Other trends revealed by the results of the National Food Survey are an increased purchase by the housewife of all convenience foods and an increased purchase of alcohol. The survey is also of use in that analysis of results can be made separately for groups of the population who might be considered to be at nutritional risk, i.e., the large families and the poorer families. To date (i.e., 1973) available results do not show any cause for alarm.

These at risk groups which include pre-school children, school children, pregnant women and the elderly are also studied in depth by the Nutrition Unit of the Department of Health (NB. These studies are always made without reference to Social Security since to ask detailed questions about income and resources etc. would lower the response rate). Again so far we have found no cause for concern about the nutritional status of these population groups. In a survey made in 1967–68 of men and women over the age of 65 years who were living in their own homes, although some malnutrition was detected by the examining clinicians, almost all of it was associated with clinical disease, and for the unexplained cases poverty was not a cause. More recent surveys still await analysis of the information collected in the field.

It can of course never be true to say that there is no malnutrition among any section of our people. There are always those who have language problems, or who cannot accommodate to our way of life, or who are socially inadequate. Such people can only be reached individually by health visitors and health educationalists. We are aware at the moment for example of the problem of rickets almost exclusively among the immigrant population, and surveys have been made by the Department with a view to finding the extent of the problem and considering how best to get these people to take advantage of the available foods and supplements which would ensure health.

Food technology is now so advanced that plant proteins, e.g., from soya or field beans, can be processed to resemble animal foods such as meat, fish or cheese, and cows' milk can be modified to resemble human milk more closely. It is the business of the Department of Health to ensure that the 'novel' protein foods and the milk substitutes do indeed resemble the natural food in all essential respects. Technology still has far to go when one remembers the antibodies and immunoglobulins which are specific to human milk, and the haemoglobin iron and Vitamin B_{12} found in meat but not in soya-protein simulated meat.

Discussion

Mr. D L Haxby (Chairman, Public Health Committee, British Veterinary Association): My Lord Chairman, I should like to congratulate Sir Henry Yellowlees on a most comprehensive and informative paper. The veterinary surgeons are particularly interested in the microbiological aspects. As you stated in your paper, biological contamination is probably the most important thing. Judging from the figures for food poisoning which does arise in this country, this is often associated with meat and meat products. I should like to ask Sir Henry Yellowlees whether he considers that microbiological examination should be carried out in slaughterhouses as a monitor of the likely status of the products and the premises.

Again, I was interested in the methods used for pesticide residues especially, as applied to the veterinary field. Here you envisage monitoring under EEC regulations for residues of these important chemicals; would you like to see statutory regulation of some pesticides in current use, especially organic phosphorus compounds?

With reference to EEC Directives with a view to veterinary inspection in both the red and the white meat industries, have you any idea of how this could be implemented and the steps that may be taken in the future? As you are well aware, there have been two reports in the last 11 years, first the Verdon-Smith Report of 1964 and, secondly, the Swann Report of 1975, both of which recommended a centralized meat inspection service, or at least a meat inspection service under central control.

I would agree with you that education is a most important factor, and I would extend it from the industry and the food handler to the actual consumer. I am sure that most of the food poisoning outbreaks could have been avoided by adequate cooking and safe handling within the premises or within the home.

One final question, do you favour the annual medical examination of people consistently handling food?

Sir Henry Yellowlees: You have asked quite a few questions, but perhaps I can start from the bottom and work upwards. The last one was, are we in favour of annual examination of food handlers. This is a difficult one at the moment, as the speaker knows well, in relation to the EEC. Our view of this is really that we do not know where we would find the resources that would be needed for this, we do not know how we should be able to keep a check on all food handlers in this kind of way or where the laboratory resources are; this is not something with which we would go ahead at the moment. Clearly, when there is an epidemiological situation developing, one goes in and does a full study. We feel that probably a sensible move would be a pre-employment check on food handlers and that they ought perhaps to be asked to fill in some basic form which would give essential information. As a result of the perusal of that, they might then be required to undergo medical examination.

You did comment on education, and I could not agree with this more. The central role, of course, is played by the Health Education Council and, as in every area, we have not got all the money we should like to have, to try to assist the Council in its work. Locally it is a different situation and we rely on the local authority activities, the DHOs. There again, these are in short supply and again it is a question of available money.

We have been thinking recently that there may be a case for suitably qualified, but less highly qualified, technicians to try to help in this, until we can train more DHOs.

Hygiene in slaughterhouses is another vexed question and, I think, relates to EEC problems. I do not think that we have enough people, of whatever discipline, to do all the inspection that we should like to do in this field and for the moment I do not see any real hope of achieving what we should all like. However, the implication that has been put forward is of course unanswerable; yes, we ought to see this eventually, but I do not know how we come to do it.

With regard to statutory controls for pesticide residues, the difficulty here is one of setting exact limits. We have always really, in this country, gone away from this. We are here for a centenary celebration to pay tribute to an era of co-operation on a voluntary basis, and it has been remarkably successful. I am not keen at the moment to go too far away from that general principle.

Mr. R F Giles (MAFF): So far as pesticides are concerned, particularly in agriculture, we have always worked in this country on a voluntary basis;

manufacturers do not put pesticides on the market until they have been cleared under our voluntary pesticides scheme. Lord Zuckerman had a lot to do with this way back in 1951 and 1953 and 1955 when the Ministry of Agriculture published three reports on the use of pesticides. As Sir Henry said, we have the usual hundred-fold safety factor in assessing the toxicity of a pesticide.

Mr. C T Ashton (Senior Scientist, Scot Bowyers Ltd): Quite rightly there has been much said about co-operation and communication this morning and my first point is one of communication. There is much microbiological analysis done in abattoirs and on fresh meat within industry. No doubt Mr. Haxby wants this to be extended to examination by official bodies, but many of us are setting increasingly stringent standards within industry.

On the other question, that of co-operation, Sir Henry referred to the fact that we do not have any microbiological standards laid down in this country, and yet increasingly I am coming across local authorities who are seeking to lay down microbiological standards for products at the point of sale. It seems to me that this shows some lack of co-operation, some lack of co-ordination, between central authorities and local authorities. I was wondering if Sir Henry would like to comment.

Dr. G A H Elton (Chief Scientific Adviser (Food), MAFF): In reply to Mr. Ashton, in many cases quantitative microbiological methods are not available, and there is need for research on methodology, especially on quantitative methods for pathogens. Until these are available, there is little point in trying to set statutory quantitative standards.

Dr. P H Berben (Chief Health Inspector, Ministry of Public Health and Environmental Hygiene, The Netherlands): Sir Henry Yellowlees said quite boldly that, for dangerous substances in food, even very dangerous substances, he proposes to use a risk analysis and not to forbid these substances on a rigorous basis. I think that this is a sensible thing to do and we try to do it in the same way in our country. However, the difficulties in doing these things are enormous because it is necessary to balance things of absolutely different weight. I want to ask a specific question and see whether the speaker comes out with the same weighing as we do, and that is the weighing of the risk that is attached to a substance such as aflatoxin. We all know the difficulties and the dangers attached to aflatoxins in our foodstuff and, in our country, we take at the moment a level of 5 points per billion in peanuts and peanut products as the acceptable level, but other people argue that we should go down from 5 ppb to even 1 ppb. Our analytical people have shown that it is possible to go down as far as that.

We are in this dilemma at the moment, and I wonder if you have the same dilemma in your country and if you have a solution to it.

Sir Henry Yellowlees: I would say that this requires an expert answer and my viewpoint is rather more generalized. I am afraid I cannot answer this in terms of the proportions which you are quoting, but perhaps Dr. Elton can take that up.

Dr. G A H Elton: A problem that we have in every advanced country in the world is to assess the risk/benefit situation in relation to food additives and, particularly, with regard to carcinogens. Aflatoxin is a powerful liver carcinogen, but we have the same basic problem with nitrosamines, poly-cyclic aromatic hydrocarbons and other carcinogens. Most people would agree a lot more research has to be done before we can say that, as a result of permitting 1 ppb of aflatoxin or nitrosamine in the national diet nobody is going to die, or 10 people are going to die in a year, or 50 people are going to die in a year. We cannot answer that question at the moment but a lot of work on dose response relationships is going on in the UK, in the United States and in Europe. Even when we can quantify the risks, we still have to make the judgment. In this country at the moment we know that 7000 people a year are killed on the roads, but we do not say there should be no more motor cars; we make a judgment about it. I do not think that we can make the same quantitative judgment with regard to food, because people have special feelings about food, naturally enough. However, I think we must recognize that there is no such thing as 100 per cent safety in any activity in this world; just sitting here as we are today we could fall down dead, or get run over when we go out and cross the road. I think that we need agreement not just nationally but internationally on risk/benefit analysis, but we are only at the start of the road.

That probably does not answer your question, but I hope it shows that we and many other people are well aware of the problem and are working towards trying to answer it in, perhaps, 10 or 20 years' time.

Dr. G F Wilmink (Cabinet Adviser, Minister of Agriculture and Fisheries, The Netherlands): I have some questions on the same lines, if I understood the speaker correctly. Am I right in thinking that you said that you were not in favour of numerical values in microbiological examination of foods? If so, might this not give a lot of embarrassment to those who have to control the hygiene situation with regard to food as it is? I am in complete agreement with you that, in handling food hygiene, it is a matter not for the policeman but for the sanitarian. On the other hand, the microbiological examination of food seems to be a kind of an art and each microbiologist has his own way of handling it. How can we, then, prevent differences in judgment of the acceptability of food?

Sir Henry Yellowlees: I think the answer is that it is an art and that the various people concerned do produce very many differing results. This links up with a point that Dr. Elton made a moment or two ago, that until one can get agreement on methodology and methods of analysis, etc. it is very difficult indeed to lay down legal standards. We can give plenty of guidance as to what is permissible within limits, but I do not think that in this country at the moment we would go towards any legal standards of that kind.

The Nation's Diet: A Century of Change

G A H Elton

Chief Scientific Adviser (Food), Ministry of Agriculture, Fisheries and Food

Introduction

Within a few years of the introduction of the first effective Food and Drugs Act in 1875, three people were born in this country who in their different ways were to have a profound influence on the pattern of the nation's food supplies and the growth of the science of nutrition during the period we are to consider: Sir Winston Churchill, the statesman and wartime Prime Minister; Lord Boyd Orr, who, in 1945, became the first Director-General of the Food and Agriculture Organization; and Dame Harriette Chick, whose main scientific concern was with the function of vitamins and vitamin deficiency diseases. In 1875 Benjamin Disraeli was Prime Minister; income tax was 2d in the £. The household telephone, wireless and the aeroplane had not yet been invented, and refrigeration had not been applied to the transport of meat.

At that time little was known about the causes of the nutritional problems that existed or the essentials of a nutritionally adequate diet, but advances were being made in nutritional research. Liebig had reported his theories on the functions of foods and their constituents in the middle of the nineteenth century and by the close of Queen Victoria's reign in 1901 the classical studies of Rubner, Atwater, Benedict and Voit on the calorific value of foods, energy metabolism, and the digestion of food by man had laid the foundations for the rapid growth of nutritional knowledge which was to occur in many different countries during the next 50 years.

Between 1875 and 1880 the mid-Victorian prosperity in British agriculture came to a rather sudden end. For the first time in history a British harvest failure could be made good by North America. This was to the consumer's immediate benefit; but at the same time the increasing use of proprietary starchy foods and sweetened condensed skimmed milk were considered to be partly responsible for an increase in infant malnutrition and the prevalence of scurvy and rickets among infants and young children. There were great contrasts between the foods eaten by the poorer labouring classes and by the wealthy, and between the diets of the people in the congested industrial towns and the scattered rural areas. It seems likely that the major dietary problem among the rich upper classes was frequently one of over-consumption. A review of Dobell's Handbook on Diet and Disease in the *British Medical Journal* of 22nd May 1875 contains an interesting comment: 'Some remark is necessary in reference to the now prevalent custom among the upper class of . . . taking an afternoon tea. Unless cautiously arranged it is apt to lead to dyspepsia. The rule should be that the tea should precede the dinner by three hours, and not come sooner after lunch than three hours, assuming the lunch to have been a good meal. . . .' Such a warning seems appropriate, since many of you will be familiar with the elaborate dinner menus advocated by Mrs. Beeton in her famous cookery book which was in use at that time.

During the last hundred years, the population of the United Kingdom has increased from about 29 million to 56 million. Accompanying the changes in the distribution of the population between town and country, it is estimated that there has been a concurrent fall of about 65 per cent in the total number of people engaged in agriculture and horticulture, forestry and fishing in Great Britain. In 1974, the total number of persons engaged in agriculture and horticulture was only 678 000 (*Annual Review of Agriculture* 1975)[1]. This is one indicator of the great changes and developments which occurred both in agriculture and the sources of food supplies, and in food technology and the food industry, which will now be examined in greater detail.

Changes in United Kingdom food supplies

Official statistics relating to food supplies are available from 1934-39 onwards. These estimates are shown in terms of major commodities in Table 1, together with reasonably comparable figures for 1880, derived from the records of the British Association for the Advancement of Science[2] and from Greaves and Hollingsworth[3], and for 1909-13 based on a report of the Royal Society Committee[4]. Since the Second World War total supplies of food from all sources have been assessed in each year [5-7]. To arrive at the total food moving into human consumption, deductions are made for exports, waste and non-food uses, and this total is then divided by the mid-year population to give average consumption per head. The figures are all national averages, representing not what any particular individual obtains, but what, on average, is available to the whole population for consumption. They are the only available figures for total consumption, and the only means of comparing the overall food position in different periods of time. The single years presented in Table 1 include the end of the Second World War (1945), which illustrates the effects of food shortages; the first complete year after the end of food rationing (1955); and a year representative of post-war prosperity (1965).

Table 1 *Trends in United Kingdom food supplies (lb per head per annum)*

	1880 (i)	1909–13 (ii)	1934–39 (iii)	1945 (iii)	1955 (iv)	1965 (iv)	1973 (v)
Liquid milk	213	219	217	314	325	321	310
Meat[1]	91	136	138	105	137	153	150
Eggs	11	16	28	30	29	34	33
Fats[2]	12	26	53	42	53	54	55
Sugar[3]	64	79	96	68	108	108	108
Fruit	na	68	104	55	96	108	111
Potatoes	296	243	190	260	234	222	216
Other vegetables	na	78	127	142	127	136	147
Wheat flour	280	211	194	241	182	155	142
Other cereals	na	26	16	17	13	16	19

na = not available.

From 1934–39 onwards:

[1] 'Meat' which includes bacon, ham, poultry, game and rabbits, is obtained by adding the quantities of constituent items, and thus does not refer to edible weight. Similarly for 'other vegetables' and fruit which thus do not refer to 'fresh equivalent'. 'Other vegetables' includes pulses and tomatoes; 'fruit' includes edible nuts.

[2] 'Fats' is the sum of butter, margarine (net), lard, compound cooking fat, and other edible oils and fats.

[3] 'Sugar' figures refer to 'total sugar content (net)', representing total human consumption of refined sugar, including the sugar content of honey and glucose, but excluding that used in brewing and distilling and in products covered elsewhere in the table.

Sources:

(i) Levi *et al* (1882); Greaves and Hollingsworth (1966)
(ii) Royal Society Committee (1917)
(iii) Ministry of Agriculture, Fisheries and Food (1968)
(iv) Ministry of Agriculture, Fisheries and Food (1973)
(v) Ministry of Agriculture, Fisheries and Food (1974)

In 1880, we were largely dependent on cereals and potatoes as staple foods and sources of dietary energy. However, during the present century, the expansion of overseas trade has resulted in a general improvement in the palatability and variety of the national diet. The main point of interest is the continuous upward trend throughout the century in the consumption of meat and meat products and fats, and the downward trend in cereals and potatoes, both of which were interrupted only by the two World Wars. Much of the rise in meat consumption was due to the growth of intensive methods of poultry husbandry and the consequent fall in the retail price of poultry meat, which had traditionally been a luxury; between 1955 and 1973, consumption increased by nearly 20 lb per head per annum. The upward trend in the refined sugar content of total food supplies levelled off in 1962, and since 1966 has slightly declined, but this has been offset by a larger increase in the amount of glucose so that the total sugar content of food supplies has not decreased. Since 1965, the gradual decline in the consumption of potatoes has continued, but the consumption of potato products, expressed in terms of fresh equivalent, has increased from 15 to 46 lb per head per year, which now represents 20 per cent of the total.

The contribution of home produced food

By 1909–13, that is by just before the First World War, the United Kingdom had come to depend on imports of most of the major food commodities with the exception of milk and potatoes; thus all sugar, at least three-quarters of the supplies of cereals, fruit and cheese, about half the margarine and carcass meat and rather more butter, were imported. In the years before the Second World War the United Kingdom imported considerably more than half her food supplies. The changed share of imports during the last war is compared with the pre-war percentages and with the position in 1973 in Table 2 in terms of the energy contribution of the major commodities. In 1972–73 55 per cent of the total United Kingdom food supplies were home produced[8].

Table 2 *Contribution of home production to United Kingdom food supplies (a), (b)*

	Pre-war	1944	1973
	per cent	per cent	per cent
Dairy products	82	81	90
of which liquid milk	100	100	100
Meat	43	32	64
Poultry, game and fish	72	50	83
Eggs and egg products	65	49	95
Oils and fats (c)	12	6	10
Sugar and syrups	22	28	30
Tomatoes and citrus fruit	6	26	6
Other fruit	18	29	18
Pulses and nuts	11	29	10
Potatoes	94	100	94
Leafy salads and greens	99	100	97
Other vegetables	81	98	86
Grain products	14	44	42

(a) Percentages based on calorie equivalents of supplies for consumption as food in the United Kingdom
(b) Partly dependent on imported inputs
(c) Including butter

Expenditure on food

The general rise in the standard of living during the last 100 years has been accompanied by a decrease in the percentage of income spent on food.

Although the somewhat unsystematic information obtained by Seebohm Rowntree in the City of York in 1899 is not directly comparable with the national budgetary surveys of household expenditure in 1937–38 and 1953–54[9–10] or with recent estimates of consumer expenditure [11] it is quite clear that whereas nearly half a labourer's income was spent on food at the turn of the century, the average expenditure on food in 1973 was only 22 per cent of the total (see Table 3).

Table 3 *Proportion of income spent on food*

1900	Rowntree	Labourer	46 per cent
		Railway employee	44 per cent
1936	Boyd Orr		30 per cent average expenditure
1937–38	Ministry of Labour budgetary survey of weekly expenditure of working-class households in the United Kingdom		40 per cent Industrial households 48 per cent Agricultural households
1953–54	Ministry of Labour and National Insurance budgetary survey		34 per cent (29–37 per cent different occupations)
	(All households used to provide expenditure pattern for Index of Retail Prices)		
1965	Ministry of Agriculture, Fisheries and Food		26 per cent All households[1]
1973	Ministry of Agriculture, Fisheries and Food		22 per cent All households[1]

Derived from National Income and Expenditure 1963–73, Central Statistical Office Report, HMSO, London (1974)

Effect of income on food consumption

The nutritional problems of the poor families at the opening of the twentieth century have been vividly described by Seebohm Rowntree in his detailed enquiry into the economic and social conditions of the wage-earning class in York[12]. He calculated that for nearly 10 per cent of the town's population the total earnings of the family were insufficient to obtain the food required to satisfy hunger or to maintain physical efficiency, and in consequence the standard of health was often very low. In comparison, families belonging to the servant-keeping class in the town, but nevertheless living simply, had a varied diet and the amount of food eaten was often in excess of their requirements. Some examples of typical menus are shown in the Appendix.

A detailed historical account of the events between the two World Wars which led to a concentration of interest on the scientific aspects of food and nutrition can be found in *The Englishman's Food*[13]. During this period great advances in nutritional knowledge led to an understanding of the important effects of vitamins and trace elements in the diet. While it is not possible in a paper of this length to review these in detail, I should like as one example to mention the classical work of Dame Harriette Chick and her colleagues in Vienna in 1919, which contributed so largely to the identification of vitamin D. From their studies they were able to demonstrate conclusively that the prompt healing of rickets could be brought about either by antirachitic food (cod liver oil) on the one hand or by sunlight or ultra-violet rays on the other.

A study of food consumption in urban, rural and mining areas of Scotland carried out over nearly five years from 1919[14] showed that immediately after the First World War the majority of those surveyed were getting sufficient calories, but in the depression of the 1930s following the short-lived post-war boom, the diets of the poorer working-class households again became almost as bad as in the worst years of Queen Victoria's reign. In 1931, the Minister of Health appointed a small Advisory Committee on Nutrition, and in 1935 a larger Committee made a comprehensive survey of the food supplies, diets and state of nutrition of the population[15]. Comparison with earlier estimates showed that while there had been a general improvement in the national diet since before the War, the national average consumption of milk and some of the other protective foods containing vitamins and minerals had remained low.

In the 1930s, the conflict between a profitable home agriculture and the benefits of cheap food to the urban poor was uppermost in the minds of the economists and nutritionists. Agricultural development in North America and in the southern Hemisphere in the two decades between the World Wars had led to an abundant supply of cheap imported foods, and in spite of improved yields and new methods of cultivation, British agriculture was quite unable to compete with the fall in prices. It was against such a background that Sir John (later Lord) Boyd Orr published, in 1936[16], 'Food Health and Income: A Report on a Survey of Adequacy of Diet in Relation to Income' in which he attempted to show the extent to which inadequacy of diet was reflected in ill-health and poor physique in the community. He tentatively concluded that a diet completely adequate for health was not attained at the income level of 50 per cent of the population, and that as income increased disease and mortality decreased, children grew more quickly, adult stature was greater and general health and physique improved. To make the diet of the poorer groups the same as the first group whose diet was adequate for full health, Boyd Orr's Group IV, would have involved increases in consumption of a number of the more expensive foods such as milk, eggs, butter, fruit, vegetables and meat.

In the late 1930s, with the growing demand for general improvement in standards of nutrition, and the alleviation of poverty, there was an increasing likelihood of changes in patterns of food consumption, and the shopping habits of the British housewife became potentially of great economic importance to food manufacturers and food producers alike. Crawford and Broadley[17] attempted to determine the effect of the changes taking place in the national diet and to forecast future trends by means of a food consumption and budget enquiry covering 5000 homes. It is of interest to compare some of their findings on the consumption of major commodities in 1936 with the results obtained by the National Food Survey in 1955 and 1973[18-19]. The latter provides a continuous source of information on the consumption of individual foods by private households, both for the population as a whole and for different socio-economic and regional groupings. In 1936 large differences were found between the lowest and the highest income groups; because of rationing, these were to a large extent eliminated, and have not reappeared, so that family size now has a more important influence on the level of food consumption than income. Differences between large and small families were also much compressed by rationing, but (unlike income effects) these differences promptly reappeared after rationing ended in 1954.

1939–45

During the Second World War, the curtailment of imports inevitably led to a lack of variety in the diet, and many of the less essential foods disappeared. Nevertheless, in contrast to the previous decade, very few people were unable to obtain the nutrients which they required, and the general health of the nation was good. This was largely due to the influence of scientific advice and to the development of a scientifically-based nutrition policy. Hammond[20] in his 'History of the Second World War' described the general nutritional strategy outlined in 'A Survey of Wartime Nutrition' which was appended to the draft import programme of the Select Committee on National Expenditure for the second year of the war. It was recognized that while there was a sufficiency of energy-producing foods and probably of protein available to everyone, many people were going seriously short of calcium, iron, and the vitamins A, B and C. War conditions were likely to lead to a steady deterioration in the quality of the national diet, more particularly in that of the poor. It was suggested that 'shortages of vitamin C and iron might be offset if people would eat more potatoes and bread made from high extraction flour. If it were desired to retain white flour in deference to public and trade preference . . . vitamin B_1 could be synthesized and added to flour. Loss of vitamins A and D could readily be made good by adding them to margarine. Calcium deficiency . . . should be met by encouraging milk production and importing cheese in large quantities. Increased home production and consumption of potatoes, green vegetables and oatmeal were all (nutritionally) desirable, as were imports of canned fish (particularly salmon), condensed and dried milk and pulses. Fruit (other than oranges and lemons), nuts and eggs in shell were uneconomic ways of using shipping'. And also that 'there was no prospect of reducing to a worthwhile extent the amount of energy-providing food consumed by the population at large, and attempts to persuade people to eat less might have disastrous effects on health'.

The agricultural industry had to adapt to the loss of imported animal feed and in particular to provide feed for cows to maintain the supply of liquid milk. Great emphasis was placed on increasing the output of wheat, potatoes, sugar beet and vegetables. The restricted food supplies necessitated a general system of rationing which provided for all persons equal domestic rations of bacon, fats, sugar, preserves and sweets, and with certain exceptions (e.g., children under five years and some classes of workers) of meat, cheese and tea. There were also schemes for the allocation of eggs and milk and points rationing for non-perishable canned and dried foods.

Imports were concentrated on those foods which had the greatest energy of protein value per ton, such as dried eggs and milk, sugar and fats. The prices of essential foodstuffs were kept down by Government subsidy, the largest amounts being paid on bread, flour and milk. Certain other measures designed to improve the nutrition of the population were superimposed on the general system of rationing. These included the addition of calcium to flour, the vitaminization of margarine, the extension of communal feeding (including a Rural Pie Scheme for agricultural workers), the expansion of the Milk-in-Schools Scheme and the School Meals Service and special allocations for the vulnerable groups of the population. Other measures included the 'Dig for Victory Campaign' to encourage the production of home-grown vegetables (which made an important contribution to the vitamin C content of the diet), and the introduction of a Waste Order by which it was made a punishable offence to waste any food fit for human consumption.

The general policy of the Ministry of Food was to explain to the consumer, as fully as security permitted, what was happening to the food supplies and why; from 1940 onwards, a small team of dietitians and cookery specialists advised the housewife on wartime cookery and food values by means of advertisements, leaflets, broadcasts, lectures and films and by practical demonstrations in Food Advice Centres all over the country.

A concise account of the development of wartime food policy and the measures which were taken to protect the consumer from the consequences of food shortages has been published with the title 'How Britain was Fed in Wartime: Food Control 1939–1945'[21].

The energy and nutrient content of the National Diet

The energy content of the national diet has remained very stable since before the Second World War at just over 3000 kilo calories (about 13.0 MJ), despite the considerable increase in the variety of foods which have been purchased by the British public. There has been a continuous increase in the proportion of calories derived from fat with an accompanying fall in that from carbohydrates, but little change in the calories derived from total protein. However, the proportion of protein from animal sources has increased from 54 per cent before the Second World War to 61 per cent in 1973.

In general, changes in the provision of calcium and iron and the major vitamins in the diet reflect Government policies with respect to the fortification of foods and the extraction rate of flour. The addition of creta praeparata to flour during the Second World War, together with increased consumption of milk, accounted for the greater consumption of calcium compared with pre-war (see Table 4). The use of higher extraction flour (85 per cent) was not made compulsory until 1942. Since 1953, the extraction rate of flour has not been controlled but flour has been fortified with iron, thiamin and nicotinic acid in quantities sufficient to raise the total levels to approximately those in flour of 80 per cent extraction. The addition of calcium carbonate to all flour other than wholemeal or self-raising flour has also continued.[22–23] From 1940 the fortification of margarine with vitamins A and D became compulsory and, in 1954, the amount of vitamin A added was raised to approximately the same level as in butter.

Table 4   *Minerals and vitamins in total food supplies (per person per day)*

	1909	1934–38	1945	1955	1965	1973
Calcium (mg)	608	696	1040	1100	1120	1120
Iron (mg)	12·6	13·0	14·9	14·2	15·1	14·8
Vitamin A (iu)	2560	3690	3620	4310	4600	4340
Vitamin C (mg)	81	96	109	99	108	99
Thiamin (mg)	1·3	1·3	1·8	1·7	1·9	1·9
Riboflavin (mg)	1·5	1·6	1·8	1·8	2·0	2·0
Nicotinic acid (total) (mg)	14·0	13·2	15·0	15·3	16·9	20·8

Sources of selected nutrients in the National Diet

At the beginning of the century *milk and dairy products* (excluding butter) provided about 8 per cent of the energy and 15 per cent of the protein in the diet. This contribution has steadily increased throughout the century, the use of milk in manufactured products having increased dramatically since the Second World War.

Meat of all kinds, including poultry, has provided about 25 per cent of the dietary protein throughout the period apart from the war years when its contribution was less than 20 per cent.

Oils and fats have contributed between 17–18 per cent of total energy since the end of rationing, which is about double that in 1909–13.

Before the First World War *cereals* provided 37 per cent of the energy in the diet; this fell to 30 per cent between the wars but rose again to 38 per cent in the Second World War. Since then there has been a steady decline in the consumption of bread and flour, and cereals supplied only 23 per cent of the total energy in 1973. In addition to energy, cereals supplied 26 per cent of the protein and 40 per cent of the carbohydrate in the diet in that year. During the Second World War these proportions rose to 42 per cent and 59 per cent respectively.

Fifty-one per cent of the vitamin C in the diet was derived from *potatoes* before the First World War and other vegetables provided 29 per cent; by 1973, equal amounts of vitamin C (37 per cent) were derived from both these sources. During the same period the contribution from fruit rose from 16 to 20 per cent.

The importance of fibre in human nutrition is a subject of some disagreement. It has been suggested that a low intake of dietary fibre (i.e., that part of plant material which is resistant to digestion by the secretions of the human gastro-intestinal tract) can lead to certain disorders, such as diverticulosis and cancer of the colon, which have become more common in Britain during this century. This is one of the areas where there is a need for more information, both on the components of the broad spectrum of compounds or substances which are embraced by the term 'dietary fibre' and on the functions of the different components. The main dietary sources are cereals, vegetables (including potatoes), and fruit and nuts. The use of high extraction flour caused by the shortages of wheat in 1918, in the Second World War and for a short period in 1946, was accompanied by increases in the amount of cereal fibre in the diet but, with these exceptions, the decline in the average consumption of bread and flour has led to a gradual fall in the amount of cereal fibre ingested. An increase in the fibre contribution from fruit and vegetables (other than potatoes) since the Second World War has also led to a decline in the relative importance of cereal fibre. Thus while flour and grain products contributed a quarter of the total crude fibre in the diet in 1909–13, by 1973 the proportion was only 12 per cent.

Detailed information on trends in food consumption and sources of nutrients in the average *household* diet of families of different size and income group has been published annually since 1950 in the Reports of the

National Food Survey Committee[24-27]. In 1973, the Survey results showed that intakes of all nutrients continued to be in excess of the recommended intakes[28] in almost every type of household, size of family being a more important determinant of *per capita* nutrient intake than the income of the head of the household. There was a similarity between the dietary patterns of all household groups except those at the extremes of the income range. The families in the highest income group (A1) had a greater intake of fat and protein (and a higher ratio of animal to vegetable protein) than any other income group, but the lowest intake of carbohydrate. In terms of foods, Group A1 has a relatively high consumption of liquid milk, cream, cheese, carcass meat, poultry, eggs, butter, cooking and salad oils, fresh green and quick-frozen vegetables, fresh fruit and juices; their consumption of sugar, potatoes and bread was relatively low. By contrast, in Group D1 (the lowest income group containing earners) the consumption of margarine, meat products (not carcass meat), lard and compound cooking fat (not cooking oils), potatoes and white bread and sugar was relatively high.

Factors influencing food choice and the pattern of the diet

The transition from the labourer's simple and often restricted diet of the 1870s to the great variety of both fresh and processed foods which is now available to the great majority of households all the year round can be attributed to many factors, but the primary stimulus for this fundamental change in food habits was the great increase in population and the rapid urbanization which accompanied industrial growth in the 1900s.

The increasing need for the storage of both home produced and imported foods during transport and distribution which was accentuated by two World Wars has been met by technological and nutritional research resulting in new and improved techniques for the preservation of perishable and seasonal foods by chilling, refrigeration, quick-freezing, canning, pasteurization and dehydration. This in turn has contributed to the great improvements in the purity and safety of the foods offered to the consumer which are to be discussed in this Symposium: the pasteurization of milk is one of the earlier and perhaps more notable examples.

It has been estimated that retail expenditure on quick-frozen food in the United Kingdom was about £43m in 1960; by 1973, it was about £452m, including broiler chickens[29], and some 14 per cent of households owned home freezers. One consequence of this growth of the quick-freezing industry has been that the seasonal pattern of the diet is tending to become less distinct. This can be illustrated by the average quarterly purchases of fresh and quick-frozen peas and beans in the National Food Survey (see Table 5).

Table 5 *Seasonal purchases of peas and beans: National Food Survey
All households (oz per person per week)*

		Jan–March	April–June	July–Sept	Oct–Dec
1955	Fresh	0·04	0·20	11·45	0·39
	Quick frozen	0·19	0·26	0·07	0·14
1966	Fresh	0·03	0·69	7·78	0·68
	Quick frozen	1·12	1·47	0·87	1·09
1973	Fresh	0·13	0·34	5·19	0·45
	Quick frozen	1·73	1·95	1·66	1·86

Changes in social structure and developments by the food industry in production methods and technological processes have led to progressive changes in the methods of selling and preparing foods which have had a fundamental influence on food choice. In the 1890s food was sold in the local market or in the family shop; by the First World War chain stores with national coverage were becoming popular. In the 1950s and 1960s food retailing entered a new phase with the growth of the supermarket and the self-service shop and more recently we have seen the introduction of other innovations such as the hypermarket and retail outlets specializing in the sale of frozen foods.

In the last 25 years the food industry has increasingly assumed a greater role in the responsibility for food preparation which was formerly carried out in the home. It is, therefore, perhaps appropriate to remind you that some of the older 'convenience foods' which are now widely accepted in their own right were unknown at the turn of the century. Among these are prepared breakfast cereals (average consumption of which increased from 1.8 to 7.3 lb per head per annum between 1939 and 1973), canned and bottled baby foods, fish fingers, potato crisps and instant coffee. During the last decade special plastic films and foil laminates have been developed for packing a wide variety of convenience foods; while quick snack meals are popular it is likely that the demand for pre-cooked and quick-cooking products will continue.

As to the future and what the next 100 years will bring, it would be fool-hardy to try to predict the situation in the year 2075. By looking forward on a shorter time-scale of a decade or two, one can foresee the wheel turning full circle towards a higher degree of agricultural self-sufficiency in this country, and indeed in Europe as a whole, as the world food surpluses on which we have drawn so freely in the past begin to disappear. The food processing and distributing industries, and their supporting research organizations, will no doubt continue to improve our ability to store, preserve, process and distribute a wide range of food commodities in good condition, and to maintain and improve the safety and nutritive value of food which so many of us have come to take for granted. Novel types of food, such as simulated meats, derived from non-meat proteins and fats, are useful and are already being developed; their popularity will depend on their appeal to the customer and their price in relation to competing foods. Further advances in medical knowledge will help us to understand even better than we do now the importance of various food components in relation to health. We have come a long way in the last hundred years, but we still have a long way to go.

I am grateful to my colleague, Miss Jean Robertson, for her help in the preparation of this lecture.

Appendix

Typical menus from Rowntree's study

A. Labourer: Family consisting of two adults and three children
Weekly income under 26 shillings. Forty-six per cent spent on food

	Breakfast	*Dinner*	*Tea*	*Supper*
Friday	bread butter tea	fish bread coffee	bread butter teacake tea	
Saturday	bacon bread tea	brawn bread butter coffee	bread butter teacake tea	
Sunday	bread butter tea	rabbit potatoes Yorkshire pudding	bread butter currant cake tea	

B. Servant-keeping class: Family consisting of three adults and three children

	Breakfast	*Dinner*	*Tea*	*Supper*
Friday	porridge eggs bread butter toast boiled milk tea	beefsteak potatoes cauliflower sponge pudding stewed rhubarb cream dates	bread butter teacake pastry tea	bread butter teacake Bengers food cocoa

Saturday	porridge	minced beef	bread	bread
	beefsteak	potatoes	butter	butter
	bread	cauliflower	buns	sweet cake
	butter	rhubarb pie	tarts	cocoa
	toast	cream	pastry	
	hot milk	oranges	tea	
	tea			
Sunday	bacon and	roast beef	bread	bread
	fried steak	potatoes	butter	butter
	bread	asparagus	teacakes	Bengers food
	butter	cornflour	fruit	hot milk
	toast	stewed rhubarb	cake	
	tea	cream	queen cakes	
			cream cakes	
			lettuce	
			tea	

References

[1] *Annual Review of Agriculture* 1975, Cmnd. 5977, HMSO, London

[2] LEVI, L., BOURNE, S., BRITTAIN, HANCOCK, JEVONS and FELLOWS, F. P. *Report of the Fifty-first Meeting of the British Association for the Advancement of Science*, 1882, 272. John Murray, London

[3] GREAVES, J. P. and HOLLINGSWORTH, D. F. *World Rev. Nutr. Dietetics* 1966, **6**, 34. S. Karger, Basel

[4] ROYAL SOCIETY COMMITTEE. *The Food Supply of the United Kingdom*, 1917, Cmnd. 8421, HMSO, London

[5] MAFF. *Bd. Trade J.* 1968, **194**, 753

[6] MAFF. *Trade and Industry*, 1973, **12**, 459

[7] MAFF. *Trade and Industry*, 1974, **16**, 515

[8] CENTRAL STATISTICAL OFFICE. *Annual Abstract of Statistics*, 1974, HMSO, London

[9] MINISTRY OF LABOUR GAZETTE, 1942, 49, (January 1941), 9, HMSO, London

[10] MINISTRY OF LABOUR AND NATIONAL SERVICE. *Report of an Inquiry into Household Expenditure in 1953–54*, 1957, HMSO, London

[11] MAFF, 1963 et seq, unpublished

[12] SEEBOHM ROWNTREE, B. *Poverty, a Study of Town Life*, 1900, Thomas Nelson, London

[13] DRUMMOND, J. C. and WILBRAHAM, A. *The Englishman's Food*, 1957. Revised edition by Hollingsworth, D. F., Jonathan Cape, London

[14] PATON, D. N. and FINDLAY, L. *Poverty, Nutrition and Growth*. Medical Research Council Special Report No. 101, 1926, HMSO, London

[15] MINISTRY OF HEALTH. *Advisory Committee on Nutrition, First Report*, 1937, HMSO, London

[16] BOYD ORR, J. *Food, Health and Income*, 1937, Macmillan, London

[17] CRAWFORD, SIR WILLIAM and BROADLEY, H. *The People's Food*, 1938, William Heinemann, London

[18] MAFF, National Food Survey Committee. *Domestic Food Consumption and Expenditure*, 1955, HMSO, London, 1957

[19] MAFF, National Food Survey Committee. *Household Food Consumption and Expenditure*, 1973, HMSO, London 1975

[20] HAMMOND, R. J. *History of the Second World War: Food* 1, *The Growth of Policy*, 1951, HMSO and Longmans Green, London

[21] MINISTRY OF FOOD. *How Britain was Fed in Wartime: Food Control* 1939–1945, HMSO, London, 1946

[22] MAFF. *The Bread and Flour Regulations*, 1963 (S.I. 1963 No. 1435)

[23] MAFF. *The Bread and Flour (Amendment) Regulations*, 1972 (S.I. 1972 No. 1391)

[24] MINISTRY OF FOOD, National Food Survey Committee. *Domestic Food Consumption and Expenditure*, 1950, HMSO, London 1952

[25] MINISTRY OF FOOD, National Food Survey Committee. *Domestic Food Consumption and Expenditure*, 1951, HMSO, London, 1953

[26] MINISTRY OF FOOD, National Food Survey Committee. *Domestic Food Consumption and Expenditure*, 1952, HMSO, London, 1954

[27] MAFF, National Food Survey Committee. *Domestic Food Consumption and Expenditure*, 1953–1964; *Household Food Consumption and Expenditure*, 1965–1973, HMSO, London, 1955–75

[28] DHSS. *Recommended Intakes of Nutrients for the United Kingdom*, Reports on Health and Medical Subjects No. 120, 1969, HMSO, London

[29] MAFF, unpublished

Introductory remarks by Dr. Elton

Although the population of the United Kingdom has approximately doubled in the last 100 years while the farmed acreage has decreased slightly, the yield of crops per acre has greatly increased, often doubled or more, due to the breeding of better plant varieties, the improved control of pests and diseases etc. Although we were virtually self-supporting for indigenous foodstuffs until the early nineteenth century, a rapid expansion in imports of wheat, bacon, sugar, butter and cheese occurred after 1850 and, after 1882, refrigeration techniques led to a corresponding increase in meat imports. At present 54·5 per cent of the total food supply by value is home produced and 68 per cent of indigenous food materials.

The average diet in the past hundred years has become richer in milk, eggs, meat, fats, sugar and fruit with a lower consumption of wheat flour and, to a lesser extent, of potatoes. The average intake of energy from food has increased by about 10 per cent between 1909 and 1973; there has been a small increase in protein intake and a large increase in fat intake. The percentage of energy from alcoholic drinks has increased rapidly in recent years and is now 5 per cent: leaving out young people, teetotallers etc. the average drinking person probably derives 10 per cent of his energy intake from alcoholic drinks. Very few people today are undernourished due to eating too little food and, as the Chief Medical Officer said earlier, the incidence of obesity is probably the most serious nutritional disorder.

As to the future, most forecasts predict an increasing imbalance of world population and food supplies. There is clearly a need for increased

97

agricultural production in the world at large, and less reliance can be placed on this country's ability to buy in the world market the materials which make up nearly 50 per cent of our total food supply. The recent White Paper *Food from our own Resources* concludes *inter alia*:

1. That the world situation with respect to supply and prices of foodstuffs justifies a policy of expansion of food products in the United Kingdom.
2. That the agricultural industry should be capable of continuing expansion at about $2\frac{1}{2}$ per cent per year on average.

In the *next* hundred years therefore we may find ourselves moving back towards a situation of greater self-sufficiency for food than has been the case in the recent past. Furthermore, where we do have to import food, we may well import from our partners in the EEC rather than from other parts of the world, a trend which has been accelerating recently.

Discussion

Dr. B D Powell (Director, Cadbury Ltd): I should like to raise just one aspect of what Dr. Elton said. He has dealt most ably and interestingly with the nation's overall diet in the past, which indeed was his remit, but I think that we need to look in nutritional terms at what the individual is eating, what the individual diet is, if we are to identify any particular persons or group of persons who are at risk.

Also I think that, in collecting data on the nation's diet, we must consider what use we can make of it for the future. Clearly, if one takes the total nation's diet and divides it by the number of people, one only gets this rather artificial figure of what the average man consumes; it takes no account, naturally, of individual variations. I think that this is recognized to some degree in the Food Survey, where there is an attempt to look at families and data appear on large families and small families. However, what we really need to know is how the housewife's purchase is divided once she gets it home. One suspects that, in many families, the father of the house—especially if he is a heavy manual worker—will take perhaps an undue proportion of the meat and the bacon, the children may take an undue proportion of the carbohydrate and the mother, as usual, is left to eat rather what is left. Do we take account of what happens to the food when it is in the home, whether it is well cooked or whether it is badly cooked and what, in fact, is the nutrition that is getting to the particular individuals?

The Survey tells us a lot about past trends. Assuming that we can refine it in terms of the individual, what are we going to do with the fresh data? How can we influence people, if in extrapolating we do not like what we see? Do we know how to influence people in terms of food choice when we are talking of nutritional factors? I should be interested to hear comments on these questions.

Further, do we have enough information? Should we be doing more research work to determine what influences food choice and how we decide what we really eat and drink?

Dr. G A H Elton: Dr. Powell is quite right in saying that the main food surveys only tell us about averages. The Consumption Level Estimates which are based on the total amount of food coming into the docks or out of the farm gate can be divided by the number of people in the population to give us an average number of calories per head. The National Food Survey analyses data in terms of income groups, in terms of family size and in terms of location within the country, so that we know, for example, how much bread people eat in Wales and how many kippers they eat in Scotland. However, when it comes down to individuals this is something which is difficult to do. It requires a lot of willpower to determine precisely how much food you eat yourself in the course of a week—I do not know how many people here have tried it. Nevertheless, there are a number of surveys which have been published on this subject in recent years. Apart from independent medical studies by Drs. Passmore and Durnin at Edinburgh, there have recently been studies by the Department of Health particularly on groups of people which might be thought, *prima facie*, to be at risk— the elderly, for example, There was a recent study by a Committee of COMA on the nutrition of the elderly; there have been several studies on the nutrition of schoolchildren; and there have been recent studies on the nutrition of nurses, so we are gradually acquiring more information on food consumption patterns for individuals.

How one influences people's choice is a difficult business. In wartime there is no problem; you say to everyone, 'You have two ounces of cheese a week and four ounces of meat and there you are, you get on with it.' Fortunately, we are not in that situation. It comes back partly to education, and the food industry itself has a responsibility here which is discharged with great enthusiasm in terms of convincing the public of the value of its own products. It would be interesting to know more about the psychological motives which cause people to eat one kind of food rather than another, although I would not myself put that problem very high on my list of priorities if I had a limited amount of money to spend on research. I would prefer to spend it on studies on food safety.

Professor A E Bender (Department of Nutrition and Food Science, Queen Elizabeth College, London): I should like to take this further. The legislation we have been speaking about today controls food as far as the front door. The question is, what happens after that where we cannot legislate? We have spoken of hygiene, for example, and any dirty person at home can cause far more harm to himself and his family than anyone outside. Pesticide residues are controlled, yet do we know how much pesticide is being put on our own pure, natural, fresh vegetables in our own garden? The legislation makes sure that the manufacturer of fruit juices retains all the vitamin C in the bottle on the shelf in a shop for a year or two perhaps, but once the bottle is opened at home it can disappear in a week. If overheated fats are toxic, the manufacturer can ensure that he does not overheat them, but do we know what is happening at home? This is not a question of nutrition education or health education. This we have little faith in ourselves; we do not think that we can change people's habits very much.

My question relates to one that was asked this morning, how far do we get less and less return for our money spent on increased legislation? In other words, how much should we be or are we legislating, and how much are we losing on the wrong side of the front door because we do not know what is happening there?

Dr. G A H Elton: I am surprised to hear you say that you do not have much faith in spreading the gospel on nutrition; I am sure that you do it very well with your own students and one hopes that they will go into schools and colleges and pass this on down the line to their students, and so on. Admittedly, however, it is very difficult to get nutritional information over to the hard-pressed mother in the home, and I would agree that that is where many of the food hygiene problems may exist. The Food and Drugs Act has helped to improve hygienic practices in the food processing industry, who now pay very great attention to making sure that they produce safe, clean products, and in the distribution industry where, as appropriate, they use cold chains to make sure that their perishable products get to the shop in good condition; in retailing, the old-fashioned food store where you could take your baby in and sit it on the boiled ham has disappeared. Most shops nowadays are reasonably good in respect of hygiene, although there is sometimes still something left to be desired. However, in the home it may well be that the standard of hygiene in the preparation of food is sometimes poor, in some households at least.

How we get information about this I do not know, because whenever one does a survey one has an inbuilt uncertainty because the fact that a survey is being made changes the result; everybody is very clean and washes the cups out three times before they do anything with them, while they are being watched.

So I do not know how you establish the hygiene situation in individual homes, and if anybody can make a suggestion I should be interested to hear it.

The Chairman: Would anyone like to respond on how little we are getting for our increased legislation?

Mr. R F Giles: I am afraid I am still of the opinion that we try to legislate perhaps too far, and we really must rely on education and advice to improve standards in the home. If Professor Bender can do anything towards making his students spread the gospel, I shall be only too grateful.

The Chairman: I wonder if Dr. Pereira has any comment to make on the need to increase our agricultural output by 2½ per cent per annum in order to meet the predictions which our colleagues in the Ministry have put before us.

Dr. H C Pereira (Chief Scientist, Ministry of Agriculture, Fisheries and Food): My Lord Chairman, the 2½ per cent in the White Paper was based largely on the estimate of the economists as to what it would make sense to grow in this country. The farmers of this country can only grow what they can sell and, therefore, can only plan to produce what we cannot import very much more cheaply from the rest of the world. That still dominates our agriculture, but I have no doubt at all that the world position that Dr. Elton has sketched is going to make it steadily more difficult for us in the future to be able to rely on getting what food we need as and when we want it from overseas. For a long time we are going to have the situation in which supply and demand are so closely equal that the ordinary fluctuations, particularly of the monsoon climate in which a very large proportion of the world's subsistence agriculture exists, will give us quite big changes in availability and price. It makes a great deal of sense to me that this country should steadily work towards the maximum self-sufficiency in food.

Mr. C Stanfield (Public Control Committee, Mid-Glamorgan County Council): I was interested in what the speaker said dealing with the policies of wastage. This is a tremendous moral and ethical problem. You dealt with the question of cooking waste and industrial processing but you never touched upon the tremendous waste that takes place as far as price fixing is concerned. I am just wondering whether you have any solution to this problem that you could offer this audience. I understand that now in the EEC there has been tremendous over-production of apples so that they are pulping them and throwing them down the drain; in this country even, last year many thousands of gallons of milk were thrown down the drains. On the other hand, we hear from the speaker the tremendous problems that are facing the people of the world with regard to expanding population, not only in this country but in the world at large.

101

What contribution can we make in terms of utilization of the land of the world and in cutting down this waste?

My question is, have you got any figures on the amount of waste that is taking place and, if you have, is there any solution to this problem?

Dr. G A H Elton: Occasionally we do get widely publicized cases of this kind of food wastage, not only in this country but in other parts of the world. I do not have any figures of how much this represents, but I should think that only a very small fraction of 1 per cent of our nation's food supply gets wasted in this sort of way. Of course, under the new EEC arrangements some food gets sold into intervention storage if it is in excess. One reads from time to time about butter mountains, wine lakes and things of this kind. They are big lakes and mountains, but small in relation to the total food needs of the population of Western Europe.

If we are going to try to plan at all we have to recognize that we are dealing with a biological situation; sometimes we shall get a bigger harvest than was expected and sometimes a smaller one, so that there will sometimes be surpluses. In fact, if we are wise we shall always plan to have a surplus; otherwise we may find ourselves with a deficit.

It is a considerable economic and administrative problem to try to balance what you want to produce against what you can consume bearing in mind the demands of the world market. Furthermore, if we have a quantity of skimmed milk powder available in this country at the moment and somebody in India would dearly like to have it, it does not necessarily follow that we can get it to him over the thousands of miles between, up jungle tracks and so on. There are questions of international economics and logistics involved in all these things.

Professor H M Sinclair (Director, International Institute of Human Nutrition): My Lord Chairman, Dr. Elton repeated a monstrous statement made this morning by Sir Henry, and I quote: 'If there is a nutritional problem, it is obesity.' Dr. Elton's figures showed that, from 1934 to 1938, the *per capita* calorie consumption was 3050; in 1973 the *per capita* calorie consumption was 3050. Unless we are sitting more and more on our bottoms, which is probably true, obesity cannot be a major problem and it is doubtful if obesity has really increased very much.

Dr. Elton stated that food has become cleaner and safer in the last 100 years. Safer? The expectation of life of a middle-aged man 130 years ago was almost exactly the same as it is today; there is 2·7 years difference between the expectation today and in 1843. Yet in 1843 middle-aged men were dying of pulmonary tuberculosis, lobar pneumonia, and the chronic degenerative diseases that now kill us were very rare. Those chronic degenerative diseases

102

are nutritional. Coronary heart disease has risen at least two times, or deaths attributed to coronary heart disease in middle-aged men have risen twice in this country since 1939. Atherosclerosis and dental caries are universal in this population, or almost universal, over the age of two. They are nutritional.

Now this is no fault of the food industry that I admire enormously; it is the fault, my Lord Chairman, of people who stalk, as you stalked, the corridors of power and divert no money into human nutritional research.

The Chairman: I am extremely sad that the bad light prevented me from seeing my old friend, Hugh Sinclair. He may recall that, many years ago, before I stalked any corridors of power, we both spoke the same language and, during the early part of the Second World War, I think that he and I, and one or two others, were responsible for putting some jolly good goads behind the authorities in order to see that what should be done was done.

Unfortunately, Sir Henry Yellowlees, the man to whom this question should have been addressed, has left. The last thing I would do would be to take on Hugh Sinclair on his interpretation of the statistics that he has given us, and I do not think it would be fair to Dr. Elton to ask him to discuss atherosclerosis and one or two other such matters today. However, I think that another occasion should, indeed, be arranged on which we can take up this point of whether or not the quality of nutrition is such that food has become safer as well as more wholesome when one takes into account all the variables that have to be considered when discussing the expectation of life in different age groups.

Reference was made this morning by the Chief Medical Officer of the Department of Health and Social Security to this carafe of water, which I see has been changed. Once upon a time, if I remember correctly, British legislation had it that water had to be 'pure and wholesome'; then the word 'pure' was dropped, though it still has to be 'wholesome'.

However, the point is very well made. Let us find out whether we should be as complacent and self-congratulatory as we are about the wholesomeness of food which is associated with the apparent increase in the general health of the population. But I do think that this is a matter which should be taken up in the presence of the Chief Medical Officer.

Dr. Elton (communicated): In my brief remarks on obesity, I was quoting what I regard as two very good sources, namely the Chief Medical Officer of the Department of Health and Social Services and the Report of the ARC/MRC Committee on Food and Nutrition Research (Neuberger, 1974), which states (p. 123) that 'obesity is probably the most serious nutritional disorder with which we are faced in this country . . .'. Although energy

103

intakes are about the same now as they were 40 years ago, energy *requirements* have probably fallen for a variety of reasons, including a lower average level of physical activity in the population.

A discussion of the many factors which affect expectation of life (including cigarette smoking, environmental hazards, etc. as well as nutrition) would, as the Chairman has said, probably merit another Symposium.

A Century of Food Analysis

H Egan
Government Chemist

The role of food analysis

The chemical analysis of food is widely used today as an index of nature, substance and quality control and consumer protection, being secondary only to the main sensory responses such as appearance, odour and taste. Indeed, for some aspects of quality such as safety, and for some compositional aspects of consumer protection, analysis today is the basis of standards which are either in parallel with, or in some cases (for the purposes of day-to-day control) take the place of, sensory aspects of acceptability. In these areas, two main kinds of analysis may be distinguished, compositional analysis and trace analysis. Compositional analysis relates to the amounts of the different major constituents water, fat, protein or carbohydrate which are present in the individual basic food products of agriculture, animal husbandry and fishery such as milk or meat, flour, fish or fruit. Compositional analyses can also be applied to processed foods, such as cheese or sausage, bread or jam; the results may then be used for the estimation of the amounts of the ingredient basic foods used in their preparation, although other analytical evidence may also be required before reliable estimates can be made. Compositional analyses are thus primarily of use in quality control; and in the protection of consumer interests in so far as the type and amount of food ingredients are concerned. Trace analysis relates to minor constituents, normally those present to the extent of less than 1 per cent (but often less than 10 mg/kg or 10 parts per million) and can be similarly used.

Trace analysis is widely used in the context of adulteration and the health of the consumer, for the detection and estimation of small amounts of additives and contaminants which may be present. The history of food adulteration and food analysis was reviewed by Filby in 1934[1], who describes analytical chemistry as the great enemy of adulteration. Although the origins of analytical chemistry can be traced back to ancient times, applied analytical chemistry was almost unknown at the beginning of the nineteenth century. By 1875, however, compositional analysis had developed to the point where it provided a general knowledge of the proximate composition of most basic food commodities, and had begun to find useful and practical applications to everyday problems of fraudulent substitution or adulteration. Detailed compositional knowledge was still lacking in many areas however, but progress in this aspect was being made. Indeed, developments continue in this field today, with specialist areas such as plant chemotaxonomy extending well beyond the immediate area of food analysis. The report of the Food Standards Committee on Novel Protein Foods[2] published earlier this year, for example, contains a detailed appendix illustrating the analytical aspects of the estimation of non-meat proteins in mixed meat products. Trace analysis on the other hand has developed more recently, many of the methods which are in wide use today being based on practical principles which have become established only in the past 30 or 40 years. Trace analysis, too, is a developing subject. Microanalysis, the analysis of small amounts of sample, has also developed considerably in the past century[3] but is of less importance in the context of food.

There are many facets to the contributions of food analysis to public safety and commercial quality control today. These include the estimation of acceptability, nutritional value, storage life (a matter of increasing importance with the development of consumer interest in open date-marking of pre-packaged retail produce) and value-for-money considerations. Quality control is important for both raw materials and the processed food manufactured from these; analysis is one of the key factors in standardization, important to industry (and the consumer) in the maintenance of 'brand image' and to government (and the consumer) as a practical basis for standards of acceptability in international as well as national trade. Analysis also plays a part in the identification of products: apart from the consumer protection aspect this is also of economic significance in the operation of import restrictions and quota controls. Finally, analysis plays an important part in many aspects of food research, for example in the provision of a rapid index of nutritional value of new varieties of cereals in the course of plant breeding studies.

Early analytical chemistry

The beginnings of analytical chemistry can be traced back to ancient times, eventually to become more clearly recognized in the case of organic chemistry in work of the French academicians of the seventeenth and early eighteenth century and taking on the semblance of an exact science in the hands of men such as Berzelius and Liebig at the beginning of the nineteenth century. Thus the original basis for much of qualitative and quantitative analytical chemistry today was laid in the decades around the year 1800, although the essential knowledge of the chemical composition of the substances (or of their individual constituents) to be analysed upon which this in turn is based was developed through studies which continued well into the nineteenth century. Indeed the search for such knowledge continues in various forms today, for example as the possible basis for alternative (and better) methods of examining fruit or meat products for compositional characteristics. The basic compositional aspects upon which food analysis is still broadly based were recognized by Liebig in 1846. Foods are composed largely of carbohydrates, fats and proteins. These together with water and smaller amounts of other substances more recently recognized such as mineral salts, vitamins, colouring and flavouring substances still form the essential foundation for food analysis.

Adulteration is probably nearly as old as food itself. The maintenance of quality in former times became the responsibility of the professional guilds and officers who were responsible to the crown or were specially appointed by civic authorities to protect ale and bread. O'Keefe[4] refers among others to the Guild of Garblers, concerned with the detection of impurities in pepper (used as a preservative), a duty which in 1429 passed to the Grocers Company; and to the Bakers Company, incorporated in 1307. By the beginning of the nineteenth century the microscope had become a useful and often effective means of detection of substitution and gross adulteration; and it was largely relied on by Frederick Accum in his famous *Treatise on Adulteration of Food and Culinary Poisons* published in 1820[5], as well as later by Dr. A H Hassall[6] and Dr. H Letheby for their reports and publications on extraneous matter in staple foods, published in the *Lancet* between 1851 and 1854. These reports, published in collected form in 1855, were directly responsible for the appointment by Parliament of a select committee of enquiry which resulted eventually in the passing of the first 'Pure Food' Act in 1860.

By about 1850 such basic processes as precipitation, filtration, titration and volumetric gas analysis were well established, though in a form dependent very much on *ad hoc* equipment made in individual laboratories for the purpose and with a specificity or exactness of a different order from that now regarded as proper to qualitative (or quantitative) analysis. Some of the purely physical methods, especially those based essentially on the measurement of basic properties, such as the precise weight (mass) of solids or the precise volume of liquids, became well established in advance of more sophisticated methods such as colorimetry, the precursor of spectrophotometry in its various forms. Writing in 1857, the author of Loftus' *Handbook for Officers of Excise*[7] comments that the method of ascertaining the original gravity of wort was then regularly practised by chemically qualified officers stationed in the principal ports of the United Kingdom. This is an analytical process which essentially depends on laboratory distillation and the ability to measure mass and volume accurately.

Chirnside and Hamence have surveyed the state of analytical chemistry as applied to the work of Public Analysts a hundred years ago[8], by which time the main classes of the organic components of food were recognized as acids, albuminous matter (proteins), colouring matter, fats and oils, fibrous matter, gums, starches, sugars and tannins. However, there were still no reliable methods for the estimation of the proportions of these various components and no general textbooks of food analysis. There was in consequence no full understanding of the variation in proportions which occurred naturally in foods and the limits of composition which in consequence could be regarded as characterizing genuine produce. At the same time there was only a limited ability to distinguish individual substances within a class of substances such as fats or sugars.

Analytical background to the 1875 Act

In addition to the developments in chemical analysis outlined above, analysis by examination under the microscope also played a large part in the detection of food adulteration in the first half of the nineteenth century. Much of Hassall's pioneering work was based on microscopy[6]. Earlier legislation dating from 1787[a] relating to the strength of spirits was based on the purely physical concept of specific gravity, from which had developed the hydrometer; the definition of proof spirit in 1818[b] still holds today. Filby[1] cites all the statutes which bear on the adulteration of food from the Assize of Bread of 1266[c] to the 1875 Sale of Food and Drugs Act[d]. The first of these to feature analysis (or analysts) as such was the original 1860 Food and Drink Act[e] which provided that any purchaser of an article of food or drink in an area in which an analyst had been appointed under the Act could, for a prescribed fee, have the article analysed. The appointment of analysts was not compulsory, however, and many authorities empowered to do so made no such appointment. Even in the City of London in 1861 Dr. Letheby, the first analyst to be so appointed, stated that he received only four applica-

---

(a) 27 George III, C.31 (1787)
(b) 58 George III, C.28 (1818)
(c) Assisa Panis 51 Henry III (1266)
(d) An Act to make better provision for the Sale of Food and Drugs in a pure state, 38 and 39 Victoria, C.63 (1875)
(e) An Act for Preventing the Adulteration of Articles of Food and Drink, 23 and 24 Victoria, C.84 (1860)

tions for analysis in the previous quarter[9]. The amending act of 1872[f] again left exercise of the power of appointment of public analysts optional, except that the Local Government Board could require individual authorities to make appointments. The Board had in any case to approve all appointments. The 1875 Act essentially repeated this position, except that it required inspectors to procure samples of food or drink suspected to be adulterated and to have them analysed, if not by an analyst appointed by their own authority, then by one appointed by another.

The essence of the 1860 Act was freedom from adulteration, a concept which basically was unaltered by the 1872 Act. The 1875 Act introduced the additional concept of prejudice to the purchaser in terms of the nature, substance and quality of the food; or in particular by any undisclosed change in composition by way of abstraction of any part of it.

The question of qualification for appointment as public analyst became a major issue. One aspect of the controversy which developed related to the question of referee analysis in cases where the opinion of the public analyst was challenged. Using the correspondence columns of Sir William Crookes' *Chemical News*, various public analysts in 1874 disagreed with the proposals of the Select Committee on the Adulteration of Food that referee analysts should be appointed to help reach a decision in disputed cases[10]. When the Adulteration of Food and Drugs Bill was laid before Parliament, the view that analysts at Somerset House (the laboratory of the Inland Revenue) should be so appointed was not well received[11]. Mr. George Phillips, who had been in the Revenue service since 1826 and principal of the Inland Revenue Laboratory since 1842, had recently retired; he stoutly defended the competence of the staff from the columns of *Chemical News*[12].

When later in the year the Bill became law, Section 22 appointed the chemical officers of the Inland Revenue Laboratory as referee analysts in the event of a dispute in court. Phillips had long been an advocate of a single laboratory service available to all government departments and his view had obviously been taken into account in framing the Act. And at the same time, the Public Analysts, employed by the larger local authorities since about 1860 and many of them medical men, now assumed a much greater responsibility in safeguarding the quality of food on sale to the public.

The story of the formation of the Society of Public Analysts has been fully documented recently in a book published on the occasion of the centenary of the Society for Analytical Chemistry[8]. In the early years of the Act about half of the referee analyses carried out at the Inland Revenue

---

(f) An Act to amend the Law for the Prevention of Adulteration of Food and Drink and of Drugs, 35 and 36 Victoria, C.74 (1872)

Laboratory (often referred to simply as 'Somerset House' in the contemporary literature) failed to confirm the findings of the Public Analyst concerned and for some 20 years a state of open hostility existed between Public Analysts and the Inland Revenue Laboratory. One of the causes of this acrimony was almost certainly the question of qualifications, since Public Analysts were expected to possess professional qualifications, although it was not until 1900 that the Branch E certificate of the Institute of Chemistry became a legal requirement. The staff at Somerset House were taken entirely from the Excise service; they were given scientific training 'on the job' and at special classes at London University but were not legally required to be qualified at all. But whatever criticisms there may have been of the calibre of the junior staff, these could not have been levelled at the new principal, Dr. James Bell. At the time of his appointment, he had had 28 years' service with the Excise and had produced new editions of the Compendium of General Excise Orders[13]. As a consequence of the Laboratory's new involvement with food, a full study of analytical methods was initiated and volumes describing methods of food analysis were published in 1881[14] and 1883[15]. Shortly after the publication of these, Dr. Bell was made a Fellow of the Royal Society and in the following year he read a paper on the chemistry of food and drugs at a public conference on Food Adulteration at the International Health Exhibition in London[16].

In addition to the analytical functions assigned by Section 22 of the Act to the Inland Revenue Laboratory, Section 30 directed that from 1st January 1876 all tea imported as merchandise into Great Britain or Ireland should be subject to examination by persons to be appointed by the Commissioners of Customs (not then merged with the Excise Department), for which purpose samples might 'be taken and with all convenient speed be examined by the analysts to be so appointed'. Section 22 also directed that 'an officer should be appointed to analyse samples of tea when deemed necessary by the Inspector'. The appointment of three Inspectors, two Assistant Inspectors and an analyst was announced by the Board of Customs in September 1875. The appointment of Mr. J B Keene as Tea Analyst marked the formal setting up of the Custom House Laboratory, although a Wine Testing Station had been in existence for some years in the same building. The new laboratory was for some time maintained separately from the testing station and for several years the annual reports of the Board of Customs gave separate returns of samples examined in 'the Laboratory established at Custom House under the Sale of Food and Drugs Act, 1875' and for 'the gauging department' or 'the Testing Room' at the Custom House. In making the new appointments, the Treasury stipulated that 'these gentlemen in addition to their new duties will still have to perform those appertaining to them as Officers of

Customs' and each was granted an allowance of £50 per annum. This probably meant that Keene, in addition to running the new Laboratory, also retained some connection with the Wine Testing Station at the Custom House. The distinction between the two establishments must have been rather artificial, as the 1879 return shows that the wine station also examined imported beers, spirits and fusel oil for spirit content, while the Tea Laboratory also examined some 900 samples of other imported goods to determine whether they contained, or had been manufactured with, spirit.

The 1875 Act commanded the interest of analysts from the beginning. The newly formed Society of Public Analysts did not then have its own journal but used the columns of the *Chemical News* to keep its members informed of the progress of the Bill, the full text of which was published with discussion immediately after it was read a second time in the House of Commons on 19th February 1875[17]. A month later, *Chemical News* carried a report applauding the remedy of defects of the Bill as a result of the Society's representations[18]. Throughout this period it also published notes of interest in the context of the analysis of adulterated foods (mainly milk, bread, butter, but also including other fats, tea and wine), together with reviews of the new textbooks of food analysis then becoming available. All of these contributions were subsequently drawn together and published as a single volume of proceedings[19]. The *Analyst*, the journal of the Society of Public Analysts, was first published in 1877 and was very largely devoted to matters relating to water and food analysis. The new journal was the first of its kind in the world and indeed a pioneer. So far as analysis in general was concerned, reliable methods for the estimation of the proportions of many of the main organic components of food[8] had still to be developed and there was no proper understanding of the variation in proportions which occurred naturally in foods, or of the limits of composition which in consequence could be regarded as characterizing genuine produce. At the same time there was only a limited ability to distinguish individual members within a class, such as fats or sugars. The establishment of the proximate composition of food upon which to judge the genuineness or otherwise of suspect samples was one of the first tasks of the analyst and this process is faithfully reflected in the pages of the new journal, which still flourishes under the same title today.

Food analysis 1870–95

Filby[1] has described the development of food analysis during the period 1820–1930 but is mainly concerned with the period to the turn of the century. Techniques have developed very considerably in the past hundred years and although reliable and fully developed methods were rarely available in 1875 many of the basic operations upon which the compositional analyses of today are now based were by then well advanced and in some cases reasonably well established. Much of the work of chemists in the early part of the nineteenth century had in fact been of an analytical character. The period from 1860 to 1900 was largely devoted to the application of the techniques which had already been developed to problems of economic and public health importance[20, 21], and this is still one of the roles of the Laboratory of the Government Chemist[22]. The widely used Kjeldahl method for the estimation of organically bound nitrogen, still one of the basic methods for proximate food analysis today, first appeared in 1885. Hamence has described the development of techniques for the examination of milk and butter[20], indicating how these have themselves influenced the standards for these commodities. Thus until the introduction of the Adams coil method for the determination of fat in which the milk sample is first absorbed onto a coil of filter paper and dried and the subsequent ether extraction done by the Soxhlet process, the standard for fat in milk adopted by public analysts had been only 2·5 per cent. The better appreciation of the physical basis for the analysis led to a fuller understanding of the true composition of milk and the limits within which it was reasonable to set standards; and also provided in later years a sounder basis for the standardization of the methods, so improving substantially the value of the compositional standards themselves. A similar situation applied to many other everyday food items and the need to develop standards by which, in analytical terms, the purity and wholesomeness of food could through the process of law be judged was well recognized. The Society of Public Analysts put forward limits indicative of genuineness for many of these, which were eventually brought together in 1902 by Moor in his book 'Suggested Standards of Purity for Foods and Drugs'[23]. This dealt mainly with drugs but simple standards were included for bread, butter, cheese, cocoa, coffee, condensed milk, cream, flour, honey, jam, meat preparations, milk and sugar, some (but not all) of which were in due time given statutory force.

As regards basic quantitative analytical processes, by 1875 titration had already gained considerable benefit from the development by Mohr in 1853[24] of the precursor of the modern burette. His design of apparatus was substantially more precise and controllable in everyday use in comparison with the earlier designs, including the fragile Gay-Lussac tube with a long narrow side-arm. Gravimetric analysis was also improved and its application was extended in 1878 with the introduction of the Gooch asbestos crucible.

Few general textbooks of food analysis were available before 1874, when the precursors of the present day compendia were just beginning to appear as slim, pocket-sized volumes devoted to individual foods. Among the first of these were Wanklyn's 'Milk Analysis'[25] and 'Tea, Coffee and Cocoa Analysis[26] and Hehner and Angell's 'Butter'[27], all published in 1874 and Wanklyn and Cooper's 'Bread Analysis' 1881[28]. Many went through subsequent editions. They were joined at a later stage by contributions from authors in industry[29] such as Droop Richmond's 'Laboratory Book of Dairy Analysis' 1905[30]. Whilst written with proper scientific aspirations for truth and precision, the earliest textbooks clearly displayed the limitations of the analyst and his equipment at the time. Wanklyn, for example, aware of the limitations of the calibrated laboratory glassware then commercially available, was most careful to instruct his readers how to check this. It was necessary to give precise catalogue and agency details for the acquisition of a suitable analytical balance and one reads with some nostalgia of 4 cm platinum dishes costing 70p, '14s a piece'. The quantitative basis of the chemistry of butter analysis, for the purpose of ascertaining its genuineness or otherwise, was developed between the first edition of Hehner and Angell's book published in 1874[27] and the second edition three years later. This became possible by the simple expedient of using an alcoholic solution of alkali for the preliminary hydrolysis in place of aqueous alkali, an improvement attributed to the Medical Officer of Health and Public Analyst for Portsmouth, Dr. G Turner. Thus modified (to quote from the second edition of Hehner and Angell), 'the original, tedious, troublesome and inaccurate method was at once rendered quick, exact and even elegant'.

Gas analysis was in a sense a precursor of gas chromatography, although the methods of separation and isolation of individual gases and the methods for the detection and measurement were vastly different. Techniques in the nineteenth century were concerned mainly with carbon dioxide and such permanent gases as oxygen and nitrogen, not with vapourized liquids or solids; separations were based on combustion or the use of chemical absorbent solutions. Another important separation technique in both trace and compositional analysis is solvent extraction. The means for achieving this in 1875 were relatively imprecise, depending basically on removal of the upper phase by mouth-pipette. Specially designed glass separators were developed in the later years of the century, the separating funnel in its present form being introduced in the 1890s. The basic laws of optical absorption had already been established by Beer and Lambert earlier in the century and there had been an important contribution to the improvement of techniques for trace analysis in the Duboscq colorimeter[31]. This was further developed during the latter half of the century and improved the means for the colorimetric estimation of trace metals such as lead and iron. Similar instruments also provided the basis for the development in the late 1930s of the photoelectric spectrometers, the precursors of a whole range of infrared, visible and ultra-violet spectrophotometers and their counterparts in the still developing fields of nuclear magnetic and electron spin resonance spectrometry today.

Analytical developments 1895–1950

It might be said that the developments in methods of analysis up to the turn of the century paved the way for firmer legal control of the composition and purity of food. Something of the converse process began to develop around 1895–1905, however, and increasingly the law began to make stronger demands on the skills of the analyst so that today there are areas where problems of analytical control arise.

Much of the development of food analysis during the first half of the twentieth century was by way of the consolidation of techniques of the previous decades. The basic principles of gravimetry, titrimetry and colorimetry were already well established. Commercial laboratory equipment became available more easily, designs improved and standards were developed for calibrated glassware and the purity of reagent chemicals. Until the First World War, the United Kingdom had come to rely upon the European Continent (particularly Germany) for the reagent quality chemicals essential for reliable food analysis. As a result of a joint initiative of the Society of Public Analysts and the Institute of Chemistry (now the Royal Institute of Chemistry) in 1915 a new range of Analar chemicals (still available today) was launched in Britain. Improved reagents and apparatus then made it possible, through collaborative study, to standardize the analytical methods themselves, so facilitating agreement between analysts and between laboratories. This in turn led to the acceptance of quality criteria based on direct analytical evidence for such aspects as nutritional value. The Analytical Methods Committee of the Society of Public Analysts (the predecessor of the present day Analytical Division of the Chemical Society) was set up in 1935 but there had been earlier studies of methods standardization, dating back to 1882[8]. Similar developments in the central standardization of analytical methods followed in the United State of America in the early years of the present century[44]. Whilst as in Britain these centred on methods of food analysis, the organization took place at federal government level and the Association of Official Agricultural Chemists (now the Association of Official Analytical Chemists) was founded in 1886. This body has had a strong influence on the philosophy and development by collaborative study of standard methods of food analysis and although the problems of food adulteration did not become its concern initially, a strong analytical interest in this area began in 1896[32] which is still sustained today.

Sampling is an integral and important part of all analytical processes, but neither this nor the actual analytical methods to be used in the laboratory are normally specific in the law. The 1955 Act[g] does however make specific provision in Section 93 for the division of samples taken by a Food and Drugs Authority into three portions, whilst Section 96 provides that samples, taken under direction of the Minister, shall be divided into four parts. The problem of dividing samples was originally dealt with in the 1899 Act[h].

I have mentioned the hostility towards the Somerset House Laboratory which arose because of analysts there, coming from the revenue service, were not required to have any formal qualifications in chemical analysis. This was not entirely true, however, although it is true that there were no ready-made training courses for them to attend. But special courses were arranged for these analysts at South Kensington; and at the conclusion of a course the officers were duly and impartially examined. Papers were set annually; copies of these still exist. In the event, the candidates acquitted themselves well.

The formal examination in food, drug and water analysis of the Institute of Chemistry did not become available until 1898, although as far back as 1890 the Society of Public Analysts had suggested that proof of adequate training in food analysis should be available when local authorities appointed public analysts[33]. The Local Government Board had accepted the Fellowship of the Institute of Chemistry (now the Royal Institute of Chemistry), founded in 1877 and incorporated by royal charter in 1885, as sufficient evidence of competence in chemistry for such appointments. But it took some years for the Institute to persuade all the authorities concerned to discontinue the practice of making appointments jointly to the office of Medical Officer of Health and Public Analyst[34]. In 1898 the Institute established a professional qualifying examination in the analysis of water, food and drugs[15]. Since 1900 the diploma which is awarded to successful candidates has been accepted as evidence of the statutory requirement of competency for the appointment of Public Analysts, now embodied in the Public Analysts Regulations 1957[i]. The examination in later years became known as the 'Branch E' Fellowship examination. The Royal Institute of Chemistry still holds a postgraduate examination in the analysis of food, drugs and water, leading to the award of its Mastership in Chemical Analysis, the regulations for which have recently been revised to bring it into line with

---

(g) Food and Drugs Act, 3 and 4 Eliz. II, C.16 (1955)
(h) Sale of Food and Drugs Act, 62 and 63, Victoria, C.51 (1899)
(i) The Public Analyst Regulations, Statutory Instrument No. 273 (1957)

the present day needs of law enforcement agencies in the light of reorganizations in local government and the needs of contemporary environmental interests.

Food analysis and the law 1895–1950

A major influence on the application of analysis to the control of the purity and composition of food in Britain has been the development of standards, both legal and voluntary.

Analytical methods do not usually feature in the law itself and have only occasionally done so in the law relating to food. Most if not all of what I have to say on this subject applies equally to England and Wales, to Scotland and to Northern Ireland, although separate Acts or regulations may apply. Compositional standards for food are normally dependent on the availability of suitable analytical methods. Many such standards have come into force since 1900. These were relatively few in number at first: those which had been in operation prior to 1940 have been listed by Wood[35]. Regulations relating to purity, for example the limit of arsenic or lead, apply to all foods; those relating to composition normally concern individual foods or groups of foods. Section 7 of the Food and Drugs (Adulteration) Act 1928[j] empowered the Minister of Agriculture and Fisheries to make compositional regulations in respect of milk, cream, butter and cheese although presumptive standards for the composition of milk had been made in 1901 and for butter in 1902, whilst the Minister of Health had exercised such powers under the Public Health Act 1875–1907[k] and the Milk and Dairies (Amendment) Act 1922[l] in respect of condensed milk in 1923.

A committee appointed by the Ministry of Health to consider matters relating to the composition and description of food reported in 1934[36] in favour of alterations to the law to enable definitions or standards to be prescribed or declarations of composition to be required for food. The Committee, while indicating that it did not think that such considerations should apply automatically to all foods, was clearly in favour of such an extension of powers; but thought that they should only be exercised if the question of conformity with the requirements or the declaration could be checked by chemical analysis or otherwise. It was no doubt in consequence of this that the Food and Drugs Act 1938[m] which repealed the 1928 Act, consolidated the previous powers to make compositional regulations and

(j) Food and Drugs (Adulteration) Act, 18 and 19, George V, C.19 (1928)
(k) Public Health (Regulations as to Food) Act, 7 Edward VII, C.21 (1907)
(l) Milk and Dairies (Amendment) Act, 12 and 13, George V, C.54 (1922)
(m) Food and Drugs Act, 1 and 2, George VI, C.56 (1938)

116

extended them to all foods, thus setting the scene for the many compositional and labelling regulations which now operate today. The 1938 Act was in turn repealed by the Food and Drugs Amendment Act 1954[n], which however re-enacted the powers and further extended them to the prescription of methods of analysis the results from which should be preferred in evidence to those from any other analysis or test. Perhaps the most important of the methods of analysis which were subsequently prescribed in this way was that for vitamin A in margarine set out in the schedule to the Food Standards (Margarine Order) 1954[o]. Many of the wartime standards for food were made under Defence (Sale of Food) Regulations 1943[p], several of which (together with the earlier standards) were taken over under the present powers of the Food and Drugs Act 1955. Many of the standards which are set by these regulations have resulted from recommendations by the Food Standards Committee (and later by the Food Additives and Contaminants Committee), which was first appointed in 1947.

Food analysis today

It is fair to say today that analytical chemistry is not now what it was. The chemical 'wet' techniques are still used and frequently play an important part in the preparation of the food sample for the eventual analytical detection and measurement operations. These latter however are less frequently the classical volumetric or gravimetric procedures of former days. Instead they usually now depend on the use of more or less complex equipment, very often embodying electronic signal amplification circuits and chart recorder or digital displays, which go to make up such techniques as spectrophotometry or gas-liquid chromatography. In some cases, as for example in mass spectrometry, they may also involve the aid of a dedicated computer for their full interpretation. It is in this general context that Meloan, for example, has discussed the extent to which 'chemistry' is going out of 'analytical chemistry'[37]. As with analytical chemistry, so with food analysis. Under the Agriculture Act 1970 the word 'analysis' includes any process for determining any fact as to the nature, substance or quality of any material. Whilst the Analytical Methods Committee of the Analytical Division of the Chemical Society has not been concerned solely with methods of food analysis, much of its work is of direct interest in this area. The factors accepted for the calculation of lean meat from the organic nitrogen levels

---

(n)   Food and Drugs Amendment Act, 2 and 3, Eliz. II, C.67 (1954)
(o)   Food Standards (Margarine) Order, Statutory Instrument No. 613 (1954)
(p)   Defence (Sale of Food) Regulations 1943

found analytically for a wide variety of animal meats have been established by the Committee and it has developed many standard methods for the detection and measurement of trace metal contaminants and veterinary food additive residues in food. These in recent years have been gathered together in a single volume[38], which also contains separate bibliographies of the various standard methods which have been established by other organizations for the main types of foods, including cereals and flour confectionery, coffee, dairy products, fish and fish products, meat and meat products, sugar and sugar products, tea and vitamins. The Analytical Methods Committee now has strong links with the Association of Official Analytical Chemists in North America, this being but one manifestation of the international character of food analysis at the present time. The United Nations joint FAO/WHO Codex Alimentarius Commission, the main objectives of which include the furtherance of international trade in food and food products, is developing a large number of food commodity standards an integral part of which are the referee methods of analysis which are to be used in the event of dispute as to the choice of method. The Codex Committee on Methods of Analysis and Sampling has given considerable thought to the manner in which such methods should be selected and has laid down criteria for this purpose[39].

The referee analytical function which the 1875 Act imposed on the Inland Revenue Laboratory at Somerset House also extends beyond the United Kingdom Parliament, for example to the *Acte des Etats* of the States of Jersey, entitled the Food and Drugs (Jersey) Law 1966 and to the Tynwald Food and Drugs Act 1963. As in the United Kingdom, the precursor of the Jersey Food and Drug Law, the *Loi touchant la Falsification des Denrees*, had in 1886 designated the Principal of the Inland Revenue Laboratory as referee analyst. They have all been transferred, through successive laws, to the Laboratory's direct descendant immediately across the River Thames, the Laboratory of the Government Chemist. Indeed, the Government Chemist also inherits the Customs Laboratory role, although this no longer includes the statutory examination of tea. The certificate of analysis which was issued in connexion with referee functions under Section 22 of the 1875 Act was not final and no special provision was made to enforce the subsequent attendance of chemists in court. Today Section 112 of the 1955 Act provides that the certificate of the Government Chemist 'shall be evidence of the facts stated therein unless any party to the proceedings requires that the person by whom it is signed shall be called as witness'[38]. The number of reference samples examined by the Government Chemist has declined over the years[40]: the open publication of analytical methods and their standardization through collaborative experimental study is one of the principal reasons for this. The relevant Section of the 1955 Act, S.112, requires that ' . . . the court before which any proceedings are taken . . . may, if it thinks fit, and upon the request of either party shall, cause the part of any sample produced before the court . . . to be sent to the Government Chemist, who shall make an analysis and transmit to the court a certificate of the result thereof'. It does not necessarily require the court to indicate a reason for requiring the analysis and whilst the 'third sample' is normally only sent to the Government Chemist in this way where analytical evidence conflicts, there is no requirement that analytical results should disagree before a Court can so act. The number of statutory referee analyses of food samples in the period 1875–1974 is illustrated in Table 1. This shows an increase to an average of about

Table 1 *Statutory referee analyses of food samples by the Government Chemist during the period* 1875–1974

Period	Samples Analysed
1875–1884	227
1885–1894	466
1895–1904	1203
1905–1914	931
1915–1924	707
1925–1934	287
1935–1944	161
1945–1954	143
1955–1964	66
1965–1974	31

120 per year at the turn of the century, falling subsequently to the present level of about three per year. This perhaps is some measure of the extent to which agreement among analysts has improved over the period concerned.

Having spoken at some length about the rivalry which earlier existed between Public Analysts and those in central government, and the part which these interchanges played in the development of food analysis and enforcement in the early days of modern food law, I would like here to pay a tribute to the work, both then and now, of public analysts who today take the main brunt of law enforcement, whether in relation to purity, quality or identity. There is today the widest area of mutual understanding and respect between industry, local authority and government service. The public analyst today plays a very diversified role, not only in law enforcement but also (for example by way of evidence to the Food Standards Committee) in helping to shape the law.

The attitude in the United Kingdom towards analytical methods required for the enforcement of legislation is such that, as indicated above, detailed methods are (with some notable exceptions) seldom laid down by statute. The exceptions are mainly in the field of fertilizers and animal feeding-stuffs analysis but include a few analytical processes where the constituent or property being measured is defined by the method of measurement itself. This state of affairs seldom occurs in trace analysis. In compositional analyses it is most evident where it became necessary to measure (or estimate) groups of substances which are closely related chemically, such as fats or proteins, that is in so-called proximate analysis; or where such analyses are used as the basis for the estimation of food constituents such as fat or lean meat. But even for these it is not usual to lay down statutory methods of analysis. Instead the basis is the acceptance, by trial over a prolonged period following open publication and often in addition by collaborative or other study, of basic procedures which are then, where appropriate, embodied in recommendations published in the scientific literature. Thus when in 1940 it became necessary to control the meat content of sausages, the Society of Public Analysts published details of the method to be employed in the laboratory[41], based on procedures which had first been published some 20 years earlier[42].

In several major statutes in Britain, provision is made not for a referee method of analysis but for a referee analyst and in most instances the referee has a completely free choice of the method of analysis which he uses. This is the case under the Food and Drugs Act 1955. Where in Britain an official method is prescribed, it is generally recognized that its use is binding for the examination of formal samples and in cases of dispute; however, for general day-to-day purposes less rigorous methods may (at least in the first instance) be used. There are a number of points of principle which must be borne in mind when considering the choice of methods which may ultimately be given statutory force. These may be summarized as in Table 2[43]. The analyst who is required to use an official or otherwise designated method may, on ethical and professional grounds, be forced to qualify his report by reference to a more accurate but unofficial method. Adoption of the above principles would minimize the risk of this occurring. With the law as it stands in Britain at present, the Government Chemist, whether as referee analyst or not, and in fact all other analytical chemists, is normally free to choose from the whole field of available methods that one, or that modification, which in his judgment is most suited to the analytical problem in question. The analytical chemist is free to take the fullest advantage of all the experience of a century of food analysis and is free, if he so decides, to use the most recent development not yet perhaps recorded in the general literature. This freedom is essential since the analytical

Table 2 *Principles to be observed in selecting mandatory methods of analysis*[43]

---

1 Preference should be given to methods the reliability (accuracy and precision) of which has been established in collaborative or similar studies in several laboratories.

2 Preference should also be given to methods which have already been recommended or adopted by relevant international organizations.

3 Where such an international organization has made provision for a two-tier structure (e.g., reference and routine methods), or for acceptable equivalent methods, these provisions should also be adopted.

4 Where appropriate, methods of analysis which are uniformly applicable to various substrates should be selected in preference to those which apply only to individual substrates.

5 Where possible, methods of analysis should be published in separate form and not incorporated in the body of a Directive, Regulation or Act.

6 Provision should be made for up-dating the methods.

7 Adequate attention should be given to the description of the nature of the sample to be examined and to the mode of sampling.

8 Analytical specifications which imply the use of a particular method should not be accepted unless the details of the methods are also agreed.

---

approach to proximate analysis which has been perfected during the past century now faces challenges which raise fundamental questions of compositional standards in terms of the acceptability of the basic constituents of foods such as meat, or fruit, or fat. This applies particularly to processed foods, including the wide range of convenience foods now available. Perhaps unexpectedly, the analytical chemist has come off particularly well at the other end of the scale, with an ability to detect, identify and measure minute traces of contaminants, some of them very complex substances, in a complicated organic substrate such as food. Nothing, in the long run, will take the place of the palate and the basic need for a nutritious and healthy diet. But analytical chemistry has come a very long way during the past hundred years to providing the practical means for the control of these and economic aspects in the production, distribution, processing and sale of food not only in Britain but throughout the world.

References

[1] FILBY, F. A. (1934), *A History of Food Adulteration and Analysis*. Allen and Unwin, London

[2] Food Standards Committee Report on Novel Protein Foods. HMSO, London (1974)

[3] BELCHER, R. (1975), *Proc. Soc. Anal. Chem.*, **12**, 77–83

[4] O'KEEFE, J. (1968), *Bell's Sale of Food and Drugs Act* pp 1–3. 14th edn. Butterworths, London

[5] ACCUM, F. C. (1820), A Treatise on the Adulteration of Food, Culinary Poisons etc. London

[6] HASSALL, A. H. (1861), *Adulterations Detected in Foods and Medicines*. 2nd edn. Longman, Green, Longman and Roberts, London

[7] ANON (1857), *Handbook for Officers of Excise*, pp 149–150. Loftus, London

[8] CHIRNSIDE, R. C. and HAMENCE, J. H. (1974), The 'Practising Chemists', pp 27–33. The Society for Analytical Chemistry, London

[9] JONES, E. G. (1930), *Food Fakes, Ancient and Modern.* Institute of Chemistry, London

[10] *Chemical News* (1874), **30**, 10

[11] *ibid.* p 11

[12] PHILLIPS, G. *ibid.* p 39

[13] BELL, J. (1858), *Compendium of General Orders 1700–1857.* Loftus, London

[14] BELL, J. (1881), *The Analysis and Adulteration of Foods, Part I; Tea, Coffee, Cocoa, Sugar.* Chapman and Hall Ltd, London

[15] BELL, J. (1883), *The Analysis and Adulteration of Foods, Part II; Milk, Butter, Cheese, Cereal Foods, Prepared Starches.* Chapman and Hall Ltd, London

[16] PILCHER, R. B. History of the Institute of Chemistry 1877–1914

[17] ANON. (1875), *Chemical News*, **31**, 90

[18] ANON. (1875), *Chemical News*, **31**, 125

[19] Proceedings of the Society of Public Analysts, Vol 1, London (1876)

[20] HAMENCE, J. H. (1974), *Proc. Soc. Anal. Chem.*, **11**, 321–33

[21] PEDEN, J. D. (1975), *J. Assoc. Public Analysts*, **13**, in press

[22] EGAN, H. *et al.* (1975), *Chem. Ind.*, 490

[23] MOOR, C. G. (1902), *Suggested Standards for Purity for Food and Drugs.* Ballière, Tindall and Cox, London

[24] SZABADVARY, F. (1966), *History of Analytical Chemistry*, p 243. Pergamon Press, Oxford

[25] WANKLYN, J. A. (1874), *Milk Analysis.* Trübner and Co., London

[26] WANKLYN, J. A. (1874), *Tea, Coffee and Cocoa Analysis.* Trübner and Co., London

[27] HEHNER, O. and ANGELL, A. (1874), *Butter: Its Analysis and Adulteration.* Churchill, London

[28] WANKLYN, J. A. and COOPER, W. J. (1881), *Bread Analysis.* Trübner and Co., London

[29] HUGHES, E. B. (1960), in *Pure Food and Pure Food Legislation* (ed. A. J. Amos), p 24. Butterworths, London

[30] RICHMOND, H. DROOP (1905), *The Laboratory Book of Dairy Analysis.* Chas. Griffin and Co., London

[31] IRVING, H. M. N. H. (1974), *The Techniques of Analytical Chemistry.* p 23. HMSO, London

[32] HORWITZ, W. and REYNOLDS, H. L. (1967), *J. Assoc. Offic. Anal. Chem.* **56**, 1024–32

[33] MARKLAND, J. (1974), *Analyst*, **99**, 810–6

[34] CHIRNSIDE, R. C. (1973), *Chem. Britain*, **9**, 295–6

[35] WOOD, E. C. (1967), *J. Roy. Soc. Health.*, **87**, 317

[36] Report of the Departmental Committee on the Composition and Description of Food. Cmnd 4564, HMSO, London (1938)

[37] MELOAN, C. E. (1967), *J. Assoc. Offic. Anal. Chem.*, **50**, 1044–6

[38] HANSON, N. W. (ed.) (1973), *Official, Standardized and Recommended Methods of Analysis.* Society for Analytical Chemistry, 2nd ed., London

[39] Procedural Manual of the Codex Alimentarius Commission, 3rd edn. pp 67–8. FAO Rome (1973)

[40] 1972 Report of the Government Chemist, pp 9–10. HMSO, London (1973)

[41] Analytical Methods Committee (1940), *Analyst*, **65**, 257

[42] STUBBS, G. and MORE, A. (1919), *Analyst*, **44**, 125

[43] 1973 Report of the Government Chemist, p 6. HMSO, London (1974)

[44] IHDE, A. J. (1974), *J. Chem. Educ.*, **51**, 295

Discussion

Mr. G B Thackray (Public Analyst, Hampshire County Council): My Lord Chairman, Dr. Egan, Ladies and Gentlemen, the historians tell us of the animosity which did exist between the Government chemists and the public analysts in days gone by. Let me reiterate what Dr. Egan has said, that no such animosity now exists. We have the highest regard for Dr. Egan and his staff and we do thank him very much for his very interesting exposition this afternoon.

The second thing I want to say refers to Dr. Egan's written paper, which you all have. It refers to a George Turner, one of the old public analysts. Mr. George Turner was, in fact, a medical officer of health who, nevertheless, proved himself to be a very competent public analyst, and I have on the wall of my office a portrait of Mr. Turner. What does not appear in Dr. Egan's paper is the fact that, although he was proving himself a very competent public analyst, Mr. Turner seemed to think better of it and went to help the lepers in Africa. Subsequently he died of leprosy. He was knighted and became Sir George Turner, and he was known as 'the Portsmouth martyr'.

There are two aspects of the work of the public analyst to which Dr. Egan has not referred and to which I am sure that he would wish me to draw your attention. Apart from the two main divisions of analysis so far as food is concerned, there is the aspect of labelling problems and the list of ingredients. It is part of the duty of the public analyst to make sure that that list of ingredients is correct and is in the right order. This does sometimes pose very complex analytical problems.

The second aspect which I believe to be worthy of mention is the part that we have played as public analysts in the pesticide residue problem. A very large nationwide survey was organized jointly between the Association of Local Authorities and the Association of Public Analysts, and the first year of that survey, in fact, resulted in the voluntary withdrawal of two of the organo-chlorine pesticides which were evidently very persistent in the ecological system.

The present changing situation involving a very great increase in the complexity of analysis to keep up with changing food technologies, problems arising from entry into the Community, and problems arising from the very expensive instrumentation required, prompts me to my question to Dr. Egan. It is, how does he see the work of the chemist in food control in the future and, in particular, the work of the public analyst?

Dr. Egan: First of all, Mr. Thackray referred to the complex problems of labelling, and I will come to those in a moment.

On the problem of pesticide residues, I should say that so far as the analyst is concerned there are two broad approaches to the problem. This is so whether they are pesticide or other environmental residues like lead or mercury. There are residue surveys by central Government and these approach the problem in two ways, looking firstly at those areas which are thought most likely to be at risk. That is not to say that there is a risk, but the areas most likely to be a risk. Then, at the other end of the scale, there is the total diet, which is a measure of what people on average eat. The surveys to which Mr. Thackray referred which were conducted by the local authorities and the public analysts were a most valuable complement to the two central Government survey approaches in that they related largely to individual foods on the retail market, and so they help further to shield the position and to give reassurance across the board, the areas most at risk, the total diet, and then the whole range of individual food products from the retail market.

The complex problem of labelling really is part and parcel of the same question which Mr. Thackray asked at the end of his contribution. The more sophisticated apparatus such as mass spectrometry, coupled with dedicated computers, could be necessary for the specific identification of things like nitrosamines. There does seem to me to be a need to share equipment of this sort. Whilst I think most people would agree that government should be devolved as much as possible, there is a financial barrier which makes it difficult to operate mass spectrometers and computers within each and every local authority. So there must be some kind of resolution along the lines of sharing pieces of equipment like that. That is going to be very important in order to control situations requiring them.

At the same time, there is a heavier demand for surveys of what I might call ordinary things like lead, mercury or cadmium. Much more information is needed and I think that part of the answer to that, at least, lies in the development of mechanized or automated methods of analysis. I had the privilege earlier this year of attending the annual meeting of the Association of Public Analysts and describing there the development of a system for the automation of one of the key stages in such analysis, one which it has been very difficult up to recently to get a hold on, and that is the digestion of the food sample itself. Once one solves that problem, there are many simple and established automated trace analysis techniques for doing lead, mercury and so on.

Dr. A R Johnson (CSIRO, Sydney, Australia): You mentioned refinements in analytical techniques and the ability to measure compounds at lower and lower levels of detection, particularly in regard to carcinogens. This has led to the concept of zero tolerance where you should not be able, in fact, to detect any part of a particular substance. What are your views on this? Is it reasonable? Or do you have to accept the practicality of the situation that you can always find something if you look hard enough?

Dr. Egan: We do not have such a concept in law in the United Kingdom. In fact, we have no pesticide residue tolerances, there being at present no need for these. Certainly the idea of a zero tolerance is not a scientific concept at all. We were speaking this morning about aflatoxin, about the ability of an analyst to detect and estimate 5 µg/kg, and we were asking ourselves whether it would be reasonable to do this because it is now possible perhaps to go down to 1 µg/kg. One answer to that in the context we were then discussing lies in a consideration of the cost/benefit aspects of the situation. It is going to cost a good deal more in terms of manpower, equipment, time and money to achieve a limit of detection of 1 µg/kg than it is to be satisfied with 5 µg/kg. There is a judgment to be made, based on the toxicological risk involved. I certainly think it necessary to resist the temptation automatically to ask the analyst further to improve analytical methods so that these can respond to (say) 1 nanogram/kg. This is not the only consideration so far as zero tolerance are concerned. The limit of sensitivity also depends to some extent on the size of the sample taken for analysis.

Mr. E Hopkin (International Organization for Standardization): Dr. Egan did refer in passing to sensory analysis. Does he see any room for this in the legislation?

Dr. Egan: I am not quite clear what the question is. Does it relate to restriction of the number of different additives which may be used to colour or flavour food; or to the analytical control of these aspects in terms of standardization of the final product?

Mr. Hopkin: What I meant was, do you see requirements in legislation based on sensory analytical techniques?

Dr. Egan: I think I said at the end of my presentation that analysis did not itself replace such things as sensory values, although analysis was very often the basis for the day-to-day control of some things which control sensory aspects such as colour, or texture or even flavour. However these are the aspects which predominantly make their mark in the consumer market, and it is a matter perhaps more for industry if it wishes to control by laboratory means any of them. I think the simple answer to your question is 'No'.

Dr. H C Pereira (Chief Scientist, Ministry of Agriculture, Fisheries and Food): Would Dr. Egan feel that the sampling techniques, particularly for large bulks of food, are in any way commensurate with the accuracy of the laboratory analysis? I ask because I was in Africa at the time when aflatoxin blew up, and trying to look for one diseased groundnut in a 200 lb sack really did stretch the statisticians.

Dr. Egan: Sampling is always an important consideration but the example quoted by Dr. Pereira represents one of the extreme situations where sampling is at least as much a problem as the analysis. It is still a problem even given that it is possible to detect aflatoxin at a level of 1 µg/kg. The problem relates also to animal feeds and it is worth remarking that in the United Kingdom more attention has been given to animal food than to human food in this context. The Agriculture Act 1970 lays down by regulation not only methods of analysis but details of the manner of sampling feedingstuffs.

Lord Zuckerman (Symposium Chairman): I wonder if I might ask a question. Is it really true that in 1875 public analysts had to take an examination which lasted five hours? If so, what were their nutritional requirements at the time?

Dr. Egan: There were no formal examinations for public analysts until 1898 but annual examinations were conducted for entry into the Inland Revenue Laboratory from 1881, possibly earlier. The time allowed for the papers was seven hours, with no indication of any break.

Mr. T McLachlan (Thomas McLachlan and Partners): The Institute of Chemistry's early examination, Mr. Chairman, was a full day, but you were allowed to say whether you would like lunch brought in to you, and you paid for it, or you could bring sandwiches and they would supply coffee or tea.

Professor A G Ward: It is always difficult to cap Mr. McLachlan's stories, but there is the story of a practical examination at Cambridge for which the students demanded ice at the start of the practical. The demonstrators knew that ice was not required for any chemical experiment in the course of it, but the candidate had the right to have anything he wished. When the ice came, a bottle of champagne was produced.

Enforcing the Law

F J Evans

County Consumer Protection Officer for the Northamptonshire County Council

In 1960 a 'Pure Food Centenary' was held at the Royal Institution in commemoration of the passing in 1860 of an 'Act for Preventing the Adulteration of Articles of Food or Drink'. During the course of the proceedings speakers referred to the introduction of the 1860 Act as heralding the era of pure food and to the development from that time of analytical chemistry. Certainly the Act made it an offence to sell an article of food or drink 'which is adulterated or not pure' but probably one of its most important provisions was the power given to local authorities to appoint an analyst. Without doubt the emphasis at this earlier centenary related to the analysis of foods and to developments in the study of modern food chemistry. Yet in the opening paper Dr. J H Hamence wrote[1]:

'Historians tell us that this Act and the succeeding one were failures but was this really unexpected?'

He suggested that these failures were due to lack of knowledge of the composition of foods and to the state of analytical chemistry at the time but it is also a fact that the only method of bringing an offending seller to task was by the action of a complainant who had purchased an adulterated article of food or drink. The unfortunate 'Purchaser', after giving due 'Notice of Intention' to the seller of his intention to have the article analysed, would have to bring his complaint 'before a Hearing by the Justices'. I would contend that the failure of the 1860 Act was at least equally due to the absence of an efficient system of enforcement and this may in fact have been the major cause.

In this respect, therefore, although still not making the appointment of a public analyst mandatory, the Sale of Food and Drugs Act of 1875 can be acknowledged as a major advance in food legislation and can be fairly claimed to have provided the basis for the modern system of enforcement. From this early start has developed, in a typically British manner by adaptation and compromise, a scheme of enforcement which originally rested almost solely in the hands of local authorities. With advances in food technology and in the scale of food preparation the central government became more and more involved until, with the changes resulting from local government reorganization, enforcement in this country, although possibly unique in structure, can be considered as being at least as efficient as that of any other country and perhaps more capable of adaptation to meet changing circumstances.

The Act of 1875 may therefore justly be hailed as the real base on which the present UK food and drugs legislation was built and thus most appropriately the reason for this centenary symposium.

Section 13 of the Act must for this reason be considered as being particularly important in providing for the appointment of and the allocation of enforcement powers to 'any medical officer of health, inspector of nuisances or inspector of weights and measures, or any inspector of a market, or any police constable under the direction and at the cost of the local authority . . .'.

Of these, the only officers still involved with food and drugs enforcement are the inspectors of nuisances, now called public health or environmental health officers, who have general control over the hygiene aspects of food production, and inspectors of weights and measures, now known as trading standards or consumer protection officers and for the most part responsible for the composition, labelling and advertising provisions of food and drugs law.

Other speakers will have dealt with the hygiene and safety requirements enforced by environmental health officers but my experience and background mainly qualify me to refer to the development of control by county council trading standards/consumer protection departments of composition and labelling, a task shared until the recent reorganization between the public health departments of the larger borough councils and the weights and measures departments of county councils.

At this point, therefore, I propose to trace this development through four stages from the Act of 1875 to indicate briefly the changing pattern of the officers' duties.

Early stages

Although the full impact of the appointment of enforcement officers did not make itself felt until the establishment of county councils by the Local Government Act of 1888, their officers, usually inspectors of weights and measures, had the more or less easy task of keeping an eye on those engaged in the production or sale of relatively few staple foods. Adulteration was on a fairly standard scale and was readily detected by the public analyst.

Straightforward addition of water to milk or whisky and of flour to spices or the introduction of sand into sugar or alum into bread presented few analytical problems, whilst an experienced officer usually knew where to look for likely offenders. It is surprising how quickly county officers got into their stride and it may be of interest to set out from an early prosecution record of the Northamptonshire County Council a few of the infringements and the fines awarded for typical offences:

Trade	Selling	Fine
1890 Licensed Victualler	Brandy 32° under proof	£3
1890 Licensed Victualler	Whisky 40·6° under proof	£2
1890 Baker	Bread containing 43 g alumina	£2
1891 Grocer	Coffee containing 23 per cent chicory	Dismissed
1893 Grocer	Margarine as butter	£1
1893 Grocer	Unlabelled margarine	2s 6d
1893 Milk Seller	Milk with 22 per cent added water	£2
1894 Milk Seller	Milk with 22 per cent added water	£5
1896 Milk Seller	Milk 15 per cent deficient in fat	£1

These extracts give a useful indication of the types of adulteration dealt with and, bearing in mind the relative value of the money in those days, show fines which can only be considered as substantial. It should be noted that the milk seller who was fined £2 in 1893 was also responsible for the repeated offence in the following year, when he was fined the very large sum of £5. Spirits, milk, bread and margarine were the main foods appearing in the list but a little later, in 1902, there was a prosecution for the sale of sweet spirits of nitre 30 per cent deficient in ethyl nitrate, whilst in the following year a grocer was fined for the addition of 10 per cent starch to mustard.

Two points of importance arise from a further study of the record. The first is that more than 30 years later milk and spirits remained the foods most subject to adulteration. The second, which could have had a significant influence on the first, is that the fines had tended to decrease rather than to increase to keep pace with modest inflation. In 1933, for example, a milk dealer convicted for the third time within two years for adding water to milk was fined only £2.

The changing patterns

One more signpost to the future may be discerned from the table of prosecutions given in the preceding section. The two cases in 1893 dealing with margarine give a very early warning of the need for firm control over the use of names and descriptions and of the importance of adequate labelling for the guidance of the consumer. From the point of view of the enforcement officer these examples foreshadow the eventual change from concentration on adulteration of simple foods to the complex problems of description, labelling and advertising which form the major part of his duties today.

It is certainly to the credit of the government of the day that it acted with such remarkable speed and efficiency in dealing with the problems arising from the introduction of margarine as a butter substitute.

Following the marketing of this product around 1880 manufacturers were inclined to take advantage of the demand for butter and of its relatively high price to describe the new food by names such as 'butterine' on the basis that people were more likely to buy a new product if it had a familiar-sounding (even though misleading) name. There was also the added danger that the unscrupulous shopkeeper might sell this new substitute as butter. The passing of the Margarine Act in 1887 was the first and most important step on the road to controlling the sale of this food under a suitable name and requiring appropriate labelling to safeguard the consumer. This was an exceptional piece of consumer protection legislation for the times and was a great incentive to the very few inspectors engaged in the enforcement of food and drugs legislation.

Margarine was, however, unparalleled in its development as a substitute for a food in normal use and for quite a long time after its introduction there was little other change in the types of food being produced and distributed. As the sale of food was firmly in the hands of retailers who had usually had a long training in a particular line, it was possible for the consumer to rely on the expertise of the seller; the duty of the enforcement officer, therefore, was mainly to keep an eye on the less honest shopkeeper and particularly to safeguard sales of milk and spirits.

The first signs of a change in this pattern came during the First World War, with the advent of rationing and the consequent introduction of food substitutes. By and large there had been little scientific study of the composition of foodstuffs and analytical food chemistry was in its infancy. As a result the food substitutes, and these included margarine, tasted very little like the originals and were used only as a last resort. There was little likelihood of any major 'passing off' since the taste of the substitute itself was a positive indication that it was not the original food.

Nevertheless, rationing and the introduction of substitutes called for more attention to be paid both to the supervision of sales from shops and also to the labelling of articles prepacked ready for sale. It could be said that the stage was now set for the introduction of new consumer legislation and more effective enforcement.

Between 1920 and 1930 there appeared on the statute book a succession of items of legislation dealing with controls over the sale of food and drugs, imposing restrictions on the use of preservatives, even providing for special designations for certain foods and culminating in the passing of the Food and Drugs (Adulteration) Act of 1928. During this decade enforcement officers steadily increased their rate of sampling, reaching something like

3·5 samples per thousand of population by 1930, although the records were not necessarily as precise and accurate as they ought to have been and the action taken in respect of the incorrect foods was not as uniform as might have been desired.

In addition, foods were beginning to be manufactured on a much larger scale and distributed over steadily increasing areas. Advances were being made in the production of foods such as self-raising flour, baking powder and compound fats and with increasing sophistication came the need for more effective control of labelling and advertising, although government action to provide a positive guide in this direction had to await the next World War. It was at this point that the development of the enforcement service had become a vital need.

The evolutionary stage

By the time of the Second World War the pattern of legislation had already changed and had developed a more positive consumer protection emphasis; this had without doubt resulted from an increasing awareness of the problems caused by technical advances in the production of food and prepackaging and the increasing influence of advertising, particularly in the introduction of new foods. During the war period, with the shortage of foods and the growing interests of the food industry in adapting scientific procedures to the production and development of new products, there came the first of the really progressive measures to establish controls.

Although the main purpose of the emergency legislation was to regulate distribution, composition, price and marking for the purposes of wartime rationing, the 1943 Defence (Sale of Food) Regulations set a pattern for future labelling measures and introduced food and drugs officers to the complicated requirements which resulted. By 1955 food and drugs authorities had acquired responsibility for the legislation which had evolved from this enforced beginning and had assumed their present duties in the control of the advertising and labelling of foods.

This development in the legislation, as will have been explained in previous papers, had a great effect in safeguarding the consumer but also resulted in a considerable increase in the duties of the enforcement officer, not only in his sampling work but also in dealing with the problems arising from the application of the regulations to the steadily growing flow of newly developed foods.

During the period of rationing the licensing system organized by the then Ministry of Food led to the establishment of a section of the Department charged with responsibility for approving labels and advising on labelling matters. This was of great assistance to the food industry and was of course an essential control at a time when adulterants had to be legally permitted in certain circumstances. It undoubtedly made the work of the enforcement officer easier in some respects but it did leave a legacy of problems for later years.

In a paper presented at the Annual Conference of the Institute of Trading Standards Administration in 1973[2], after referring to the assistance given by this labelling advisory section, I commented:

'This section, of course, had to work under extreme difficulties. First, there was a need to permit the sale of substitutes for foods in short supply. Secondly, its personnel may have had experience in the making of laws but they had little knowledge of their enforcement. And, thirdly, although they had effective scientific support, their views were a little remote from those of the consumer. Whilst providing much valuable advice to the food industry, the section gave what appeared to be official approval to many unfortunate opinions and to far too many names of doubtful validity.'

This may be a little harsh but it does indicate the dangers which attend the setting up of any central advisory bureau on labelling and emphasizes the importance in dealing with labelling problems of effective advice from the standpoint of both enforcement authorities and the consumer. A number of codes of practice were developed at the same time which were of a depressingly poor standard and had the negative result of encouraging a decrease in compositional quality and rendering all negotiated codes subject to suspicion. Codes of this type dealt with such foods as cocoa powder, fish paste, canned soups, soft drinks, tea, coffee, vinegar and biscuits. Many suspect biscuit names appeared to receive Ministry approval as a consequence and are with us to this day, although subsequent appeal cases have removed from these codes the adverse effects of definitions applied to foods such as vinegar and champagne.

In spite of these wartime setbacks the new legislation nevertheless was the basis of the modern system of food enforcement and formed the foundation of the further controls over food composition, labelling and advertising which food and drugs authorities are now attempting to interpret and employ to deal with an enormous number of newly introduced foods or older foods being produced to new formulae.

The need for effective and informative labelling becomes greater as each new food is marketed and as more and more of these are sold in self-service stores and supermarkets. Enforcement patterns must change to provide protection for the consumer who may not have the time or the knowledge to study carefully each of the foods he buys. The duty of a modern enforcement officer must include the close supervision of the names and descriptions applied and the lists of ingredients added to the vast range of foods now sold prepacked in self-service stores. There is, too, one further aspect of modern food production which must be borne in mind and this is the influence of contamination by pollutants of one form or another, such as heavy metals from the atmosphere or the sea or pesticide residues resulting from modern agricultural techniques, and from this point of view also the enforcement officer's sampling programmes must be effective.

Local government reorganization

In its early years the enforcement service was mainly occupied in dealing with the local trader who was, on the whole, helpful and efficient but who needed protection himself from unscrupulous competitors. It did not matter greatly that the enforcement officers were appointed locally and may have been little concerned with national aspects, provided always that the local unit was large enough to ensure that the officers acted with complete impartiality and independence. Over the years, therefore, public health officers in boroughs and county boroughs and inspectors of weights and measures in counties maintained a service of reasonable efficiency at a remarkably low cost to the community. For a time, in fact, its very localized nature was an advantage in permitting the maximum use to be made of the knowledge of the officer about his area and its inhabitants.

With the change in trading conditions came the need for a change in the methods of enforcement. The regulations had become highly complex; food supply and advertising was rapidly developing into a large-scale operation conducted nationally rather than from a purely local point of view. It had become apparent that the enforcement officer must have considerably increased expertise, with even more emphasis being placed on impartiality and independence.

Extensive local knowledge of traders and the trading community was no longer a prime requirement and the large number of food and drugs authorities operating on a purely local basis was proving an embarrassment in dealing with the labelling and advertising problems of a food industry distributing its products very often on a national scale. Lord Aberdare, speaking in the House of Lords in 1972[3] and dealing with the question of the very large numbers of food and drugs authorities at that time, said:

'At present there are 235 of these food and drugs authorities outside Greater London. This has led to divergencies in enforcement and lack of uniformity in the application of these complex regulations.'

With the introduction of local government reorganization, therefore, the tasks set by the Food and Drugs Act 1955 were clearly divided into two

133

sections. Food hygiene, which benefited from a greater knowledge of local conditions, became the responsibility of district councils, whilst the county councils became exclusively the food and drugs authorities dealing with composition, labelling and advertising. The effect was to reduce the number of authorities outside Greater London who were concerned with this aspect of enforcement to only 47 counties and six metropolitan counties in England and Wales. A reduction of this order must without doubt lead to greater uniformity of action, greater ease of consultation both between authorities and with the members of the food industry, and also much closer links with the central government.

The change-over has not been without problems. Reorganization has resulted in a number of experienced food and drugs officers in the public health service being diverted to other duties, whilst a rather large number of extremely efficient chief officers in the pre-reorganization weights and measures service have been lost owing to early retirement provisions. Nevertheless, every effort is being made to provide the training necessary and to encourage senior officers to specialize in the highly complicated food and drugs field. As soon as appropriately qualified staff becomes available there is no reason why the present enforcement service should not be capable of handling all the calls made on it to provide protection for the consumer whilst being in a position to offer to industry professional advice of a high order.

Into the future

The pattern of enforcement must change again with the introduction into the United Kingdom food and drugs legislation of the regulations and directives of the European Economic Community. These could prompt a refreshingly new look at some of our ancient customs and might help us to take a rather more sensible view of the unfortunate habit of choosing inappropriate names for new products and applying descriptions which are either meaningless or misleading.

It may be that some of the draft directives of the EEC tend to introduce a certain rigidity in the application to products of the names and descriptions prescribed. Nevertheless, there is much to be said for the requirements of the proposed EEC legislation which are more definite than those of the present UK regulations. Any new look introduced by the Common Market may ultimately be to the benefit of both the consumer and the enforcement officer.

There is no doubt that with the changing trends of food production and the introduction of the Common Market laws enforcement must become less insular and inward-looking, more in touch with central government requirements and more effective in dealing with national problems.

Although for many years there has been liaison with the central government, it has tended to be on an *ad hoc* basis and there has not been a very efficient system of disseminating information on any matters which have been discussed. Action has been taken by the Institute of Trading Standards Administration to pass on to trading standards/consumer protection departments details of agreements reached on matters affecting national products, but this cannot be a satisfactory substitute for more direct contact with the Food Standards Division of the Ministry of Agriculture, Fisheries and Food.

One advance in this direction came in 1966 when on the initiative of the Ministry of Agriculture, Fisheries and Food there was established an informal consultative committee consisting of representatives of the Ministry and the Local Authority Associations. The purpose of this new body, which came in time to be known as the Food Standards Liaison Committee, was to arrange for discussions on matters of mutual interest concerning the administration of food and drugs legislation between Ministry officials and enforcement officers nominated as the representatives of the Local Authority Associations. These meetings were not intended in any way to replace the normal consultations between the Ministry and the Associations on proposals for regulations and were not necessarily meant to lead to any standardization of enforcement procedures. It was considered by the Ministry, however, that a general exchange of information with officials who were directly responsible for enforcement would be of mutual benefit. The Committee was instrumental in bringing to the notice of the Ministry some of the administrative problems which have faced food and drugs authorities and has also enabled enforcement officers to be made aware of impending legislation, particularly during the period when EEC draft directives were being considered. Although its contribution has been a valuable one and it could still have an important part to play, the time has now come for a more direct link between the government and local authorities.

The Local Authority Associations are ideally situated to forge this link and in fact the first steps have already been taken to this end. In 1960 the Local Authority Associations and the Association of Public Analysts together formed the Local Authorities Joint Advisory Committee on Food Standards. The purpose of this committee was to discuss with food manufacturers the setting up of codes of practice in the case of foods for which there were no statutory regulations, establish standards for their composition and make recommendations as to good practice in the labelling, description and advertising of food. This body had a limited success but with the advent of negotiations for joining the Common Market changes were made to produce a new and more effective joint advisory committee, on which the enforcement authorities and the central government would be represented and which would be in a position to provide an essential bridge between them. The new committee, renamed the Local Authorities Joint Advisory Committee on Standards, was a purely transitional unit and in fact new negotiations are now in progress for the establishment of a permanent advisory committee, the main purposes of which I would consider to be as follows:

To encourage co-ordination of enforcement policies and especially to assist in the enforcement of EEC controls in a uniform manner.

To provide advice to the government on the enforcement aspect of legislation.

To provide a venue for negotiations with national trade associations on matters concerned with consumer protection legislation generally.

If it were possible to establish the new style Local Authorities Joint Advisory Committee on consumer services matters in this manner, it could provide a most helpful service as the link between central government and enforcement and a reliable channel for the exchange of information.

Because it has always been the custom of the local authorities who enforce the composition, labelling and advertising provisions of the Food and Drugs Act 1955 to disregard for other than statistical purposes samples which are reported as genuine or are properly labelled and advertised, much of the good work done has not been fully utilized. The information gained is not used to maximum advantage when recorded only at a local level but if sufficiently detailed and collected on a national scale it could be of great assistance in safeguarding the welfare of the general public. That more effective use has not up to now been made of the information is one of the defects of the present local authority system of enforcement. Possibly a major share of the responsibility for this must be borne by the Ministry, who could have arranged for collection of data in a form in which it could be used for assessing trends in food composition on a national basis, and for compiling details of additives or contaminants found locally in foods sampled. Such particulars could be invaluable in reaching decisions on the form of further legislation and as a safeguard against the over-enthusiastic use by manufacturers of additives which may not always be to the benefit of the consumer.

The present procedures must now change and the Local Authority Associations and the Ministry are already discussing means by which this valuable information can be collected and utilized. Computer processing is one obvious way in which the sheer volume of results can be handled to enable details to be extracted in a prearranged manner.

There can also be advantages in arranging that at least part of the programmes of local authority sampling should be carried out on the basis of a nationally organized scheme of surveys. The analytical data required should be determined in advance by consultation at regular intervals between the government, the public analysts and the Local Authority Associations representing the enforcement authorities. The first steps in such a programme are already being discussed but there are so many practical advantages that its successful implementation must be ensured.

The sophistication of these plans is indicative of the vast changes which have taken place. In the years following the passing of the Act of 1875 enforcement consisted of the relatively straightforward matter of the taking of samples. The food was either genuine or adulterated; both the offence and the duty were simple. The skill of the analyst probably counted for more than the expertise of the sampling officer. Now, however, with the change in emphasis from adulteration to the problems of the labelling and advertising of foods with resounding nutritional claims of one type or another, the point must be made that the roles of the analyst and the enforcement officer are complementary. They require quite different skills but each must be recognized as being essential for the establishment of an efficient system of enforcement.

Successful administration of modern food and drugs legislation after its years of development from 1875 depends, therefore, on teamwork. Increasingly analyst and enforcement officer must work in close contact. They must plan and prepare together surveys designed to produce the maximum of information. The data so obtained must then be made available to the central government, either direct or through the organization developed by the Local Authority Associations so that all the members of the enforcement team work harmoniously together. In this way the local authority system which has functioned so well in the past can operate even more efficiently and with greater flexibility for the benefit of the community.

References
1 Papers of the 1960 Centenary Conference, edited by Amos, A. J. and published by Butterworth, p 16
2 Supplement to 'The Monthly Review' of the Institute of Trading Standards Administration, March 1973, volume 81
3 Hansard Reports, House of Lords, 19th September 1972

Introductory remarks by Mr. Evans

History is full of laws passed with the very best of intentions to achieve public good which have failed, owing to the absence of any effective means of putting the intention into practice. This was true of the early laws dealing with the adulteration of food (produced at regular intervals from a time not much later than the mid-thirteenth century). These were largely unsuccessful because they contained no facilities for uniform enforcement, even though punishments were specified for the few flagrant offences which came to light.

This was also the reason for the comparative failure of the Act of 1860, attractively entitled 'An Act for Preventing the Adulteration of Articles of Food or Drink' and referred to in the opening paragraph of my paper. In fact the two events at the end of the nineteenth century which really gave impetus to the dramatic history of food legislation in this country were the Sale of Food and Drugs Act of 1875 and the Local Government Act of 1888, which between them provided for some measure of enforcement. The first authorized the appointment of public analysts to examine suspect foods and named officers who might be given the duty of obtaining samples. The second extended the facility for the appointment of sampling officers to the areas for which the county councils thereby established were responsible.

The effective policing of food and drugs legislation is clearly dependent on the employment of officers trained and experienced in inspection procedures as well as in the taking of samples, operating in close liaison with an analytical service which has up-to-date equipment for carrying out increasingly complex analyses.

In the early days of the 1880s the work was simple once the public analyst was equipped to deal with the adulteration of the staple foods. The sampling officer, at least in the county areas, was a figure of some importance and many amusing stories are told of somewhat unorthodox methods of control and sampling.

What is important to note, however, is the size of the fines imposed on some of the offenders. In the table in my paper, for example, a fine of £3 was imposed for watered brandy and the milk seller received a penalty of £5 for added water. At present-day prices these fines would be equivalent to about £40 and £70 respectively, far higher figures than would normally be awarded for similar first offences nowadays. In addition, in the closed communities of the early days the disgrace of appearing before the justices of the peace for offences of this type would be considerable and would be known to all the members of the community. The position today is quite different—the lists of cases at the magistrates courts are so extensive that publicity is rare and the multiplication of offences, particularly motoring offences, has greatly reduced the social stigma of an appearance in court.

Nowadays straightforward adulteration is possibly of less significance and is certainly less common than the problems which arise from the labelling and advertising of nationally produced and packaged commodities. It may be that the modern magistrate has a very much more difficult job in evaluating the relative importance to the community of the many crimes with which he has to deal, compared with the old-fashioned adulteration of foods such as spirits and milk which was the most common offence of the 1890s, as instanced by the cases shown in the table in my paper.

Labelling and advertising have now become so complicated and scientific that they offer almost unlimited scope for misrepresentation or excessive 'puff'. Doubts are therefore now felt about the effectiveness of dealing with disputes over matters of this type by a simple estimation by a magistrates court of the facts as they would appear to the 'man on the Clapham omnibus'.

Manufacturers producing new products are faced with a mass of legislation dealing with standards and the reluctance of the consumer to try out new packs and food substitutes with new names. A complicating factor is the unwillingness of the buyer to accept the addition of substances such as phosphates, however they may be explained as adding to the 'succulence' of the product. There is therefore a tendency to use old and familiar names for foods developed in an entirely different manner and a marked aversion on the part of the manufacturer to specifying prominently the additives employed.

Another factor which may exercise an unfair influence on the unwary consumer was illustrated in a recent article on 'Conning in Colour', in which a research psychologist came up with the theory that careful and scientific use of colourings can affect the apparent size of a food pack or the apparent strength of the contents or otherwise beguile the customer into buying.

In the light of all these considerations it is suggested that some other means ought to be found of settling disputes between the manufacturers and the enforcement officer on labelling or advertising problems than the somewhat hit or miss method of the magistrates court. What is called for is an adjudication by an independent authority who should have a wide and comprehensive knowledge of food legislation and of the difficulties which face the manufacturer in this field.

In this context, of course, one might point to the effective action by the Government referred to in my paper in dealing with the introduction of a substitute for butter. This is now controlled reasonably firmly by legislation which has developed from the Margarine Act of 1887. One way of dealing with part of the present-day problem would be to pass individual laws to control the description and sale of major food substitutes but it could be that the Food Standards Division would have difficulty in arranging for prompt legislation on this basis in view of the consultations required and the shortage of parliamentary time.

In my paper I refer to some of the changes resulting from local government reorganization but it might be useful to consider for a moment the system of delegating enforcement to the local authorities in this country. Our system has always depended on control at the retail level, an obvious development in view of the origins of the legislation and the nature of the communities in existence in 1875.

This is in distinct contrast to methods employed in some other countries by the use of a nationally controlled service, but even now the local authorities possess distinct advantages in this field. Provided that the areas covered are of reasonable size—as they are in the new counties—the local knowledge of the officers involved and their ability to liaise effectively with the food producers in the area result in as efficient a means of law enforcement as any other. It has the advantages of adaptability and a certain freedom from rigid direction by a remote head office which more than compensate for any disadvantages. Any additional EEC requirements for more specific control at the factory level can easily be incorporated to achieve uniformity with the Community. This should not, however, be to the exclusion of some form of enforcement at the retail level, a point of some importance for the welfare of the consumer.

Of the disadvantages, the main one is the difficulty of securing an adequate degree of uniform administration and it is suggested that the steps now being taken by the Local Authority Associations in consultation with the Government can assist greatly in this direction.

Provided some means can be found to establish a reliable appeal procedure operated through some form of special court or by some national agency, it is suggested that no system can work more effectively than our present one.

The present pattern of administration has grown, as in the case of so many British institutions, in a haphazard way by compromise and adaptation. Possibly because of this it works very well but, partly for financial reasons, enforcement has to struggle to keep up with the technological progress of the food manufacturers. Certainly economic considerations must always tend to inhibit the development by analysts of techniques which are called for by changes in food product and they must necessarily always be one step behind the inventive resourcefulness of the industry.

The ever-increasing use of food additives and the introduction of new products such as novel proteins do bring in their wake problems of analytical technique which can seriously hinder efficient enforcement. The influence of contamination, whether as a result of accidental discharges affecting the environment or in the form of residues in human foods which may result, for example, from medicinal additives used in animal feedingstuffs, presents increasing difficulties for the analyst and the enforcement officer. They may relate either to points of technical analysis or to matters concerned with the collection of data and its interpretation and use.

It could be that the employment of part-time public analysts might need reconsideration in the light of all these circumstances and one possible solution might be the establishment of regional laboratories operating in close conjunction with small groupings of counties, which might provide the resources and the time necessary for the more effective analyses and for the indispensable research which could be unduly hampered by the systems at present in use. Nevertheless, should this idea prove a desirable solution I would consider it essential that the regional laboratory should be responsible to the local authorities which it is designed to serve, whilst retaining a measure of independence from them.

All these points, therefore, suggest the importance, as mentioned earlier in this introduction, of effective liaison between the public analyst and the enforcement officer, since each has his own part to play in the enforcement pattern and they can achieve much more by close co-operation. As long as this results, as it should, in improved scientific data and the more comprehensive collection of information, which can be made available to Government bodies which may be in need of specific advice on food composition or the incidence of contamination, then the service will continue to provide protection for the consumer capable of adaptation to all circumstances.

Discussion

Mr. E W Kingcott (Principal Environmental Health Officer, Westminster City Council): I feel that Mr. Evans has dealt very thoroughly with most aspects of the enforcement field, but I would like to draw him out on one or two points.

I was interested to hear his observations about magistrates' courts. We have heard a lot today about the need for educating the consumer and so on, and I think that there is a good case for educating the magistrate, particularly in relation to some of our food cases, as he has already indicated.

One point that I found interesting in Mr. Evans' paper was the case he made out for a central pooling of statistical information on sampling. I feel that, whilst we have done a lot of congratulating of MAFF so far today, this is possibly one field where they might be criticized in that a very recently formed organization, that of the Office of Fair Trading, has recently instituted something which I think could have been done a long time ago, that is a national system of collecting quite detailed statistics on food complaints received by local authorities. I have always been very surprised that MAFF has not done this in the past, either for complaints or for prosecutions. I should be interested to have his observations on that.

He also suggests in his paper that, instead of the public analyst simply reporting that a sample is satisfactory, he might elaborate further, which would enable the enforcing authority to collect statistics on, for example, trends in the composition of certain foods over a period of time, and this information might be passed through to the central authority. Clearly, this would impose an additional burden on the public analysts if they had to do a rather more detailed analysis on each product than they already do, and this does call into question the whole subject of the present financing of the analytical work. I would agree with Mr. Evans' suggestion that there might be something to be said for regional laboratories. However, if in fact the present situation is relying on swings and roundabouts, where the analyst makes on one sample and loses on another, and we have a flat figure of roughly £10, which is often a bone of contention with them, would it not be better if we sent a smaller number of samples and paid a realistic fee which would enable us to ask for more realistic information?

I was interested in the comments about the National Labelling Advisory Service. This is something of which I have no personal experience, but I have often heard the demise of this service lamented by members of the trade, both the manufacturers in this country and importers, who have terrible problems in obtaining an authoritative opinion on a label or description. I have had experience of this work and, although it might well be argued that the reorganization has rationalized the situation to some degree with a smaller number of authorities, I still feel that the situation is far from being as effective as it could be. I should like Mr. Evans' views on whether we might go back to having a central advisory service.

I did feel on that point that there might have been a slight contradiction in the paper, because Mr. Evans criticized the National Labelling Advisory Service for being too remote from the consumer, but on the other hand he argued in favour of food and drugs going over to the county council, saying that it was no longer necessary for it to be in very close contact with the local community. Would it not be true to say that, if he is arguing that 'big is beautiful' as far as food enforcement is concerned, the logical extension of that would be a national food regulation enforcement service? I know that he has already given some indication of his views, but that would be the logical extension of what he has said.

Another point made in the paper was that local government reorganization had created a clear distinction between food and drugs and food hygiene. I must take issue with him on this point, because I feel that it is very dangerous to try to make a clear distinction like that. Food hygiene has quite considerable implications for the ultimate quality of the food and there are dangers in trying to split the thing down the middle like this between two different forms of food enforcement.

My final point is that Mr. Evans ended his paper by expressing a good deal of optimism about the ability of the existing system for the future. If I may say so, having been in a county council for some time, I think that it may be a little biased, since the service has now been handed over to county councils in that respect. I cannot help feeling that, however far we go with unifying the laws, if we are ultimately to achieve uniformity of enforcement through the EEC the only way is to have some form of unified inspection service. Unless people have a common background of training, philosophy and so on, I feel that there could always be quite wide differences in the application of the law.

Mr. Evans: Mr. Kingcott certainly has thrown a few items into the discussion!

I am glad that he feels as I do about magistrates' courts, that this is a rather difficult area in which we have to work and that it is possibly an unfair area for both the enforcement officer and for the food industry since there is not, at a hearing of this sort, any absolutely certain way of ensuring that the results are going to be reasonably uniform.

So far as sampling programmes are concerned and the introduction into this field of the Office of Fair Trading, I am not quite sure that I go as far as Mr. Kingcott. Certainly the Office of Fair Trading provides a useful service by collecting information about prosecutions on food and drugs matters. Whether the Ministry should have done this or not I am not competent to answer, but I am sure that Bob Giles would be prepared to come in on that one. I do feel that sampling programmes are in need of organization, and I suggest that we are already at the stage of considering ways by which this might be achieved to provide more information which should be available in the analysts' offices and could be used by the Government in specific cases.

It is quite possible to devise programmes working on the basis of consultation between the Government, the public analysts and the Local Authority Associations, so that the essential details are clearly provided of the way in which samples will be obtained and the way in which they will be analysed.

Certainly, if we are taking samples and sending them in for analysis—and I accept the point that the present system of payment for part-time analysts is open to some objection—there is a need to get from the samples the maximum amount of information so that it can be collated for the benefit of either the Government or the food industry, especially if it meets a specific purpose of a previously approved plan. Time and money are needed for this, and it is only by getting together the parties involved in food and drug enforcement that a sensible solution will be achieved.

So far as the Ministry's labelling service was concerned, I did criticize it, and I have encountered problems which still remain from the advice provided at that time. I am not, however, criticizing the service as it operated then. It had to work under what were, in effect, wartime conditions. It did not have the same liaison with enforcement officers that is available in these days. I still believe that there is a need for a central organization for advisory purposes, but it must work on the basis not only of advice from people who make the laws but also from those who analyse the food and from enforcement officers who are in closer contact with the consumer and have the consumers' interests very much at heart.

I trust this answers all the questions.

Mr. T McLachlan (Thomas McLachlan and Partners): I am not a legal man, as it says on the list of delegates, nor, if I may make another disclosure, in spite of what one or two people in this room may believe, was I born when the 1875 Act was passed.

I was very interested in both Mr. Giles' paper this morning and Mr. Evans' paper this afternoon, because Mr. Giles brought out the point that the courts decide and Mr. Evans has said how difficult it is for the courts to decide. I had over 41 years as a public analyst and quite frequently I was very disappointed. I got into trouble on one occasion in an annual report for saying that, if I wanted to bring a case for milk, I would rather have it heard before a stipendiary and, if I wanted to bring a case on some food other than milk, I would rather be heard by a bench of magistrates.

When the 1860 Act and subsequent Acts were passed, it was made a criminal law, and that is still maintained. At the same time, as Mr. Evans was stressing just now and as the papers are continually telling us, most of the cases at the moment are brought on points of law regarding labelling, description, etc. rather than on actual composition. Very often there may be a strong difference of opinion between experts even on the same side as to what the interpretation should be. My own view is—and I have urged this for over 40 years in and out of print—that there should be some form of advisory service. We were not entirely happy with the advisory service set up by the old Ministry of Food, but we all bowed to it and public analysts in particular protested violently when it was done away with. I think that something on those lines should be brought back.

I should like to ask Mr. Evans whether he does not think that the time has now arrived when the Food and Drugs Act should be taken out of the criminal law and put into civil law.

Mr. Evans: Looking at Mr. McLachlan, no one would ever believe that he had been around in 1875! However, he has been an authority for a long time and he has collected a great deal of information in that time.

I do not, however, agree that it is possible or right to consider a change of the Food and Drugs Act from the criminal to the civil code. I think that what Mr. McLachlan would like, and what I would like, too, would be a greater opportunity for talking to the manufacturers involved in these disputes, possibly under the aegis of the Ministry's Food Standards Division, rather than trying to settle complicated matters of interpretation of labelling and advertising problems by legal means. It would be preferable for this to be done on a voluntary basis, rather than by going to law and using the criminal provisions of the Food and Drugs Act. However, that is a rather different thing from changing the whole aspect of food and drugs legislation which would, I think, be a retrograde step, even if it were possible. I am all for voluntary persuasion beforehand, but there is a need for the criminal sanction if this should fail.

Mr. R S Hatfull (County Analyst, Staffordshire County Council): While congratulating Mr. Evans on his paper, I feel that I must at the same time offer him my sympathy in that he is speaking on the whole subject of enforcement of the law. There are two main aspects of the Food and Drugs Act; the first is that of the inspectorate and the second is that of the public analyst. As a measure of the involvement of the public analyst, I could perhaps mention that in this theatre today we have something in excess of a quarter of all the public analysts in Great Britain, which emphasizes that we do consider this an extremely important subject and an extremely important Symposium.

Mr. Evans has rightly emphasized that the public analyst and the enforcement officer must work in close contact, and I am sure that everybody would agree. However, I would counsel caution in regard to the word he used in his circulated paper, the word 'teamwork'. The roles of the public analyst and the inspectorate are quite different and separate. The inspector takes samples and institutes prosecutions when such are deemed to be necessary; the public analyst is an expert on matters of science, in which he is exceptionally well qualified. Thus, the role of the public analyst is that of an independent expert witness giving factual evidence for the information of the court. He can, in fact, be called not only by the prosecution but also by the defence. Therefore, he is not part of a prosecution team.

Mr. Evans has talked, as have other speakers today, about labelling, and he has spoken of a change in emphasis from adulteration to labelling and advertising. Dr. Egan to some extent redressed the balance and I would draw the attention of members to the ever-important aspect of composition. In that I include additives and contaminants. There are a great many compositional regulations. There are regulations governing contaminants and additives, and more regulations are falling from Whitehall like autumn leaves. These are very important. They are very important for the work of the public analyst.

Mr. Evans has emphasized that the roles of the public analyst and the inspectorate should be complementary. I would go further than that and stress that, in these two complementary roles, each must play his full part in the task to which he was statutorily appointed and for which he is qualified.

Mr. Evans: I accept that the public analyst is a scientific expert. I accept that he needs a measure of independence if he is to assist the courts before which he may have to give evidence. I cannot, however, see why there should be any objection to my use of the word 'team'. If the word 'team' implies an objectionable official relationship, then I will withdraw it and change it for something that suggests getting together and deciding the best way to employ the expertise of both analyst and the enforcement officer. It is necessary that they work together. The system can only operate if they do work together. It is on that basis that they form a team, even if it is not a formal team.

The falling leaves will keep on falling, since the more we have of additives the more we shall have of labelling controls. Moreover, the greater the impact of EEC Directives the more, I fear, Bob Giles will have to produce his 'autumn leaves'.

Dr. L E Coles (County Analyst, Mid-Glamorgan County Council): I was going to bring up many points, but for the sake of time I will confine my remarks to what I think is important and give you, perhaps, an unbiased opinion.

Reorganization has itself created a regional type of scientific service in which the expertise is concentrated within county boundaries. In your paper you mentioned the desirability of having co-ordinated sampling programmes either regionally or nationally based. I must say that, so far as this is concerned, it is essential for the public analyst to have a central part in this organization. One of the reasons for this is that he is often employed by county councils and he has direct contact with the environmental officers of the district councils, and these have an important part to play in the overall control of the contamination of food.

The other point that I wish to bring out is about the small departments that tend to be set up in some authorities to carry out what are called 'screening' or 'sifting' tests. These lead to testing which has no legal standing whatsoever.

I put this to Mr. Evans for his comments.

Mr. Evans: I do think that co-ordinated sampling programmes are helpful, but I do not think that they should replace all random sampling. The Food and Drugs Act has operated successfully for a long time on the basis of random sampling and I think that this must continue. However, co-ordinated programmes designed for a specific end and agreed with the scientific members of the service do have an important part to play.

I agree also that there is a need for the duties carried out by the environmental health officers in district councils to tie up with the work carried out by the food and drugs officers of the county councils. As far as is possible, there should be consultation, and in the majority of areas this is already done on a most effective basis.

On the question of screening tests, I would rather not be drawn too far since I am not happy that, for what is paid for the work carried out by part-time public analysts, sufficient time is allowed for the proper testing of all the samples submitted. I suggest that public analysts themselves carry out screening tests on this basis. Whether they are carried out by the public analyst or by the trading standards department really matters very little, as long as the suspect samples are given formal treatment and are dealt with in the best possible way by the public analyst.

I am quite sure that we all need more information from the samples we send in, more details of the tests carried out, and more tests carried out. It is only on that basis that we shall achieve the maximum benefit from the complete service.

Mr. J H Shelton (Public Analyst, Leo Taylor and Lucke): I am one of the so-called part-time public analysts and, for those who do not know what that means, we are just as much qualified, have the same qualifying examination, we have the same function and we are statutorily employed in the same ways as the so-called full-time public analyst. A much better method of describing us would be as fee paid rather than salaried. But however we are described, we do the same sort of work.

I must take Mr. Evans up on his last point about the difference between screening done by a local officer who is not qualified and that done by the public analysts' department. The difference is, of course, that we have the proper equipment, we have the qualifications and we have the expertise by which to do what tests we feel we ought to do for the proper examination of the sample. Whether or not we are paid the right fee for what we do is another question.

We have also been taken to task about the lack of information that we give on samples. There are one or two very good reasons for this, one of which is that we never have any control over the use that is made of the reports we give. I personally have had reason to comment on samples, sometimes comments of a pleasant nature and sometimes of an adverse one, to my local authority, only to find that information which has been in favour of the vendor has been used in advertising. Whether he has got the information directly from the inspector concerned I know not. However, as a result of unfortunate experiences that some of us have had in our laboratories, we have naturally been a little careful about what we have had to say on the samples we examine. Nevertheless, when the proper authorities ask us to elaborate—such as the Government Chemist's Department—we are always happy and able to give a lot more information than perhaps we do in our initial certificates.

As a part-timer—and I object to this term wholeheartedly—I feel that we are sometimes in a better position than the so-called full-timer to advise industry. I say this advisedly, because we are all public analysts, we all work together for the common good, but the majority of us—and we represent about 50 per cent of the total public analysts in this country—have a liaison with industry. We act in a consultative capacity right down the middle, I would say. We have no axe to grind, we are here to produce facts and, because of our liaison with industry, we are sometimes in a position to know things which our full-time colleagues perhaps do not know. We are able then to give our expert evidence on the basis of a knowledge of both sides. Many of us, myself included, have had a number of years working in industry in fairly senior positions, and this also gives us an idea of what to do on difficult occasions.

So, in defence of part-timers, if I may put it like that, I should like to say that both salaried and fee-paid public analysts work as a whole, we are unified in our approach and we wish with all our hearts to co-operate independently with the enforcement officers whom Mr. Evans represents.

Mr. Evans: Mr. Shelton and I know each other very well. He knows, also, my high regard for the work of public analysts. What I have been trying to emphasize in my paper and this introduction is the fact that there is a need for the public analyst and the enforcement officer to work together for the benefit of the community. If this is taken in its right context there can never be any question of information provided by the public analyst being used in a way to which the public analyst could take exception. I mentioned teamwork,

148

and got into trouble for using the word 'team', but this is what is meant. The public analyst and the enforcement officer must work together if the food and drugs enforcement system is to continue to function as well as it has in the past. There is no other country which employs public analysts in quite the same way as in this country. Probably there are no other enforcement officers employed in quite the same manner either. However, as long as public analysts, as scientific advisers and enforcement officers, as trained and qualified experts for dealing with enforcement, work together the system can operate probably as well as any other in the world.

Mr. D G Forbes (President, Association of Public Analysts): I speak for the Association of Public Analysts. I think I can rightly say that I can speak on behalf of all the previous public analyst speakers and also the remaining two, one of whom introduced the discussion and is, in effect, appointed to an authority for whom I also act, and the other is a past public analyst who was my predecessor.

I should like to endorse wholeheartedly what all of these gentlemen have said. I would also stress one point which perhaps has not been brought out and that is the way in which the public analyst service has developed to its present position. It has always been of the utmost independence and integrity, and this is how I believe it is used today. Our speaker was quite right in saying that we must act with the enforcement authorities and, in fact, I believe that we do. The small altercation we had regarding the question of part-time analysts was, perhaps, a misinterpretation of what he said as I understood it. It was a reference to all the small laboratories, and I stand to be corrected if I am wrong.

I think I am right in saying that all my colleagues would agree that the system we have today, in which the public analyst service is seen to be independent and is not under the control of central government, and therefore is not of the type which a regional laboratory would represent, is one which can be seen to be acting on behalf of the consumer and on behalf of the trade interest, and also enforcing the laws which the Government has seen fit to make.

In this context, I think that what previous speakers have said about the amount of legislation in this country being a very adequate balance is quite true. We feel that if we enforce all the legislation that is laid down this is to everybody's advantage, rather than to have a tremendous amount of legislation which is what the EEC laws seem to be imposing upon us and very little of which can be taken to its ultimate extent.

Perhaps Mr. Evans would like to comment upon this.

Mr. Evans: I know Mr. Forbes also, of course. The Association of which

Mr. Forbes is President and my own professional Institute do get together, and I hope will do so even more, to discuss points of difference or points of clarification in a way that can only be for the benefit of the service as a whole.

There was never any intention, and I agree with Mr. Forbes on this, that I should in any way suggest that these rather unfortunately named 'part-time' analysts were not efficient, independent and helpful. The name may be wrong, of course; it should probably be 'consultant' analyst. If there could be a change to this description it would probably save some misunderstanding.

Food and Drug Law in the United States: A 200-year Perspective

Alexander M Schmidt

Commissioner of Food and Drugs, United States Department of Health, Education and Welfare

Thank you for inviting me to this celebration of the first century of effective national food and drug legislation in the United Kingdom. This is a meaningful occasion for the world, as well as your own country. First things always have a special significance, and this is why we celebrate anniversaries.

In the United States, we are looking forward to another anniversary—the 200th since our Declaration of Independence as a nation on 4th July 1776. And if my presentation today were to have an additional subtitle, it could well be 'From Independence to Interdependence'. For we are living in a world of change which affects us all, and makes it necessary that we collaborate, rather than to go our separate ways. In that spirit, I am honoured to be here, representing the United States Food and Drug Administration.

That our food and drug laws relate directly to yours is obvious; there is a distinct familial resemblance. Soon after the colonists arrived in New England, they were enacting and enforcing bread laws similar to the 'assizes' known in Britain since the days of King John and the Magna Carta. And in 1630, the Massachusetts Bay Colony prosecuted a newcomer from Holland, one Nicholas Knopp, '. . . for taking upon him to cure the scurvy by a water of noe worth nor value, which he solde att a very deare note'. Not only was Knopp fined £5 in this early drug misbranding case, he was also declared liable for suit by anyone who had paid money for the 'said water'.

Some of the laws enacted by the colonists were patterned after those of the home land, but very early the colonists were asserting their right as British subjects to enact their own laws aimed at specific local problems. Especially significant were rather numerous ordinances assuring the integrity of exports of food and other products. As a result of the concern for safe arrival of exported goods, it appears that consumers in Britain had more protection from the colonial food laws than did the producers in America. So we find the New York General Assembly in 1773 reacting to complaints about the poor quality of bread in New York City by requiring local bakers to use only flour that had passed the export inspection.

151

Colonial food laws, from the beginning, were quite diverse, largely indigenous and, while reflecting the heritage from English law, responded principally to the needs of producers and consumers in the 13 separate colonies. The resulting diversity in colonial laws was perhaps more apparent to the authorities of the mother country than to the colonists. Probably the first attempt to secure uniformity in these early colonial laws, including food laws, was a compilation made by the authority of the Duke of York in the reign of Charles II, and intended to be a model for all the colonies. It was not very successful.

After independence was achieved, our States individually continued enacting food, drug and other laws to suit their own conditions. One of the first was a food adulteration law passed by Massachusetts in 1785, which provided for the prosecution of 'evilly disposed persons' who, 'from motives of avarice and filthy lucre, have been induced to sell diseased, corrupted, contagious or unwholesome provisions to the great nuisance of public health and peace'. This forthright and comprehensive food adulteration law was seriously weakened, however, by the phrase, 'knowing the same without making it known to the buyer', thus joining the concept of willful intent to liability—something we are still struggling to straighten out.

The first national food and drug law for the United States was passed many years after (1906) the United Kingdom's laws of 1860 and 1875. The principal reason was 'states' rights'. Many Americans, including members of Congress, thought that food and drug protection, if needed at all, was a function for the States, and most States already had laws dealing with such matters. But other Americans, as early as 1875, saw the rapid industrial development and expanding transportation and marketing systems of the country, and knew it was necessary that the central government regulate interstate commerce in foods and drugs. Only a few years after the United Kingdom adopted its first food and drug laws, Federal legislation was being proposed and seriously considered in the United States. One of these bills had an interesting history.

Then, as now, there were critical reports in the press on both sides of the Atlantic about the quality and safety of food. In America, as in Britain, the reaction of industry could be summed up as a 'qualified admission'—i.e., that certainly there was some contamination, but it was not nearly so bad as it was portrayed, and no hazard to health, else people would be sick or dying in the streets. At the same time, some in industry agreed that a Federal law to stop adulteration would be a good thing for business, as well as its customers. Reporting these sentiments, a dignified trade journal of the period, known as *The Plumber and Sanitary Engineer*, announced a competition 'for the best Act, accompanied by an Essay, designed to prevent injurious adulteration and to regulate the sale of food without imposing unnecessary burdens upon commerce . . .'. Prizes totalling $1000 were offered by the National Board of Trade, a predecessor of the US Chamber of Commerce.

The winner of the first prize, announced by the trade journal in a supplement to its December issue of 1880, was G W Wigner, not an American at all but one of Britain's leading public analytical chemists and then Honorary Secretary of the Society of Public Analysts. Mr. Wigner had written extensive critiques of the 1875 Sale of Food and Drugs Act in his own country, and he embodied in his proposed law for the United States some of the improvements he thought should be made. The Wigner bill was introduced in Congress and became one of the early ancestors of the US Food and Drugs Act of 1906. A similar bill was actually enacted in the State of Wisconsin.

A distinctive feature of the Wigner bill was the appointment of public analysts by boards of health, similar to the system adopted in your Act of 1875. Two reasons probably accounted for the failure to accept such a system in the United States—a lack of independent chemists, and the fact that the function was already being performed by the individual State laboratories.

From 1880 to 1900, more than 100 bills were introduced in the US Congress to regulate foods and drugs. While special interests managed the passage of a number of minor laws: for example, to inspect tea, and to set standards for oleomargarine and butter, not until 1906 was a comprehensive law enacted. Why did it take so long?

The opposition was tremendous. The doctrine of State rights, still powerful in 1975, has already been mentioned as an obstacle. 'Rugged individualism' was another. Many typical Americans consider themselves 'too smart' to be fooled by hucksters of spurious products. The times were not yet right. They became so only with the turn of the century leadership of Theodore Roosevelt.

Dr. Harvey W Wiley, chief food chemist in the US Department of Agriculture and the leader of the pure food and drug crusade in the United States, was aware of all this when, in 1902, he asked Congress for funds to finance a unique experiment. Its purpose was to determine and demonstrate the effects of food preservatives on the 'digestion and health' of human volunteers. Intended as a serious scientific study in toxicology, the novelty of the project nevertheless captured public interest and tremendous publicity, which Wiley turned to his advantage. His 'Poison Squad' became a major factor in getting public support for the Act of 1906.

Wiley fed his volunteers massive doses of borax, formaldehyde, salicylic acid, copper sulphate, and even sulphurous acid! The general pattern was to begin with a five-day period to secure data on the subject's normal condition, followed by 10 days of increasing dosage with the chemical, and five days of convalescence. The object was to give enough to produce overt symptoms. The case records were startling and at times amusing. The male human animal was seen to vary widely in tolerance to the various chemicals, including the effects of such accompaniments as whiskey before dinner, or cigars afterward.

Nothing could better illustrate the changes which have taken place in determining food safety than to compare Dr. Wiley's feeding huge doses to humans, with today's dosing of 50 000 mice with a few parts per billion.

The law of 1906 provided regulatory definitions of 'foods' and 'drugs', and prohibited their introduction into interstate commerce if misbranded or adulterated. It stopped the use of many harmful chemicals and brought great improvements in sanitation and labelling, but the next quarter century of change made it obsolete. The great depression of the 1930s aggravated the weaknesses of the 1906 law, and there were many. Debased foods and spurious drugs again became the target of public criticism. A book titled *100 000 000 Guinea Pigs* became a best seller.

In 1933, the Commissioner of Food and Drugs sought the cooperation of Franklin Roosevelt's 'New Deal' administration to sponsor a new and stronger law. Again, strong opposition was expressed by business interests, particularly to the possibility that FDA, rather than the more lenient Federal Trade Commission, would regulate the advertising of food and drugs. Finally, after a five-year struggle, the Federal Food, Drug and Cosmetic Act was passed, in 1938. Reacting to a drug manufacturing error that cost over 100 lives, Congress required in the new law that the safety of new drugs be established by scientific studies performed prior to, and as a condition of, FDA approval for marketing. In addition, cosmetics and therapeutic devices were, for the first time, placed under FDA jurisdiction.

The 1938 law is still the bedrock of our regulatory system. It provided, among other things, that the FDA could set standards of composition for foods—known formally as standards of identity and quality. The law prescribed ingredient labelling for those foods not standardized. It prohibited the addition of poisons to foods, but if addition to food of a 'poisonous or deleterious substance' was necessary or could not be avoided, FDA could set safe limitations on the permissible amount of the substance.

The 1938 law did not remain unembellished for long. Unforeseen loopholes needed to be plugged, and new scientific discoveries mandated new approaches to the control of 'poisonous substances'. Particularly, there was still no requirement that the safety of pesticides or food additives be demonstrated before marketing. Any chemical could be used until the government proved in court that it was harmful. Toxic chemicals were turning

154

up in foods with disturbing regularity, and hundreds of widely used sub-stances lacked scientific evidence of their safety. The burden of proof was entirely on the government. Again, the FDA brought a bad situation to the attention of Congress; and, in 1949, a Select Committee of the House of Representatives, the 'Delaney Committee', was appointed to investigate the use of chemicals in food and cosmetics. Out of their deliberations came three major amendments to the 1938 Act: the pesticide amendment of 1954, the food additive amendment of 1958, and a colour additive amend-ment in 1960. Patterned after the new drug approval section of the 1938 Act, all three amendments applied the principle that the safety of ingredients and products should be determined before the public is exposed to them.

This fundamental change was one of the most important advances in social legislation during the past century. It made the manufacturer respon-sible for establishing the safety of his product and the government responsible for evaluating the evidence submitted. The burden of proof was shifted from government to the manufacturer.

Mandatory pre-marketing clearance is today the dominant feature of the US food and drug law, and we expect before long it will be applied to medical devices and cosmetics as well.

Tremendous benefits have resulted from pre-market testing. It prevented the drug thalidomide from becoming a major disaster in the United States. It stopped the use of overtly toxic and untested chemicals in foods, such as thiourea, monochloracetic acid or lithium chloride—to name three of the 'horrors' exhibited in the 1950–51 Delaney Committee hearings previously mentioned. The requirement that effectiveness, as well as safety, be shown, added to the law in 1962, made it possible to clear the market of hundreds of questionable or worthless products, and to improve the label claims of thousands of others.

And although some critics disagree, pre-market control seems to have had little adverse effect on the progress of technology. Thousands of new com-pounds and products have reached the market after passing the required safety examination. In fact, there is evidence that pre-marketing regulations have been a stimulant to technological progress. But there is also abundant evidence that technological developments continue to generate regulatory problems.

Just 15 years ago, you were commemorating the 100th anniversary of the United Kingdom's first general food law, the 'Act of Preventing the Adulteration of Food or Drink'. At that anniversary meeting, Commissioner George Larrick reviewed the FDA's effort to remove from the American market cranberries contaminated by an improperly used herbicide which had been found to cause cancer in laboratory rats.

The cranberry caper was but the first in a series of actions stemming from a proviso in the 1958 Food Additive Amendment. This proviso is the section which declares that 'no (food) additive shall be deemed safe if it is found to induce cancer when ingested by man or animal'. Now known as the 'Delaney clause', this section was initially opposed by the FDA and by scientists who argued that a food additive used at low levels need not be banned automatically simply because it had caused cancer when very great amounts were fed to test animals. Proponents of the section justified it on the basis that cancer experts have not determined how much or how little of a carcinogen will trigger the cancer process in a susceptible individual. Thus, they argued that no amount of such a substance could be judged safe for human use.

In 1962, the US Congress amended the Delaney clause to allow the use of carcinogenic substances, such as diethylstilboestrol (DES), in livestock feed if no drug residue could be detected by analysis of edible tissues from the treated livestock. The method of analysis used was to be approved by the government.

The original Delaney clause prevented any exercise of scientific or regulatory judgment, which was precisely its intent. But in adding the 1962 proviso, Congress obviously intended to allow the economically important use of chemicals in livestock feed, even carcinogens such as DES if the safety of humans could be assured.

As the years went by, however, our analytical methods improved greatly. For example, the ability to detect DES advanced to the degree that one could measure parts per million, and then parts per billion. Thus, in 1973, the FDA banned the use of DES in cattle production because of the detection of trace amounts in some beef livers. That ban was set aside by a court because of an alleged procedural error on the part of the Agency.

DES is again being added to animal feed in the United States, and is occasionally being detected, in very small amounts, in beef livers. Seeking to carry out the intent of the amended Delaney clause, the FDA is struggling to perfect a regulation stating how sensitive the approved analytical method used to detect chemical residues must be to ensure safe use of a carcinogen in livestock feed. The proposal has resulted in substantial scientific discussion and disagreement. It is one of the most important, as well as complex, proposals ever issued by the FDA.

The use of DES as a growth promotant in animal feed presents a classic case in which the benefits of more cheaply abundant food need to be weighed against an indefinite risk. DES is, at present, perhaps the most interesting food regulatory problem we are now facing in the United States, and how we resolve the outstanding issues will predict how we will deal with the many similar regulatory problems yet to come.

The complications are increasing. The United States Senate has recently taken the unusual step of passing legislation that would ban the use of DES in animal feed. This is a fascinating regulatory development, which poses a number of questions and alternatives. First, the legislation could make things easy for everyone. No one has to think, or to exercise scientific judgment. The substance is simply prohibited. But what of all the other known carcinogens—and suspected carcinogens, mutagens and teratogens in food? Were we able to detect only a few *molecules* of exogenous DES in beef liver, would its use still be prohibited? Would *any* substance, found to be cancer-producing when fed at *any* amount to *any* animal species, be prohibited if we could find *any* trace of it in edible tissue? Can the benefit derived from a food additive be measured at all against the risk of its use? Is a 2 per cent, 5 per cent, or 10 per cent gain in the efficiency of food production to be measured against the possibility of cancer being produced in one of a million persons eating the food? One in a hundred million? Five hundred million?

Clearly, balancing benefit and risk is a somewhat arbitrary and, therefore, judgmental practice. In the United States, we are trying to determine whether or not this judgment can be exercised and, if so, by whom. The FDA would like to find some means by which, in a publicly accountable manner, we could decide certain important risk-benefit questions. We have invited comment on this subject from the public, from scientists and from Congress. The answers we get are important and are, by and large, that most people are not willing to assume any known risk of cancer, however small, from eating food. Part of this reaction may stem from the current general distrust of the government to act in the best interest of the public, and part from the large amount of public attention being given to the problem of environmental carcinogens. But for whatever reason, the current trend in the United States is to say 'no known risk is acceptable', and to back it with legislation. The practical result is, of course, to prevent the exercise of judgment. One need not think, to implement legislation that absolutely forbids the use of a chemical.

This is obviously important to food regulation in our country, and, I would suppose, may well impact on other countries as well. The DES question is only one of a dozen or more in recent years in which definite benefits are confronted by indefinite or theoretical risks. Another we are now struggling with is whether or not bacon, because of nitrosamine formation, is an acceptable product for the American market. Far more certain, of course, is the risk of cancer from cigarette smoking, but it is an optional risk. It may well be, however, that simply the act of breathing subjects one to greater health hazards than does consumption of today's food additives.

Of one thing I'm certain. The only sure way out of the quandary is to be able to state with quantitative finality the risk posed by the use of DES, or nitrites, or by naturally occurring substances such as aflatoxins in peanuts. From quantification of risk can come a workable definition of the word 'safe', with some type of quantitative measures that will allow an obvious and therefore acceptable benefit-risk evaluation to be made. We fly in airplanes because they are 'safe', but 'safe' is defined by the low number of deaths per million passenger-miles, not the total absence of risk.

Today the abundance of our food supply permits the luxury of trying to avoid any and all risk. We can afford to seek the ideal of absolute safety. In this anniversary meeting, we are celebrating the great progress made during the past 100 years in improving food safety. We have only to look back to the days before modern food science and food law, to see the progress made. But will our successors, looking back, 50, 75 or 100 years from now, be able to see any accommodation, or compromise, with that concept of absolute safety?

My purpose to now has been to review the evolution of food laws in the United States, giving a 200-year perspective. Now we should look ahead, for one of the purposes in reviewing history, and celebrating progress, is to anticipate the future.

Forty per cent of all meals now eaten by Americans, whether consumed in restaurants, fast food service stations, or at home, have been prepared outside the home; and that percentage is rapidly increasing. Assuming this trend continues, we predict that in 10 years, *70 per cent* of all meals will be eaten away from home, or brought home ready to eat. A major fraction of the food consumed will consist of reconstituted substances, or be manufactured totally from raw material such as fish, vegetable, or bacterial protein or amino-acids. Totally synthesized food analogues will be commonplace. Raw materials may come from one country, be shipped to another for processing, and then be returned for consumption. International boundaries to commerce will be obscured, and a greater fraction of the food industry will be multi-national.

Meanwhile, scientists will be discovering toxic reactions at the molecular level. Environmental scientists will prove that chemical pollution has reached everywhere. The need to conserve limited resources will have resulted in recycling within food chains, with the attendant dangers of toxic concentrations.

These are glimpses of the next few years that came from our planning process. Our next step was to think about what the FDA would have to do, in order to deal with the future as we see it.

As a result of this effort we have identified six broad areas of hazard, and believe their future priority order will remain about as they now are.

The first of these hazards is that of *food-borne infection*. This hazard ranks where it does because of its continuing widespread incidence, and because of the high risk in some instances, such as botulism. We even predict the hazards of food-borne infection will increase, as foods are synthesized, as they are manufactured in one place, consumed in others, and stored and moved repeatedly.

Further, it may be that contaminating organisms will become more and more resistant to available antibiotics, thus increasing the hazards of sepsis. New types of toxins will be discovered—we are just now beginning to evaluate the effects in man associated with the mycotoxins. In short, we see no alternative but to continue our unremitting pressure against contamination of food by micro-organisms.

The second class of hazards in terms of present importance, and perhaps one of even greater importance in the future, is *malnutrition*. Malnutrition at present is poorly measured and poorly understood. Biochemically provable nutritional deficiencies do occur in numbers sufficient to be of concern now, and when a larger part of our food supply is manufactured, the problems may increase. It is often not readily appreciated that we really do not know everything that should be included in artificially constituted foods, and in what amounts, if the analogues are to be nutritionally equal to traditional foods. We will need to know much more about trace minerals, to give one example, before we can wisely tell someone how much of each he has to put into his artificial meat.

We would consider the *environmental contaminants* next most important. These may or may not be from industrial sources. Mercury poisoning has been both industrial and natural. But the increasing pollution of our world, the recycling of valuable resources such as animal wastes, and the new uses of previously discarded products such as sewage will increase still further the risk of serious hazard from environmental sources.

Naturally occurring toxicants are also likely to be concentrated, as we process and manufacture foods, and likely to survive future manufacturing processes that ignore the potential of this hazard. We all know, for instance, that many commonly consumed legumes contain toxic materials (which have, on occasion, been fatal) as part of their normal make-up. An example is the anti-cholinesterase found in potatoes. These foods are now safe for consumption only because the toxic materials are destroyed in cooking. At present, our best safeguard against this class of hazard is to adhere to traditional methods of food preparation and consumption, rather than to experiment too boldly with novel methods of preparation.

Pesticide residues might be made part of the earlier category of industrial environmental contaminants; but we distinguish them because of their

159

toxicity, and because they are subject to their own regulatory scheme. Our principal concern here is not with our present regulatory methods, but with the fact that in many parts of the world pesticides are poorly controlled, if controlled at all. If all pesticides become ubiquitous, as did DDT, and if raw materials and finished foods are to move easily across borders, then the hazards from pesticides may increase dramatically.

Finally, we must list the hazards of *food additives*. Our priority ranking puts additives sixth—mostly because so much is known about many of them, and all are now, and surely will continue to be, well regulated.

These hazards, then, illustrate important food safety problems facing all nations. I suspect that to deal with the underlying issues effectively, our laws and procedures will have to be flexible. They will and should be modified from time to time, as they have been during the century we celebrate today.

As administrators of food and drug law, we are irrevocably and deeply involved in the dilemma of civilized man, who must have the technology to sustain both his lifestyle and his life, while at the same time he is concerned over unwanted consequences of the same technology.

Our laws may not cross international boundaries, but problems do, science does, and scientific solutions to problems must. New information moves instantly by satellite around the world. People move around the world at twice the speed of sound.

In such a world, independence must be replaced by a greater inter-dependence, as we all work together for the common good of the human condition.

Thank you.

Discussion

Mr. F Wood (CPC(UK) Ltd): My Lord Chairman, Ladies and Gentlemen, Dr. Schmidt said that he was privileged to be here, but it is obvious from the way in which we have received his talk that it is we who are privileged to have him.

His paper dealing with the history of the food law of the United States has been most interesting, but perhaps the most interesting thing in this for me was the explanation of the Delaney clause. This is something which a lot of people in the United Kingdom know about, of course, but we could not understand how this could come to be accepted without any lower limits. Dr. Schmidt's paper has gone a long way towards explaining that situation to us.

The reference to diethylstilboestrol and the attempts to get away from the Delaney clause was fascinating, but it does seem, from what was said

160

about the current trend that no known risk is acceptable, that we have come full circle and are back again to this Delaney clause.

Dr. Schmidt has highlighted what he considered to be the six broad areas of hazard for today and there is no need for me to reiterate all six. However, I would pick out three which I think are important. His first one, perhaps surprisingly, was food-borne infection due to increased eating out, and having myself experienced a severe bout of food poisoning last year from a well-known London hotel I am disposed to agree with him. So far as new toxins are concerned, I think that this, too, is something which is causing a lot of concern to us in the United Kingdom. Most of us are familiar with the aflatoxins of the past 10 years, but now of course we hear about patulin, zearalenone and several others, and we naturally are wondering just how many more of these mycotoxins are going to be discovered in common, everyday food. When we think of that, and the other points that Dr. Schmidt has made, we begin to wonder whether it is safe to eat at all.

So far as trace minerals are concerned I think he made a very important point, because the role of trace minerals is indeed an unknown quantity. We still do not know the best way to take iron to be efficiently assimilated in 1975, and in the Codex we have had long discussions on the trace elements in breast milk which is still a mystery in terms of baby food.

So I wanted to refer to those three out of the six, but I am sure that a lot of people will want in subsequent discussion to raise other points.

I think that some people will have been heartened by Dr. Schmidt's comment that food additives are number six in his list since they are well regulated. Perhaps some people might disagree.

There is one paragraph in his paper, which perhaps you have not had a chance to see in detail, which is well worth reading several times. In it he says that, as administrators of food and drug law we are irrevocably and deeply involved in the dilemma of civilized man, who must have the technology to sustain both his lifestyle and his life while, at the same time, he is concerned over the mounting consequences of the same technology. This is a classic phrase and one which perhaps we should hang on the walls of our offices.

There are many subjects which Dr. Schmidt has not had time to discuss in his paper, and it is not often that we get the opportunity to have a word with a Food and Drugs Commissioner, so I would like just to ask one question and then leave the rest of you to ask all the others.

We know in this country, and it was referred to yesterday, that several million people cannot even read, and many more millions just do not, or even will not, read. We have read with great interest of the nutritional labelling experiments in the United States and we should be very glad to hear whether Dr. Schmidt really believes that this is of any value to the ordinary housewife.

161

Dr. Schmidt: Thank you very much for your remarks. I will answer the question, but I would just make two points relative to your remarks.

With regard to the Delaney clause, what I think will happen to it is that it will not go away. Nobody in Congress who wants to be re-elected would talk about voting for cancer. I mean, voting for cancer is not a wise political move. However, a number of Congressmen are talking about modernizing the Delaney clause, and some talk about modernizing it out of existence.

I think that the way we will modernize the Delaney clause will be to define zero, not to define or try to define the low effect level of a carcinogen; that way lies madness. However, you can define zero in practical terms and, if we can pull that off, if we can educate the citizenry of our country to accept an extrapolation down a dose response curve so that they will know that the risk from eating bacon is less than the risk of flying in an aeroplane, then we will keep bacon. It is as simple as that.

As far as food poisoning goes, one thing I am positive of is that it is one of the most unreported conditions that have stricken many. I cannot help but remark that the figures that were given here yesterday for your numbers of cases of food poisoning are low by at least a factor of 10. All of you in this room have probably been ill in your lifetime from food. It just is terribly unreported.

I think that nutritional labelling will go down as one of the things that I am most proud of the agency for. When I go into a Piggly-Wiggly store, or some other place, and walk down the aisle between shelves of canned food, I have a feeling of pride, tears steal down my cheeks as I see one-third of the label has white space—which is something different all by itself in our country—with nicely arranged very good information on the can. We did a recent survey which showed that now about 30 per cent of housewives say that they use the nutritional labelling, either in meal planning or in making comparative purchases between brands. I would think that the figure was somewhere between 20 and 30 per cent, just from talking to people.

In addition to the value that it might have for people who know what it is all about, there are two other important features. One is that it makes everybody else curious. They look at it, see that one-third of the label of the can is occupied by something, and sooner or later they are all going to get around to saying 'What's that?' If we can make our Sesame Street movies and other things and get them out, if we can do what we are really trying to do, and that is to teach the fifth and sixth graders, the purchasers, the customers, what it is all about, then in 20 years if you ask me it will be 80 per cent who will be using it.

The third thing is that people look at it and they say, 'Who's that?', and it is the Food and Drug Administration. If people are ever going to let us make benefit/risk decisions they are going to have to trust us, and one of the ways by which they will trust us is by getting to know us. If we can do things like giving them useful and friendly nutritional labelling and they say 'That's the FDA', then when we want to do something else they will say 'OK'.

So it is being useful now. It is teaching people and creating a need, or a desire, to learn. It is teaching people about the regulations, about the existence of the FDA, and about our concern for nutrition overall. For these reasons I think that the nutritional labelling is really great.

Professor Ward (University of Leeds): First, I should like to add to Mr Wood's tribute to what we have heard, but there is one point on which I should be grateful for a comment. That is how the regulatory power of the United States Department of Agriculture fits into the pattern. This is a point which I think was perhaps not fully covered.

Dr. Schmidt: The United States Department of Agriculture is more or less responsible for things growing and on the farm and for inter-state commerce. We have debated the need for good agricultural practices to combat aflatoxins. We sat down with the USDA and we both decided that they would get into that area. The United States Department of Agriculture regulates red meat and poultry, they have continuous on-site inspection of meat plants, and they have more people doing that than I have in the entire Food and Drug Administration. We do sea food, of course, and most other food.

We have, I think, very effective liaison with the United States Department of Agriculture. Our top officials meet at least once a month formally and settle the squabbles that have arisen during the month from a large series of meetings that have gone on between other people, and we have to work together.

One of the questions in the country is whether the nitrites, the curing agent in bacon, has ever been properly sanctioned by either the Food and Drug Administration or the USDA; we did not sanction curing by nitrites, but we think the USDA did and we are now trying to decide. What is decided will obviously then trigger our regulatory action.

We do come together in many different areas like that. They worry about canned meat, but every time someone gets botulism from canned meat we get a plate of meat from them and our laboratory people do all the regulatory analysis, and so on. So that the coarse division is red meat and poultry for the USDA and the rest for us, but we really work together very well the majority of the time.

Lord Zuckerman (Symposium Chairman): I understood you to say in opening your address that there was considerable opposition at the very start, because of states' rights, to the imposition of any federal laws in this field. I have always understood that the FDA really regulated inter-state commerce.

Yesterday, in the course of our various discussions, the question of centralization of control or its devolution to the periphery came up. How, at this moment, can you effectively control what happens within states, or within big cities, which I understand all have their own administrations?

Dr. Schmidt: Through the years, as the state regulatory bodies operated and the Food and Drug Administration grew, particularly since 1955, we have simply fallen into a pattern of operation which I did not understand at all when I became Commissioner of Food and Drugs, and nobody was able to explain it to me. So what I did was to ask all of the state people, asked all of our people in the states and asked all of our central people to list for me the activities that the states did and that we did. I made a big list of those things down one side, then I put 'Central and FDA' here, and 'Peripheral and states' over here, and I had a little red ball, and on each line I put a little red ball where that was being done. So I got a pattern of some things being done always by the FDA, some things being done always by the states, and some we sort of shared in the middle. When people want to discuss something, I haul that thing out and discuss whether we are going to move that ball, and everybody now understands what is going on for the first time.

The states traditionally take care of all the milk and all of the shellfish, and some others where clearly the products are in inter-state commerce but we have formal agreements with the states to do our work for us. There is a big fight in our country now. The meetings that you go to where people get up and shout are meetings where we have the state people and the industrial people, and we get talking about what we call pre-emption. There is a federal regulation that defines how the states do their business, so that everything is consistent across the different states. Of course, this really tramples on what is left of states' rights, and that is a very emotional and important issue in our country right now. The US Supreme Court has defined inter-state commerce to include everything, so really wheat growing in the field could be declared inter-state commerce, because the courts have said that any raw materials that are grown that will end up in inter-state commerce are then inter-state commerce. Similarly, right down to when it is sold it is inter-state commerce.

Clearly the federal power to pre-empt is there, we think, but we are going to be extremely careful in exercising that power, if for no other reason than that I cannot afford to do the things the states do. I have 7000 people and $250 million; the states right now have about 30 000 people in the same areas and a considerable amount of money. Every time somebody thinks that we want to get into milk regulations they say 'All right, you can have the whole thing and we will do something else', and then of course we blush, and shuffle———.

Harmonization in the EEC of National Legislation of Foodstuffs

M Barthelemy
Director, Agricultural Legislation, Directorate General VI,
Commission of the European Communities

We are celebrating today the 100th anniversary of the Sale of Food and Drugs Act 1875. Although I have not researched into the origins of British food legislation, I do know that in the Middle Ages already the authorities were concerned at the sale of adulterated food. Nor have I tried to unravel the intricacies of the legislations of the Member States in order to find out which can claim to have been the first to take action. In any case, any such claim would be open to question.

What is quite clear, however, is the fundamental relationship between the basic legislation which exists in all the Member States and what the Community is doing in the approximation of legislation. As you may well know, I am involved in this work, which has an obvious impact on the legislation of all Member States, and I should like to say how grateful I am to you for asking me to address you on this subject.

Two major principles underlie the food legislation of all our Member States—health protection and the prevention of fraud. The latter principle, of course, aims to protect both the purchaser and the honest manufacturer or seller. I believe the term 'fair trader' is used in the United Kingdom. It is because all the Member States have this common basis and because the approaches they follow and techniques they apply are so similar that laws can be approximated.

But what is the point of this approximation of legislation? Why are we doing it? Let us go back and see what Article 2 of the Treaty of Rome says:

'The Community shall have as its task, by establishing a common market and progressively approximating the economic policies of Member States, to promote throughout the Community a harmonious development of economic activities, a continuous and balanced expansion, an increase in stability, an accelerated raising of the standard of living and closer relations between the States belonging to it.'

The achievement of the Common Market is one of the key functions of the Community—so much so, indeed, that the Community is often referred to

165

simply as the 'Common Market'. But if there is to be a common market, goods must be able to move freely as within a single national market, and the movement of goods manufactured or marketed in one Community country must not be hindered by what are known as 'technical' provisions governing the nature, composition, conditions of manufacture and handling, packing and labelling of products. As long as there are differences between national rules, trade will be hindered by the need to produce separately for each market; in many cases trade may simply be prevented from taking place.

Clearly there can be no question of simply abolishing these rules. As we have seen in relation to foodstuffs, all the Member States apply such rules and it is essential for them to do so. The Commission must respect this need and take it as a starting point for its own work. It must set up Community arrangements enabling trade to develop while ensuring that consumers do not lose the protection they have already acquired in the several Member States. This is ambitious, but it is essential if European integration is to be promoted; the means used to achieve this is the approximation of legislation, sometimes also known as harmonization of legislation.

It has been claimed that the Commission regards the approximation of legislation as an end in itself, that it is approximating for approximation's sake, that it is going all out for uniformity and standardization. But nothing is further from the truth. In a Community founded on an economic union, it must be possible to enlarge the consumer's scope for choice while manufacturers, importers and exporters rightly demand the benefits of a large scale market. Hence, approximation of legislation means improving the standard of living and not depressing it. Yet it is clear that while the optimist sees approximation as a source of enrichment, the pessimist may well regard it as a source of uniformity. Hitherto, if you wished to eat Italian, German or French food, you had to go to Italy, Germany or France. Now you can do so everywhere. Our holidays may have lost a little of their excitement but the consumer's range of choice has been enhanced.

This task is being done now—in 1975. So we have to keep up to date both with new techniques and with new attitudes. There has been an enormous development in methods of assessing food safety. Today's consumers are generally better informed and they are demanding more and more detailed knowledge of the food they eat. Member States have taken account of this in their legislation and are continuing to do so. The Community must obviously follow their example.

In more strictly legal terms the Treaty establishing the EEC, the Treaty of Rome, gives the Community institutions those powers and procedures which it must have if it is to do its job of harmonization.

First, let us consider the general rule in Article 100, which provides for the approximation of such provisions of national law as directly affect the establishment or functioning of the Common Market. National rules which hinder trade between Member States are such provisions, and Article 100 is applicable to them.

Another basic provision is Article 43 of the Treaty, for this is the Article which governs the establishment and implementation of the Common Agricultural Policy. As a large number of foodstuffs are of agricultural origin, it might at first seem logical to take Article 43 as a basis for defining conditions for the manufacture and marketing of foodstuffs. However, most of the national delegations have been against applying Article 43 in this field, or at least have been reluctant to do so. Their reaction has not been the same as regards setting quality standards for products in the context of the common organization of the market; here, Article 43 is used systematically.

The usual instrument for approximation of legislation is the directive. Directives are adopted by the Council on a proposal from the Commission, and the European Parliament and the Economic and Social Committee are generally consulted beforehand. The directive is a flexible legal instrument in that it simply states the ultimate objective while leaving the Member States free to decide how they will get there. This also means that a directive only takes effect after the Member States have incorporated it into their national law. They are generally given a year to do so.

Clearly, we cannot press on with achieving free movement of goods if to do so would simply create chaos. As we have seen, national laws on foodstuffs aim to protect consumers both against health risks and against adulteration and fraud. The Community has followed the same objectives.

Public health has always been a matter of prime importance to the Commission.

Basically, our Member States have reached a sufficiently comparable stage of development for public health standards to be regarded as identical throughout the Community. In the field of, for instance, additives in foodstuffs, health protection is the predominant consideration. This is why national authorities responsible for protecting the consumer's health have considered the possible effects of using this or that additive, and it has been found necessary to subject each substance to a very strict toxicological examination before authorizing its use. Thus very detailed legislation has been adopted in the Member States, generally specifying all the additives which may be used. But the degree of difference between the list of permitted additives in the various Member States is striking, especially when it is borne in mind that there is everywhere the same desire to protect the consumer and that the methods used by toxicological experts and their professional skills have incontestably reached the same level throughout the Community.

The explanation for this lies in the fact that additives are used in order to meet very precise technological needs which may vary from country to country depending on raw materials, manufacturing processes and, last but not least, consumer preferences. Be that as it may, the fact that lists of authorized additives vary from one country to another means that the free movement of foodstuffs in which additives may be used is hindered, and it is up to the Community therefore to take measures to remove the obstacles. Action on these lines is perfectly possible and indeed it has been with additives that the first tangible results have been obtained.

Last year the Commission set up a Scientific Committee for Food to provide a firm basis for the protection of public health in the Community. The Committee is composed of the most highly qualified scientific experts in the Community. Its members have world-wide reputations and the Commission is particularly grateful for their cooperation. Most of the members of the Committee are doing similar work in national organizations of the same kind. The Committee gives its opinion on specific subjects when requested to do so by the Commission. It may also draw the Commission's attention to a subject at its own initiative. I am glad to be able to say that the results of the Committee's first year's work are more than encouraging. Its opinions will normally be published, probably in the form of a periodic compilation.

Apart from the protection of public health, the law relating to foodstuffs also aims at improving the information available to consumers and protecting consumers against fraud. In our work on approximating legislation, these aims take on added importance in that the attainment of free movement of goods entails the appearance on the various national markets of new products about which the public is insufficiently informed, if at all. The only way of avoiding confusion is to provide clear and comprehensive labelling. Indeed it can be said that the free movement of goods must go hand in hand with the provision of greater information for consumers.

As for methods, what we must do above all is to remain pragmatic and resist dogmatism. As the main purpose of approximating legislation is to permit the freer movements of goods in areas where differences between national laws make this difficult, the general rule is to preserve the characteristics of the goods produced in our various countries.

Applying this principle strictly, Community directives should list all the products now manufactured or marketed in this or that Member State and allow all goods available on any given part of the Community market to move freely throughout the Community.

However logical this may appear in abstract terms, this is an idealist approach, divorced from reality. The need for free movement is not felt as regards a number of products, which claim only local importance and do not aspire to sales throughout the Community. Other products may be rejected in one or other of the Member States on grounds, for instance, of quality. What we therefore have to do in general terms, is to decide for which products within a given sector free movement is both desirable and possible and then to confine the field of application of the Community directive to these products. This is particularly applicable to products manufactured on an industrial scale to standards which, unlike those of certain unprocessed products, are not fixed in advance once and for all.

Naturally, the same considerations apply where it is not possible to produce a standard approach to some factor (such as authorized forms of processing) for a given product specified as that product in the directive. Hence a number of approaches to harmonization of laws on foodstuffs are possible, and we have to select the best approach in each case.

One flexible approach is the optional method, under which a product may move freely throughout the Community despite minor differences between the laws of the Member States. However, if this method is applied indiscriminately, the result will be that the only product which can be traded throughout the Community will be that complying with the strictest standard set and then no progress will have been made in achieving free movement. In any case, the need for protection of public health imposes limits on this method.

In other cases it is possible to go further so that the directive can cover virtually all forms of the same product in all Member States. Harmonization here has a much more complete effect. In yet other cases a partial method may be followed. This has been found successful in the case of sugar for incorporation in foodstuffs. The directive adopted here applies to 'certain types of sugar' and not to all sweeteners.

One method of harmonization which has sometimes been used in areas other than foodstuffs is to refer to standards which have emerged from the work of other international organizations. This method has not yet been used for foodstuffs, though I see no reason why the Community should not do so where an international standard is wholly acceptable to us.

When applying these principles to which I have referred in the field of foodstuffs, account naturally has to be taken of the particular features of this sector. One important point recognized and applied by the Member States, and by the Community in the rules which have been so far evolved, is the specific description. Where a legal provision relating to foodstuffs defines a particular food product by reference to its principal characteristics, it also gives a specific description which can be used only for that product, every other product having to bear a clearly different description. This has been found to work satisfactorily under the total and partial methods but requires modification when used with the optional method. There remains the possibility of applying yet more flexible procedures whereby standards would be laid down for products in free movement, although no specific description would be adopted by the Community. With this exception, a decision as to the products in respect of which free movement is to be obtained and a decision as to their specific description have to be taken at the same time. In any case, products not meeting the requirements of a Community directive can still be marketed under the relevant national rules as long as their labelling is not likely to confuse the consumer.

The procedure for preparing a Community directive runs through several stages. The procedure begins when Commission staff consult experts from the member governments, generally at joint meetings. There is then a stage of these consultations where the opinions of the various economic and social groups represented at Community level are needed, and it is up to the Commission staff to seek their views.

In the past, drafts were circulated to the relevant organizations, which were then asked to give their views within a given space of time. But this procedure was found unsatisfactory since it was not possible for the various groups to compare their often divergent approaches. The Commission has therefore set up a Consultative Committee for Food which represents farmers, manufacturers, workers, distributors and consumers. Each of these groups has two full members appointed by the Commission and four experts, varying according to the subject for discussion. The Committee's first two meetings seem to indicate that interested circles will be better able to take part in the work of harmonization. The work itself will also be better understood by the public and, I hope, better appreciated.

After these consultations, and after consultation of the Scientific Committee for Food, if questions of health protection are involved, the Commission adopts a proposal which it lays before the Council. The Council generally consults the European Parliament and the Economic and Social Committee. The opinions of these institutions may lead the Commission to amend its proposal, and the Treaty of Rome enables it to do so.

At the Council, the Commission's proposals are first considered by the Working Party on Foodstuffs, which takes in delegates from the Member States and representatives of the Commission. The Permanent Representatives Committee then meets, with or without the appropriate members of the Permanent Representatives' staff, to consider questions which the Working Party has not been able to solve and to prepare for the Council's meeting. The Council discusses the substance only where the national delegations have still failed to agree. Once the directive has been adopted by the Council, it is notified to the governments of the Member States, and this is when its existence as a source of law actually begins.

The Community's work on harmonization can be summed up as follows. Success was first achieved with additives in foodstuffs. The directive on the use of colouring matters was adopted in 1962. It was followed by three others governing preservatives, antioxidants, and emulsifiers, stabilizers, thickeners and gelling agents. All these directives follow the positive list principle, for this is the best method of ensuring health protection in that each substance must be tested for its harmlessness and technological usefulness before it can be authorized. The Community can boast that it has speeded up and even initiated the adoption of positive lists in a number of Member States. Some of the Member States have taken the opportunity, when incorporating Community directives into their national law, to extend the positive list system to cover types of additive not yet covered by Community rules.

The directives generally confine themselves to listing authorized additives. They very rarely lay down conditions for their use, for these are generally decided on later, either in directives relating to individual food products or through additions to the horizontal directives on additives.

Additives authorized in the Community have to meet certain general and specific purity requirements. Specific requirements remain to be fixed for antioxidants, emulsifiers, stabilizers, thickeners and gelling agents. What is known as the safeguard clause authorizes the Member States to take the necessary protective measures, which can go so far as a ban on use of a given product, where it is found that an additive authorized in the Community may be dangerous. There is a Community procedure by which a solution may be adopted for the whole Community thereafter. The directives also lay down rules on the labelling of additives sold as such before incorporation into a foodstuff.

As regards food products themselves, a directive was adopted on cocoa and chocolate in 1973. This was the first vertical directive adopted in the Community and, as you will readily understand, a number of general difficulties were met. The most difficult political question was whether all products coming from all the Member States should be recognized.

To illustrate the scale of the difficulty here, a single example will suffice: British chocolate did not qualify for description as chocolate in five of the six original Member States but had to be sold under names as barbaric as 'vegecao' or 'fantaisie au cacao'. In the sixth Member State, sales of British chocolate was totally prohibited. The directive removed this anomalous situation. It regards all types of chocolate as being equivalent in the sense

171

that they may all be sold throughout the Community, and distinctive labelling is provided to ensure that the consumer knows what he is buying.

The other Member States have had to give way on this point, changing their law and changing their own consumption habits. All those of you who have ever been involved in any type of discussion will know that if joint action is to be taken and extended, the same side cannot always be the one to make concessions and no approximation of legislation would be possible without a willingness to change what exists. This is why approximation takes such a long time and meets so many difficulties, given all the economic factors involved; nevertheless, much can be achieved—for I have no hesitation in saying that all the national delegations take a very constructive approach.

Another difficult question, though more legalistic in nature, was that of the correlation between a vertical directive and the horizontal rules of food law. It was eventually decided that unharmonized national rules on health protection, fraud prevention and industrial property rights should be preserved. The directive further contains rules which have to be complied with when the relevant products are being manufactured and marketed. These cover definitions of the various finished products, the quality of raw materials, authorized forms of processing and additives and labelling.

The Commission is also taking an active part in the work of other international bodies, and particularly in the FAO/WHO joint programme on food standards (Codex Alimentarius) and certain projects at the Council of Europe. The Community has produced directives on sucrose, dextrose, glucose, syrup and honey, and these were largely inspired by the Codex Alimentarius. Commission staff are now working on a proposal for Community control of flavourings, where it is finding the material published by the Council of Europe to be extremely helpful.

As regards current work, a distinction must be drawn between work of a vertical nature and work being done on more general lines. A number of vertical proposals are now being discussed in the Council, such as those on fruit juices, preserved milk and jams. I do not propose to list all these proposals here, for you can find a list in the Council programme for the abolition of technical barriers to trade in foodstuffs and industrial products[1]. The programme, incidentally, is well behind schedule.

However, as the programme requires, priority is to some extent being given to questions of a general nature so as to ensure that the directives which are adopted are reasonably consistent. A directive is currently being prepared on substances which come into contact with food, and this directive

---

[1] Council Resolution of 17th December 1973 on industrial policy: Official Journal of the European Communities No. C 117, p 1

is based on the positive list principle. A general directive on the labelling of foodstuffs is also being drafted. It will cover all foodstuffs and will aim to provide Community consumers with the greatest volume of information possible. Finally, the 10-year-old list of colouring matters is now being revised. A number of questions which were not settled at the time of enlargement of the Community will now be dealt with. At the Commission's request the Scientific Committee for Food has given its opinion on the health aspect of every colouring matter now being studied. Legal force is to be given to its recommendations after the relevant trade circles have been consulted.

Harmonization of legislation is a tricky area which has to be dealt with imaginatively and patiently. It affects a wide range of interests, for consumers, manufacturers, workers, distributors and producers are all concerned. As with any other form of joint action, concessions have to be made and changes have to be agreed to. But at the same time harmonization is vital if economic integration is to be beneficial to the consumer. What we have already achieved shows that progress is possible. This is why I believe that no stone should be left unturned in helping our citizens to share in the abundant variety to be found in all the countries of our Community and to reap the full benefit of this common market.

Discussion

Mr. J G Grinling (Consultant, Grand Metropolitan Hotels Ltd): May I first of all thank Mr. Barthelemy for his most lucid and illuminating address on the philosophy which now stands behind the harmonization of legislation in the food and drinks sector at the Community level. Such a re-statement of philosophy is, I think, very timely. There is a real need for an overall strategy to be more widely known and understood.

Certain fundamentals are, I believe, well understood—the essential difference between vertical legislation and horizontal. One might say along with the French 'Vive la différence'. The essential difference is also understood between optional and mandatory legislation, between what you may do and what you must do, but then we begin to move into areas of inter-relationship which are sometimes more difficult to correlate.

I think that we would welcome a further view from Mr. Barthelemy on where the legislative responsibility primarily lies within the Commission and its various departments. How will past vertical Directives, for example, align and interlock with future horizontal Directives? These are, perhaps, technical questions, but at the same time they lie at the heart of the legislative effort which Mr. Barthelemy in DG VI and other departments are making.

However, may I actually take Mr. Barthelemy's side and enter something in his defence? Having worked a little on his advisory committee, I do concede that the Commission have a formidably difficult task. The Commission are, after all, the guardians of the Treaty; they cannot ignore the provisions of Articles 2, 100 and 43. Therefore, it is their task to approximate the food and drink legislation across a very considerable Community with different laws and with different tastes and regional preferences.

So I do hope that the Food Advisory Committee to which he made reference is proving a helpful debating forum, because I think that for the first time the sometimes conflicting interests of industry, consumers, farmers, unions and retailers are being debated altogether.

May I just raise one further point of fundamental principle which I know very much concerns industry? In certain vertical Directives, such as the one that we discussed only a week or two ago—the Oils and Fats Directive—the Commission are seeking to legislate for factory processes. Certain processes are specified as those which are permitted. This, I know, is of concern to industry, because if you invent a new process you then have to inform the Commission, inform the Member States, as to whether this new process may be added to the list of permitted manufacturing methods. Of course, in a free enterprise society this really means releasing confidential information to a wide range of authorities instead of perhaps reaping the benefit of enterprise initiated by a company.

We are also worried how, if these controls take place within the Community, they can also be made to apply to goods which are coming from third countries where neither the manufacturers within the Community nor the Commission have the officials to supervise the processes abroad.

I should like to take up just one remark made by a British speaker yesterday, who said in his paper that food legislation should be sufficiently flexible to allow for future technological change. So this processing point, Mr. Barthelemy, is one which I know is worrying industry.

Thank you very much, and I am sure that there will be many questions after my own.

Mr. M Barthelemy: Thank you for your questions.

The first, as I understood it, concerns the relationship between the vertical and horizontal Directives. This field of harmonization of legislation is not like Minerva who came out of Jupiter; we have a lot of things which are not complete and we are working step by step. In this situation we do not have a complete sight of all the food legislation, but we move forward pragmatically. What is certain is that we cannot do everything at once.

We have begun on two lines of approach, the vertical, that is product by product, and the horizontal, additives for example. The work on additives is now advanced and we have a positive list for many classes of them. We are quite sure to go a little further with the 'horizontal' work and we now have two important horizontal texts which are materials in contact with food, and food labelling.

For labelling it is quite sure that if there is a national general rule we could not replace it in a vertical Directive. Therefore we have made exception in every vertical Directive, for the general rules which applied to all food. There are all the general matters of the food legislation which cannot be covered by the vertical Directive. A vertical Directive may give the rules which are to apply in a particular sector without prejudging the rules which have a general application. For these rules which have a general application we are making general rules.

On the other hand it may be that, in one product, you have to make an exception for some rule which is generally applicable to other products but cannot be applied to the specific product. That is, you have every time an interaction between the general rules and the individual rules, but I think that on that point we are not so different from the situation which exists in the legislation of our Member States.

In respect of the relationship between optional and total harmonization, I feel that we have to remain pragmatic. We have to see for every case how we can attain our objectives. It is certain that if you have the details for all the products which are produced in one sector you have what is called a total harmonization, but that is difficult to obtain because very often you find a problem which is not able to be settled on a Community level. You must in that case find a way to solve the problem. That is why I think that we have to work more in the way of partial harmonization. If we take the harmonization for jam, for example, we describe the product and give it a name, and this name is reserved to the product. For example, for marmalade we have proposed that the name 'marmalade' should be reserved within the Community for the British marmalade. We have been receiving letters from trade circles which are not content with this, as the name 'marmalade' refers to another product in some Member States. However consumers are accepting this change.

Fundamentally, the name is reserved in the Directive to the one product which we define. This may not always be possible and we have to make exceptions. For example, in the case of jam we have to make an exception for the products which have a high percentage of fruit and are very low in sugar. These products do not exist in all Member States and we have left them to national legislation and have therefore only partially solved the problem. It may be that in five years this product will be better known, and we can then introduce it in the whole of the Community. We have a system which is progressive, but having heard the interesting speech this morning from Dr. Schmidt it seems that there may always be some problems in relations between states and central administration, and I think that we in the Community may have this problem for some centuries.

Using the optional approach means that we say that foods of a particular defined standard can circulate freely through the Community, and we do not say anything else. For meat products it is possible that we could adopt this solution. For mayonnaise this is the way we mean to follow. But we must also be careful in using this system because it may be that no country will make concessions and we would have in that case only the purest product which can pass freely through the Community, and in that case I do not think we have obtained very much for free trade.

Taking another example, it is difficult to see how you can work with an optional solution for the Labelling Directive. You have to make a choice. For instance in the case of date marking there are various formulae which could be used. These have to be discussed. I cannot say, I do not think anyone can say, that there is one system which is absolutely the best. It is like every aspect of human work, you have to study the various possibilities to find what is the most appropriate solution; and then try to apply it. What I could not understand, however, would be that for the same product which would go freely throughout the Community we would choose, for example, one system, for instance, the date of minimum durability, and for the same product which is produced in a Member State that Member State would adopt the date of sale. You cannot have two systems operating at the same time for the same product. That is the relationship between optional and total. As you say, we must judge case for case and see what the problems are and how we can solve them.

Now on this difficult point—and I am glad of this question—of the rules that we would impose for processes. In this case it is quite clear that there are differences in approach by the Member States. In some Member States processes are frequently defined; in some other Member States it is true that the contrary is normal. In any case we have to be careful. I am absolutely in agreement with you that we should not go too quickly or too far. In the Fruit Juice Directive we have said that fruit juice is not obtained through a chemical process. Where I must say I am not quite happy about the solution is that we have been saying that the diffusion process is, if you wish, optional. That is, the possibility of including this process was left to each Member State, but it is possible for a Member State to forbid it. I would have been happier to include the process in the Directive, thus leaving freedom to manufacturers. However, it was necessary that we obtain a result. Now we have obtained free trade for the product which is pressed; we have not

176

obtained it for the product which is obtained through diffusion. However, I am sure that in a few years, if we revise this Directive, we can find a solution for this problem, but we must be ready to make concessions to the point of view of others, otherwise we cannot have any solution.

Professor J B M Coppock (Consultant, Spillers Ltd): My Lord Chairman, Mr. Barthelemy has indicated to us the way that harmonization takes place. I am glad that he is a chocolate expert, because the Chocolates Directive has harmonized legislation, but another barrier has been erected to free trade. On the Continent British milk chocolate will have to be described as 'household chocolate', and this must be death to any marketing man who is trying to sell his British milk chocolate on the Continent. Would Mr. Barthelemy care to comment on this particular aspect of international barriers?

Mr. M Barthelemy: I must say that, even after 10 years of discussion, I know only a little of this subject of chocolate. It may be that from time to time it is not always possible to obtain the best solution we would wish. We have to try to find a satisfactory solution. I cannot say—that is why it is so difficult—that it will always satisfy all the member countries and all the people who are working in it. For example, in this case it was very difficult to obtain the agreement of all delegations, and this denomination existed already in some Member States.

It is not possible to have perfection in every point that will take account of every point of view. It is only possible to get a solution if we accept some solutions that are the best for the moment, and think that in a few years we have to come back with the result and find some better solution. We cannot do it all at once.

Mr. A J H Skrimshire (General Dept Manager, H J Heinz Co Ltd): In his paper, Mr. Barthelemy indicated that the starting point for the harmonization process was the existing laws in the Member States. From this it could be argued that those Member States that had the most extensive food law might have the loudest voice in any discussions in the harmonization programme. We understood that, at the time of the enlargement of the Community, there was a tacit agreement by Governments of Member States that there would be no great proliferation of food legislation whilst the harmonization programme was under way. We are viewing with some concern the fact that there are a number of Member States who are passing extensive food legislation which is having an undue influence on the progress of harmonization.

Our United Kingdom Government appears to have adopted the proper point of view, which is to ask its committees to review and report on many items relating to the harmonization programme, but we appear to have stopped short of legislation.

I should like to ask Mr. Barthelemy if he could give his views on this.

Mr. M Barthelemy: On that point also I would say that I have been optimistic, after having heard the speech by Dr. Schmidt this morning. The Member States must communicate their intention of doing something if they wish to change their legislation, but I understand that in the United States if there is no federal legislation a State may legislate on its own initiative, and in the Community we have similar problems. It is difficult to have a total standstill of legislation, because knowledge is changing. Public health requirements may demand changes, and also the consumer influence is changing. These are all reasons why, if we could proceed more quickly, we could insist more on the principle of the standstill in legislation of the Member States. If we go slowly we cannot be too strong on this, principally because it is not possible to stop all change. The remedy is therefore to go more quickly with our Community legislation.

Food Laws, Standards and their Enforcement in Developing Countries

G O KERMODE

Chief, Joint FAO/WHO *Food Standards Programme*

Problems of the developing countries

The major problem facing many developing countries today is the need to ensure an adequate supply of safe and nutritious foods for the well-being and existence of their peoples. The rapidly growing problems of developing countries in many parts of the world are obliging the governments to recognize that food laws and food control services are urgently needed and that they are an essential part of national economic and social development. Countries without an effective food control system cannot ensure that their supplies of foods are safe and wholesome and they are especially vulnerable to the 'dumping' of inferior or unfit foods. The absence of an effective food control service, and all that stems from it, often results in the food exports of developing countries being rejected by importing countries with serious repercussions for infant food processing industries and the economy as a whole. The trend towards industrialization and urbanization, in the absence of adequate public health controls, is resulting in widespread problems concerning foods. Contamination of the environment is resulting all too often in outbreaks of food-borne disease affecting hundreds or even thousands of people over great areas. The need to grow more food has resulted in the extensive use of pesticides. The need to keep foods for longer periods has resulted in the widespread use of food additives. Proper controls on the use of pesticides and food additives are essential if the populations of developing countries are not to be put at serious risk as well as to ensure that their food exports comply with the requirements of importing countries. Because of the susceptibility of foods to contamination, strict hygiene precautions need to be observed. The lack of proper food hygiene is one of the major problems in developing countries and is one of the most frequent causes of the rejection of their food exports.

Most developing countries are concerned to increase their trade in foodstuffs. Such an increase in trade is dependent upon the confidence of the purchaser which is best maintained by a strong food inspection service, ensuring compliance with standards. Without standards, purchasers have no assurance that foods will be of the expected nature, substance or quality. Purchasers must also be able to rely upon the genuineness of labelling. Without a food law, standards cannot be established. Without an effective food control service, there is no assurance that foods will comply with either standards or label declarations.

Food losses through wastage and spoilage are massive in some developing countries. Improved handling and storage are urgent needs. Combined with good hygiene practices, they could protect the national food supply by improving both the keeping qualities and safety of certain foods. Effective food control services, with improved food handling, could save large quantities of foods which are now being lost. A well-trained inspectorate as part of the food control service can provide guidance and incentive to make the use of pesticides, food additives, and improved hygiene practices more effective with less risk.

Gross adulteration of food is another major problem facing the authorities in many developing countries. Some of the earliest forms of food adulteration are still practised. This results in serious economic damage to individuals and countries, and those who are cheated are often those most in need of good quality foods. Developing countries need laboratories and trained analysts to detect food adulteration. Many foods which are imported are often misrepresented as to their nature, substance or quality. Making foods appear better than they actually are is an ancient art which is still widely practised in the developing parts of the world. Serious risks to the health of the consumer are often inherent in these practices. Harmful dyes or other chemicals are often employed to make stale or decayed meats and other foods appear to be fresh or of good quality. Proper inspection services are needed to check these abuses. Cases of serious illness or even deaths due to intentional food adulteration or accidental contamination occur all too often in developing countries. An effective food control service is therefore essential, not only to try to prevent such incidents, but also quickly to remove dangerous foods from channels of commerce.

Fraud, in the form of short weight, remains a widespread and persistent problem in many developing countries. The lack of uniformity or standardization of weights and measures gives rise to many abuses, and where there is no effective enforcement of weights and measures, widespread cheating can be expected. Problems of fraud and adulteration appear to be most acute in areas of the world where food is scarce and the demand for it great. Examples of practices to extend foods with cheaper or less nutritive substances are common.

Food laws in developing countries

At present, the food laws in a large number of developing countries are far from being comprehensive. In many cases various legal provisions governing production and sale of foods are to be found in a number of widely different laws, causing confusion among the food control service, the regulated industry and consumers. As many of the developing countries of Africa and Asia were previously under the control of one of the developed countries of Europe, their food laws have a tendency to resemble those of the developed country concerned. Such food laws were, however, usually introduced to deal on an *ad hoc* basis with specific problems as they arose. A comprehensive approach was hardly ever made. In some instances, the laws are extremely detailed, containing provisions that would better serve as regulations. Most of the food laws which were introduced have rarely been updated. This has led to the anomalous situation where the developed countries have since, in many instances, updated and revised their laws, whilst many developing countries, which were formerly their responsibility, have remained with an outdated or inadequate set of laws. The food laws of these countries need to be re-examined, updated, and if possible, brought together into a single code.

Concerning food legislation, developing countries can be divided, in very general terms, into three groups. First, there are the comparatively few developing countries which have a modern basic law with the appropriate general provisions. In nearly all such cases, however, the country still needs to develop detailed regulations for the composition and labelling of foods.

Secondly, there are those developing countries which have no food legislation or food control system or have ones which are insufficient for the purpose. These countries could have the advantage of a fresh start based upon the experience of other countries and the stimulus and support of expert recommendations at an international level. Their first priority will be to introduce and enforce a basic food law and then to make the detailed regulations, whilst simultaneously establishing arrangements for their administration and enforcement.

Thirdly, there are those countries which fall somewhere in between and need either to make major amendments to or to repeal their basic food law to provide adequate general provisions. The amendment or replacement of the basic law and such detailed rules as they have could profitably be done after making new regulations in line with the priorities of their own circumstances and international recommendations.

AFRICA

In the main, two basic types of national food legislation exist in Africa which often, though not always, are a legacy of pre-independence times. There are a number of countries which have food legislation similar to that of France, with emphasis being laid on the repression of fraud. Other countries have legislation similar to the Food and Drug Legislation of the United Kingdom. Much of this legislation was introduced prior to independence and is now being reviewed by a number of countries, with a view to the preparation of new national basic food laws to meet situations quite different from those for which the earlier enactments had been designed. Such legislation as exists tends to deal with basic provisions such as weights and measures, the protection of the health of the consumer in respect of toxic substances, and the prevention of fraud and adulteration of foods. National efforts to update and adjust the many variations and discrepancies in their food laws led some countries to decide that a completely new food law was the only way in which the local situation could be adequately dealt with. New basic food laws have been introduced in Kenya, Zambia and Nigeria and a proposed new food law is currently under consideration in Ghana. A number of the francophone countries of West Africa are, under their basic food laws, introducing detailed regulations relating to composition and labelling. The developing countries of Africa have many pressing problems, not the least of which is the great lack of skilled or trained personnel. There is not the local staff available in many cases to prepare food laws suited to the particular circumstances nor the scientific and technical staff necessary for their enforcement by means of food analysis, sampling and efficient inspection. There is also a shortage of materials and equipment, and many other problems exist in connection with the introduction and operation of an effective food control system. Much work still remains to be done in these fields, as well as the need to ensure minimum compositional requirements for traditional foods.

NEAR EAST, ASIA AND FAR EAST

Until very recently, many of the countries of the Near East have tended to rely upon assurances given voluntarily by exporters that food products imported into the region complied with the food laws and standards of the exporting country. In some instances, this arrangement has worked quite well. Many food products, however, go through the hands of intermediaries, and where the importing country has no food control service, this has resulted in the 'dumping' of inferior quality or substandard foods. As an interim measure, a number of countries have made it a requirement that imported food be accompanied by a certificate to the effect that the food complies with the laws of the exporting country and enjoys 'free sale' within that country.

Although such requirements may temporarily restrict 'dumping', a number of the countries of the region have decided that it is necessary to establish a national food control service to ensure adequate protection from malpractices. Saudi Arabia, Kuwait and Qatar are currently establishing modern food control services equipped with up-to-date laws, regulations, laboratories and personnel for analysis and inspection. One country of the region which has embarked upon the establishment of a food control service found that the mere knowledge of this development in international food trade circles led to a significant improvement in quality and a dramatic fall in the need to reject imports.

Countries such as the Lebanon, Iraq and Iran have basic food laws and are supplementing these with detailed regulations, including standards of composition, minimum quality and labelling. The current law of Iran was enacted in 1965 and is now supported by analytical control and numerous standards.

In parts of Asia, local or provincial control measures were developed in the second half of the last century. In most cases, the laws have been updated and are applied on a national basis. Two good examples of modern food laws in Asia are the 1949 Food and Drugs Act of Sri Lanka and subsequent amendments and the 1954 Prevention of Food Adulteration Act of India and subsequent amendments.

In the Far East, food control measures were slow to appear. Japan was perhaps a notable exception, due to its rapid industrial development. Malaysia's first food laws were introduced in 1952. Thailand has a modern Food Industry Control Act of 1964, which replaced earlier measures introduced in 1941 and 1959. Both the Philippines and Indonesia introduced food laws for the first time in the 1960s.

In the case of Asia and the Far East, from information supplied by governments and from other sources, the picture of food legislation that emerges is of some good basic laws of which a number have been made in the last 20 years. On the other hand, some countries have yet to introduce a basic food law. The provisions of the basic laws differ to some extent and the emphasis is not always the same. In this, they reflect the differences in approach and in drafting that can be found in food laws generally through the developed areas of the world. Some countries have special export laws and inspection systems, while others are establishing food standards through means of National Standards Institutions. There are some detailed food regulations and a start has been made in some countries with rules for additives, pesticides and contaminants. Information supplied by governments reflects continuing work in these fields and indicates that there would be advantage in it being done in concert throughout the region.

Many countries of Latin America enacted food laws during the 1920s and 1930s. Mexico was an early starter with some food control measures being introduced in 1891. In Argentina, Brazil, Mexico and Venezuela, owing to their federal structures, state or provincial food laws were introduced. Often these constituted an impediment to national trade, owing to differences in the legislation. Argentina and Brazil found it necessary to enact national food laws to overcome these difficulties. The basic legal systems of Latin America are fundamentally different to those of Asia and Africa, with the result that the food laws and food control systems of Latin America present notable differences to those of the rest of the world. In spite of having basically a common Spanish or Portuguese legal system, significant differences exist among the various food laws of Latin America and their enforcement. Most countries of the region have fairly comprehensive basic food laws and in a number of cases detailed regulations and standards have been adopted for foods, whether imported, exported or domestically produced and consumed. In some countries, use is made of national 'Codigos Alimentarios' as reference texts to establish whether food products comply with what would normally and reasonably be expected by the consumer as to proper designation, composition and minimum quality of the food concerned. Legal provisions concerning food hygiene are generally contained in Sanitary Codes which deal with most aspects of human and animal health and are often administered by the Ministry of Health. The authority to elaborate food standards is often delegated to specialized agencies, which may also be responsible for developing standards for many non-food items. Some attempts at the harmonization of national food laws and regulations have been made in the various economic groupings of countries of the region. It is widely recognized that, if intra-Latin American trade in food products is to expand more rapidly than at present, some of the differences in national legislations will have to be removed.

Codex Alimentarius Commission and related food control activities of FAO and WHO

It was against a background of rapidly increasing interest in finding solutions to trade problems that the Member Governments of FAO and WHO decided at the beginning of the 1960s that the time was opportune to create arrangements for international action to try to remove those non-tariff obstacles to trade in foods caused by differing national food legislations. At the same time, the Member Governments of FAO and WHO emphasized the need to ensure that proper safeguards be maintained or established for the protection of the health of the consumer. Thus the main considerations which gave birth to the Joint FAO/WHO Codex Alimentarius Commission were the need to facilitate international trade in foods and to protect the consumer against health risks and fraud. The world-wide interest in the work of the Codex Alimentarius Commission is evidenced by the continually growing membership of the Commission. When the Commission held its First Session in 1963 some 30 countries, most of which were developed countries, were members. The total membership today is 114 countries. Almost all the developed countries of the world have been members of the Commission for many years, but in recent years there has been a striking increase in the number of developing countries which have become members. Today more than two-thirds of the members of the Commission are developing countries and this may be taken as reflecting the importance which the developing countries have come to attach to the work of the Commission and of the benefits they expect to derive from it. The objectives of the Codex Alimentarius Commission are to protect the health of consumers and to ensure fair practices in the food trade; to promote co-ordination of all food standards work undertaken by international govern-mental and non-governmental organizations; to determine priorities and initiate and guide the preparation of draft standards through and with the aid of appropriate organizations; to finalize standards and, after acceptance by governments, publish them in a Codex Alimentarius either as regional or world-wide standards. The Commission has embarked on an extensive programme of work covering the compositional, labelling, additive, contamin-ant, pesticide residue, hygiene, sampling and analytical aspects of foods. It has set out to secure international agreement on the substance of food standards and then to invite governments to accept them in various specified ways. A complex working procedure has been built up designed to ensure, inter alia, that governments have the fullest opportunity to comment on standards while they are still in draft and to enable the Commission to satisfy itself that the standards are being prepared along the right lines. The im-plementation of the programme of work of the Commission is achieved largely, but by no means exclusively, through the expertise contained in its subsidiary bodies which, like the Commission, are inter-governmental in character. To the expertise provided by governments through the participa-tion of their representatives in the work of the Commission and its subsidiary bodies must be added a number of other indispensable inputs. A few examples will illustrate this. Much essential technical information on many aspects of the Commission's work is provided by non-governmental organizations specialized in various fields. The toxicological evaluation of food additives and contaminants is a very specialized field and here the subsidiary bodies concerned rely, in making proposals to the Commission, on the recommendations of Joint FAO/WHO Expert Committees. Expert consultations are also necessary for certain aspects of the work on food hygiene, for example, the establishment of micro-biological requirements and the establishment of suitable methods of analysis and sampling for determining compliance.

Health protection aspects of the work of the Codex Alimentarius Commission

The provisions in the international standards which are mainly concerned with the protection of the health of consumers are those on food additives, contaminants, pesticide residues and other contaminants, and food hygiene.

FOOD ADDITIVES

Before any additive is permitted to be used in a product, the technological need for its use has to be justified, by reference to strict criteria concerning the use of additives laid down by the Commission. If the technological need has been established, the next step is to ensure that there are no known health risks involved in its use. The Codex Committee on Food Additives, in deciding whether or not to endorse the use of a given additive at the level proposed by the Codex Commodity Committee concerned, relies on the toxicological evaluation of food additives provided by the Joint FAO/WHO Expert Committee on Food Additives and on the potential daily intakes of food additives calculated by WHO. Thus only approved additives at approved levels are included in the international standards. If one takes the number of Codex Standards adopted by the Commission and sent to governments for acceptance and the number of Codex Standards in the course of development one finds that they contain some 2000 food additive provisions which have gone or are going through the process described above. A fully referenced list of food additives evaluated for their safety-in-use in food has been published and will be followed shortly by a second list. A large number of specifications of identity and purity of food additives have been developed by the Joint FAO/WHO Expert Committee on Food Additives, and have been published from time to time. These specifications are currently being reviewed to bring them up to date, and the revised specifications will be put before the Codex Alimentarius Commission for adoption.

CONTAMINANTS

In deciding whether or not to endorse proposed maximum levels for contaminants in the international standards, the Codex Committee on Food Additives likewise relies on the toxicological evaluation provided by the Joint FAO/WHO

186

Expert Committee on Food Additives and on the potential daily intakes of contaminants calculated by WHO. Thus levels for contaminants in the international standards represent the consensus in the Codex Committee on Food Additives as to amounts which are unavoidably present in the food, but which on the basis of the toxicological evaluations and potential daily intakes are not known to represent a toxic hazard. As in the case of food additives, a fully referenced list of contaminants toxicologically evaluated, together with maximum limits in food recommended by the Codex Alimentarius Commission, has also been published and will be followed by a second list.

PESTICIDE RESIDUES

In fixing maximum limits for pesticide residues, the Codex Committee on Pesticide Residues proceeds on the principle that maximum limits proposed must be the lowest possible, consistent with good agricultural practice in the use of pesticides and with the need to protect consumers against health hazards. Proposed maximum limits are recommended by the Codex Committee on Pesticide Residues on the basis of recommendations of the Joint FAO/WHO Meeting on Pesticide Residues as to lowest possible levels arising from use to achieve the desired effect under conditions of good agricultural practice, taking into account the toxicological evaluations of the compounds by the Joint Meeting as well as the potential daily intake calculated by WHO.

FOOD HYGIENE

In the field of hygiene, protection is afforded through the inclusion in the international standards of provisions designed to guard against microbiological risks. These provisions are supplemented by a Code of General Principles on Food Hygiene and other codes of hygienic practice for specific commodity groups which have been elaborated and adopted by the Commission. Several other codes of hygienic practice are in the course of elaboration and codes on meat hygiene and ante-mortem and post-mortem inspection will be submitted for adoption in 1976 to the Commission. Increased attention is being given to the development of microbiological criteria for selected commodities.

Work of the Codex Alimentarius Commission in protection against fraud

There are many kinds of fraud, ranging from short weight to direct adulteration. The need for protection against adulteration and deception is recognized in the General Principles of the Codex Alimentarius Commission where it is stated that 'Codex standards contain requirements for food aimed at ensuring for the consumer a sound, wholesome food product free from adulteration, correctly labelled and presented'. All of the Codex Standards contain provisions designed to guard against fraud and particular mention should be made of the General Standard for the Labelling of Prepackaged Foods. As with other aspects of consumer protection, the standards need to be backed up with good food control services.

The need for protection against fraud was stressed by the recent World Food Conference in its Resolution V, which reads as follows: 'That governments take action to strengthen and modernize consumer education services, food legislation and food control programmes aiming at the protection of the consumer (avoiding false information from mass media and commercial fraud), and that they increase their support of the Codex Alimentarius Commission.'

Countries which do not have modern food laws, standards and regulations and a food control service to implement them are particularly open to the possibility of commercial fraud and health hazards. Food products which would not be permitted to be imported into countries which have modern food standards and regulations and the means of enforcing might well gain entry into countries which are not equipped to protect themselves in this field. Protection against the dumping of sub-standard products is, therefore, an important element of the work of extending Codex activities to the regional level in the developing world.

Whilst it is true that acceptance of international Codex standards, in the absence of adequate food control facilities, is of limited value, nevertheless a certain measure of protection would be afforded if all the countries of a developing region were to accept the standards. Such action would result in common requirements having to be observed by exporters of food products to a region, which, taken as a whole, would constitute a substantial market. The knowledge that exporters to a developing region would have to ensure that the products they were exporting would have to be in conformity with Codex Standards, would be a significant measure of protection against the unscrupulous exporter and would, at the same time, be in the interest of reputable exporters who maintain proper food standards for their products.

Economic aspects of the work of the Codex Alimentarius Commission

FACILITATION OF INTERNATIONAL TRADE

It is a fact that the provisions of national food standards and regulations differ from one another in a wide variety of ways, from composition to labelling. These differences often constitute an obstacle to the flow of international trade and this is particularly important for food exporting countries.

Clearly, if these national differences in import requirements could be harmonized to the point where an exporter had to comply with only one set of common requirements, it would be very much to his advantage. If market conditions in one country were more favourable than in another, he could transfer his exports quickly to that country without first having to be concerned with whether his product meets the import requirements. Also reformulation of products, different labels and other matters, involve extra costs which could be avoided.

The Commission goes about its task of facilitating international trade in foods by providing a truly international forum—the only world-wide one of its kind in the field—whereby government representatives have an opportunity on a continuing basis of explaining the reasons for their different national requirements, of noting difficulties which their national requirements may present for other countries, of considering the important technical data and assessments provided by panels of independent experts within the Codex system. The very fact that governments participate actively in the work of elaborating international food standards implies a willingness on their part to adapt their national standards, as far as possible, to what finally emerges, after detailed technical discussions, as the international consensus on the content of the standards. Thus at the stage when the international standards are adopted by the Codex Alimentarius Commission for issue to governments for acceptance they have already a wide measure of general acceptability and the different national legislative positions on the contents of the standards have been discussed fully and in most cases acceptable compromises have been agreed upon. The acceptance by governments of international Codex Standards is therefore part of the business of removing technical or non-tariff barriers to international trade.

IMPROVEMENT OF THE ECONOMIC POSITION OF THE DEVELOPING COUNTRIES

Whilst both the developed and the developing countries are very interested in improving their food export possibilities through the adoption of common international food standards in export markets, the developing countries have an additional problem—a general problem of inadequate development of their food industries and food control infrastructure. Easier access to foreign markets, achieved through internationally negotiated and accepted food standards, is necessary to enable the developing countries to earn the foreign exchange required for their general economic development and, more specifically, for the development of their food industries and food control infrastructure. The general acceptance of internationally agreed food standards would, in itself, be a significant achievement in terms of facilitating international trade, but many developing countries are not in a position to take full advantage of this because they lack the necessary infrastructure of sound food legislation and the means of enforcing it.

The Codex Alimentarius Commission is fully conscious of this problem and so also are FAO and WHO. The Commission is tackling the problem by establishing, at the request of Members of the Commission from the developing countries, regional Codex Co-ordinating Committees for their regions. These regional inter-governmental committees will concern themselves, in the first instance, with the establishment of a modern harmonized basic food law, but also with the question of standards for food commodities of particular importance in intra-regional trade. The regional committees will also have an important role to play in formulating proposals aimed at remedying deficiencies in food control infrastructure.

The work of the Codex Alimentarius Commission at a regional level is backed up by related activities of FAO and WHO in the formulation and execution of national food control projects for the developing countries. The aims of these projects are, first, to help the developing countries gain access to markets in countries which have modern and sophisticated food standards and regulations and the means of enforcing them. Without this assistance and effort on their own part developing countries may find themselves denied access to potentially good markets on purely food standards grounds, with consequent loss of foreign exchange earnings. Secondly, properly organized food control services in developing countries should reduce the risk of consumers in those countries being recipients of sub-standard products, imported or home-produced. The expenditure of hard currency on sub-standard imported foods represents a serious loss to many developing countries. This has been repeatedly confirmed by visits of FAO consultants. Exporters of reputable products are likewise concerned at the unfair trade aspects of competition from sub-standard products.

Progress in the elaboration of international food standards

To date, 70 international standards have been finalized and adopted by the Commission. These have been sent to governments for acceptance. In addition to the standards there is a large number of Codex maximum limits for the residues of a wide variety of pesticides on a very substantial number of commodities. Six codes of hygienic practice for various commodities have been adopted by the Commission and made available to governments, as have also sampling plans for prepackaged foods. Besides the 70 international standards which have been adopted by the Commission, there are the international standards for milk and milk products which have been elaborated

190

and adopted by the Joint FAO/WHO Committee of Government Experts on the Code of Principles concerning Milk and Milk Products, which is a subsidiary body of the Commission. In addition to the Code of Principles on Milk and Milk Products, some 40 international standards for milk and milk products have also been issued to governments for acceptance, together with a large number of standard methods of sampling and analysis for these products. All in all, therefore, some 110 international standards covering a wide range of food commodities and some 700 pesticide residue tolerances taken on an individual food product basis as well as a general standard for the labelling of prepackaged foods have been sent to governments for acceptance —most of them in the past four years.

Acceptances by Governments of Codex Standards

Considerable progress has been made by Members of the Commission in either accepting Recommended Codex Standards or initiating action on them with a view to giving acceptance. To date, some 40 countries have indicated, in accordance with the acceptance provisions laid down in the General Principles of the Codex Alimentarius, their acceptance of several of the Recommended Codex Standards. A number of countries have given Full Acceptance to almost all of the Recommended Standards issued to governments for acceptance so far. Whilst most of the acceptances have come from developing countries, acceptances have also been received from a number of developed countries, and many other developed countries have indicated that they are engaged in a thorough study of the standards with a view to incorporating them, as far as feasible, in their national legislations. Particular mention should, perhaps, be made of the detailed and voluminous information made available to the Commission by the Food and Drug Administrations in Canada and the United States of America on the extent of the action taken and being taken in these countries to give effect, as far as possible, to the Recommended Codex Standards. The Commission was informed that the European Economic Community (EEC) had adopted a Directive on Sugars which regulates several sugars covered by the Recommended Codex Standards, as well as a Directive on Honey based upon the Codex European Regional Standard for Honey. These Directives have been based on the Recommended Codex Standards concerned and the EEC has declared its wish to achieve the greatest possible measure of harmonization between Community Standards and Recommended Codex Standards. The Council for Mutual Economic Assistance (CMEA) is also following very closely the work of the Commission, and has indicated that it is making use of the results of the Commission's work. Several other international organizations have expressed themselves in similar terms. It should also be mentioned that the Arab Organization for Standardization and Metrology (ASMO) has seen fit to have many of the Recommended Codex Standards translated into Arabic to facilitate acceptance by Arabic-speaking members of the Commission.

As regards progress on the acceptance of both the Code of Principles concerning Milk and Milk Products and the some 40 international standards adopted thereunder, the position is as follows. The Code of Principles has been accepted by 71 countries. By and large, the compositional milk products standards have been accepted by 45 to 64 countries, the number varying with the particular standard concerned. Most of these standards have recently undergone some revision and acceptances of the revised versions are being received. As regards the 30 individual cheese standards, acceptances vary in number from four to 16 countries with the cheese concerned.

Long-term outlook

It is clear that interest in the value of the work of the Commission continues to grow. The increasing membership of the Commission, the insistence on the establishment of Co-ordinating Committees for Africa, Latin America and Asia to make the work of the Commission more meaningful for the developing countries, the recognition by governments generally of the expertise available to the Commission and the facilities afforded by the Codex machinery in reaching international agreement, all point to this.

The interest in facilitating international trade in food products and of protecting the consumer against fraud, as stressed by the World Food Conference, is stronger today than ever. So also is the interest in protecting the health of the consumer. In this respect, the World Health Assembly of WHO expressed the hope that the Commission would give high priority to the health aspects of its work.

More and more governments are recognizing the need to participate in the work of the Codex Alimentarius Commission and are doing so in a spirit of compromise, with a willingness to make concessions in order to secure international agreement. Recent acceptances of the Codex standards demonstrate the wish of many governments to give effect to the international food standards.

In the long run, the work of the Codex Alimentarius Commission will probably be judged by the degree of success in fulfilling its primary task, namely inducing governments to accept and implement the internationally agreed Codex Standards, although, aside from this, it is perhaps worth mentioning that many countries attach importance to the very fact of having a world-wide forum in which to discuss their problems and exchange views and ideas in the field of work covered by the Commission. A substantial amount of progress has already been achieved, but the business of adapting national standards throughout the world to international standards is necessarily a slow process in many countries, involving consultation with all the interests involved and compliance with sometimes lengthy administrative and constitutional procedures. It can, however, now be stated with confidence that the work of the Codex Alimentarius Commission will be of lasting value for all concerned with the international trade in food, whether they be producers, exporters, importers or consumers.

The Sale of Food and Drugs Act 1875

The Sale of Food and Drugs Act 1875 constituted a landmark in the development of food and drug legislation, not only in Britain but also for a number of other countries. The basic provisions and definitions of the Act are reflected in a number of Food Acts of developed and developing countries of the Commonwealth. Moreover, the pattern of administration and procedures for enforcement which developed as a result of the 1875 Act in Britain have been adopted by a number of developing countries of Africa, Asia and the Caribbean as being suited to the food situation and their legal and constitutional frameworks. The recent Food and Drugs Acts of Kenya, Zambia and Nigeria contain definitions and provisions closely akin to those of the 1875 Act. Similarly, the legislation of some of the English-speaking countries of the Caribbean contains a number of the provisions of the Act. The Food and Drugs Acts of India and Sri Lanka in some respects follow more closely the definitions and provisions of the 1875 Act than does the British Food and Drugs Act of 1955. The features of the 1875 Act which are perhaps most widely reflected in the Regulations of the aforementioned countries are the definition of food and the requirements of Sections 3 and 6. The effectiveness of much of the food legislation based on the 1875 Act stems from the foresightedness of the drafters of Section 6 which required that 'No person shall sell to the purchaser any article which is not of the nature, substance and quality of the article demanded by such purchaser . . .'.

Discussion

Mr. R B Beedham (Smedley-HP Foods Ltd): I believe that Mr. Kermode has been employed on this programme from its inception and, therefore, he has been able to give us a grasp and a picture of what has been carried out both in his paper and in his talk this morning which has set the whole matter in perspective.

I am also sure that we have been deeply impressed by his own personal commitment to a programme in which he believes and which will have a significant contribution to make to the problems of food quality throughout the world.

I should like if I may to put to him three points. As he said, the standards which have so far been developed, both the horizontal standards and the vertical directives, are highly sophisticated documents. In fact, in many areas they take quality control and quality factors beyond that which exists in the United Kingdom at the moment. I wonder to what extent the sophistication of the standards which already exist will, in fact, detract from a rapid progress in the developing countries by channelling time, effort and work into areas that are, perhaps, of less consequence. I would not for one moment suggest that there should be any compromise on any of the horizontal legislation which relates to public health and safety, but in many of the vertical standards a lot of the data which is contained is, in fact, data of a quality control nature, very important to a manufacturer in the quality control field in a highly developed industry, but I would suggest that the inclusion of this in a programme in the developing countries will, in fact, take technical time which would be better used elsewhere.

The second point I should like to ask is whether Mr. Kermode sees in the longer term a more direct communication between the major conglomerates of local government, by that I mean Codex Alimentarius negotiating directly with a Common Market Commission and possibly Comicon, and possibly any other internationally grouped organizations that may arise, so limiting discussion to some extent and achieving a greater rate of progress.

The third point I should like to make is one largely of detail within the standard itself. Within the vertical directives we have seen a growth of specific quality criteria which are subjective in nature. This is a significant departure from what has been, certainly in the United Kingdom, where the practice has been by and large to attempt to specify quality criteria which are analytically determinable and, therefore, enforceable. We see the same trend within the European directives which are being developed at the moment. I do question to what extent the inclusion of such subjective criteria in standards is really going to contribute toward food inspection and control in the future.

Mr. Kermode: I think, Ladies and Gentlemen, I have to be very brief, otherwise you may be facing some food and nutrition problems yourselves!

On the first point, I would say that the quality level in Codex standards is definitely a minimum level. That does not mean it is at the absolute lowest level, but it is a level which finds general acceptability among member governments, consumers and the food industry. I would emphasize that we do not go

194

into details of processing in Codex standards. We define a product, lay down the compositional criteria, and link those criteria as far as possible to well established methods of determination. We do experience difficulty regarding quality criteria, especially with the organoleptic aspects of standardization. It is inescapable with some products that you must have some means of judgment, and ensure adequate safeguards as to quality. I think you are all aware that we have spent a great deal of time on developing sampling techniques for quality criteria, mainly statistical sampling with acceptance quality levels. We believe that by these arrangements and by the averaging of results, manufacturers and consumers should not be placed at a disadvantage.

Touching upon the question of Codex relations with the European Economic Community, Comicon, LAFTA, and other economic groupings in the world, I am pleased to say that we have what I would describe as good close working relations. Naturally, each of these organizations has its own programme of work, but we do, on an informal or gentleman's agreement basis, discuss our programmes of work and try to avoid overlap or duplication. I think this is evident in the attitude of the European Economic Community's Commission in that, in certain fields, it is taking Codex work as a basis for its directives. I can say that, when we are embarking on new subject matter, we look very closely indeed at the work of any other international organization, and certainly endeavour to minimize overlap or duplication. I look forward to the day when the Community, Comicon and other bodies can speak with one voice and can give acceptance to Codex Standards, either through the means of individual membership of these groupings or on a community basis. This is a matter on which we have held discussions. It involves some constitutional and legal problems, but I believe that, once the member governments of these various bodies reach agreement on their approach, the United Nations system is sufficiently adaptable to accommodate various arrangements regarding acceptance.

Mr. W H High (Chisholm Associates): As another exile from this country who, in this case, chose to work in developing countries, I should like to thank the speaker for his paper and to echo his statement that the tasks are great. Although I would not in any way like to deride the work done by United Nations, WHO and all the other various able bodies that we meet in the developing countries, as one small piece of constructive criticism perhaps I might refer to Mr. Kermode's opening remark about all roads leading to Rome. I have always thought that perhaps if the headquarters of these worthy organizations were placed in developing countries, (a) they would not waste as much time as they do commuting round the world, and (b) they would get a great deal more feeling for the actual work which is going on in developing countries.

Although we find in the halls of power of developing countries the type of regulations being drafted which we have heard about and read about this morning, we find very little actual work going on in the field. We are safe in the bosom of technology this morning, but I am thinking one week ahead when I shall be back in the field. It is a far cry from talking about advanced technology here in London and wondering next week how we are going to get the basics of meat inspection operated in a reasonable fashion.

I should like to ask whether, while celebrating 100 years of food legislation, we are not being a little complacent, because we as Europeans, not only English people, have been responsible for a great deal of colonial development over this 100 years and we have left a very thin veneer of food technology behind us. I would ask Mr. Kermode what, as the professionals of today, are we going to do to ensure that we leave the coming generation a far better heritage than the one we have taken over in the developing countries.

Mr. Kermode: First of all, I would not agree that there are too many people in Geneva and Rome. Out of a staff of some 3000 professional officers of FAO only some 800 are based in Rome. FAO is considering decentralization to regional and country level. The World Health Organization is already organized in this way and all the field project work of the WHO is run through regional offices.

You have touched on a very sensitive subject, what is the colonial heritage? It is not as bad as you think. Many of the countries in which we are working on food control have a judicial system which lends itself to the very approach which is followed in Britain under the 1955 Act. There are basic concepts that must protect the honest trader, the right of appeal, especially when dealing with a criminal offence and justice must be seen to be done. These are valuable traditions.

On technical grounds, however, I would entirely agree with the last speaker that often I feel somewhat embarrassed when I look at what has been left in the technical sense. A great deal was done in public health. Most of the food control structure has not been updated. Public health inspectors still do quite a remarkable job, but the time has come when these legacies of France, Spain, Italy and the United Kingdom have to be looked at in a modern sense. We have to inculcate the ideas of modern food and drug administration in these countries.

100 Years of Progress in the Food Processing Industry

G K Lawrence
Chairman, Food and Drink Industries Council

It is impossible to survey in depth the whole field indicated by the title of this paper. I propose therefore to discuss briefly the most important factors of a social, economic and technical nature that have affected progress and then to illustrate them by reference to four specific food products.

Introduction

The last 100 years have seen the development of food manufacture from the scale of a craftsman/cottage industry to its present position. Today every consumer has readily available to him a complete range of fresh wholesome foods, whether he or she chooses to purchase the ingredients or the fully prepared meal. In either case his needs are satisfied by products of high guaranteed quality at competitive prices.

It is difficult to appreciate the extent of the change in the quality of every aspect of our lives in comparison with that of our great grandparents and in many respects it is fashionable today to denigrate these changes. In the field of food supplies however these changes have been to the advantage of the 'man in the street' and have made possible the greatest and most important improvement in his standard of living. This achievement is in large part the achievement of the food manufacturing and distributing industries. Today, the food industry is an essential intermediary in providing food for our large population. An indication of its current position is that 17 of the 22 largest European food companies are British, and indeed many of them have successfully expanded their business across the world.

Social and economic factors

The most important social factors involved were the rapid population growth and urbanization that took place in the nineteenth century.

These changes are illustrated by the population statistics shown in Table 1.

Table 1 *Population statistics (millions)*

	UK	Greater London
1851	22·2	2·6
1871	27·4	3·8
1891	34·2	5·6
1911	42·0	7·1
1931	46·0	8·1
1951	50·2	8·1

Other large towns like Manchester, Birmingham and Glasgow, though much smaller than London, grew in population at an even greater rate in order to accommodate the workers whose efforts gave to the Great Britain of the nineteenth century the name of 'Workshop of the World'. It therefore became necessary within a few decades to develop ways of providing food to millions who now lived remote from the agricultural area of supply and often in conditions which provided fewer facilities for home preparation. The arrival of increasing quantities of imported staple foods led naturally to the establishment of storage facilities and factories in the main ports.

The economic factor of most direct significance was the growth in purchasing power experienced from 1850 onwards, which continued up to the First World War. This was the real benefit of industrialization to the community at large.

Alongside this increase in real wages, and particularly from 1870 to 1900, the price of many staple foods fell dramatically. For example, in 1896 cereals cost about one-half and meat two-thirds of their 1873 price. These and other reductions in the cost of foods were the result of the Government policies of free trade and imperial preference, and they provided a suitable climate for the rapid growth of food manufacture. In the 1920s and 1930s the terms of trade were once again very much in favour of the UK, resulting in a further stimulus to the industry. Although unemployment was high, especially in the 1920s in heavy industry, the period was one of increasing prosperity for many employed in the manufacture of new consumer durables such as cars, radios and other electrical goods. After the First World War the desire of women to lead less domesticated lives provided the food manufacturer with a further impetus for the marketing of convenience foods which continues to the present day.

The nineteenth-century growth of towns gave greater opportunities to the retailer and led to larger street markets and to the beginnings of multiple stores. Names such as Sainsbury, Home & Colonial Stores, Liptons and the various local co-operatives were introduced to the town-dweller from 1860 onwards. At this time too the recent removal of stamp duties had resulted in a marked increase in local newspapers, and retailers were quick to make use of the newly available advertising space to publicize the quality and variety of their stocks. Intensive competition in the High Street led to keen prices, in contrast to the monopoly situation of the village shop of earlier times.

By the end of the nineteenth century the dominant force in the chain of manufacture-distribution-retail-consumer was the wholesaler. Most retailers still operated as relatively small family businesses with limited buying power, entirely dependent on the lines supplied by the few wholesalers available to them. The wholesaler would specify the product he wanted to the manufacturer and accept the most competitive tender. This often left the manufacturer with an inadequate profit margin.

The need to safeguard his growing investment in modern machinery led the manufacturer to develop branded or patented products and establish them nationally by advertising. This enabled him to operate more profitably and made him more independent of the wholesaler. In addition many of the multiple store organizations developed or acquired their own processing factories. In the period between the Wars the multiples entered into strong competition with the traditional corner shop, which fought back with the support of the large manufacturers brands. Such competition led to greater variety and keen prices, to the direct benefit of the consumer.

The present day has seen the move towards supermarkets, with their very wide range of products on open display. The customer now again has direct access to the goods in a way similar to that provided by the traditional street market. Close co-operation of retailers and food manufacturers is maintained to provide efficient service. Advertising continues to play a vital part in enabling the manufacturer to tell consumers about new products and thus obtain the quick introduction into the national market that is required. After that introduction the new product succeeds or fails on its own merits.

It is clear that the development of the food processing industry is closely interwoven with the many fundamental and irreversible changes in our way of life. In particular it is closely linked with agriculture on the one hand and means of distribution and retailing on the other hand.

The decade that saw the 1875 Food and Drugs Act also saw some very important beginnings, as will be seen in Table 2 below.

These pioneers, together with a few of the previous generation such as Alfred Bird, inventor of baking powder, Huntley and Palmer of the Reading biscuit company and the Cadburys in Birmingham laid the foundations of the food industry. Another line of progress is indicated by Lyons, which began as a catering concern, and found by the turn of the century that it was worth blending tea and baking bread and cakes, not only for its own teashops and restaurants, but also for the wider retail market.

Progress was uninterrupted until 1914, aided by cheaper raw materials,

Table 2

Initiative	Later development
1869	Margarine invented.	New Industry.
	Arthur Brook sold own blends of tea as 'Brooke, Bond and Co'.	Distribution of a Branded packaged product.
1870–1871	Hiram Codd's patented globe-stoppered glass bottle.	Carbonated drinks industry.
	J. J. Sainsbury opened retail dairy.	
1871	Thomas Lipton opened his first shop.	} Multiple retailers.
1872	Henry Tate built Liverpool Sugar Refinery.	
1875	Joseph Rank rented his first mill.	} Large scale manufacture.
1877	Frozen meat first imported from Argentine.	Integration from butcher back to ranch.
	Laval cream separator invented.	Efficient—more hygienic butter manufacture.
1880	Fried fish and chips invented by John Rouse of Oldham.	Ready to eat convenience foods.

an expanding consumer market which left room for all competitors, and the gradual introduction of larger, more efficient equipment. By present-day criteria, however, the individual food manufacturing company was still relatively small. In 1905 a survey of the 50 largest industrial concerns in terms of capital invested contained only Bovril and Huntley and Palmers in the 35th and 38th position.

The period between the two Wars saw the development and introduction of many new food products. They were backed by systematic national advertising and soon became established. Breakfast cereals, canned foods and prepared dry mixes, originally developed in the USA, were manufactured in the UK instead of being imported.

In effect therefore the range of 'convenience foods' was being extended very rapidly. This term could in a loose sense be applied to most of the products of our industry, since we undertake a varying proportion of the processes required to turn a primary product into food, and which would mostly have been done in the kitchen 100 years ago. The consumer can nowadays choose the degree of convenience she wants to pay for, as may be illustrated with reference to the humble potato. Market surveys have indicated that one of the housewife's least relished chores is the cleaning and preparation of potatoes. They are now available ready cooked in cans or as frozen fried chips, as potato crisps, as dehydrated mashed potatoes or incorporated into various fully prepared complete dishes in frozen, canned or dehydrated packs.

Among these products ice cream deserves special mention. Originally a luxury item of the home or restaurant menu, ice cream was by 1919 being sold all over the country by small manufacturers and traders, often in the Italian tradition. Then came a very rapid expansion of the market, triggered off by the introduction of modern machinery from the United States. Annual sales of 870 000 gallons in 1920 grew to 35·6 million gallons in 1938.

The inter-war years also saw many changes in the organization of the industry. Mergers and amalgamations occurred both among manufacturers and among multiple retailers. The larger units were more easily able to find capital for modernization and for new processing technology. Another advantage of size was the ability to bargain more effectively in the purchase of supplies across the world.

During the Second World War and for some years after, no growth in the industry was possible, and some food products, being regarded as luxuries, disappeared from the market. In the technical sense however a great deal of progress was made. The challenge of providing food for the nation during the war with restricted supplies was met by developing alternative formulations by many products. Supplies were allocated by the Ministry of Food and often the valued individual characteristics of national branded products had to be sacrificed, but the essential nutritional qualities of the food were maintained, although a great deal of variety was lost.

After 1953 wartime controls of supplies to the manufacturer were lifted. This resulted in a rapid increase in the variety of processed foods available and in competition in the market place. This has intensified with the arrival and growth of the supermarkets, the end of retail price maintenance and the systematic use of TV and radio advertising.

One of the most important new convenience foods, now accepted across the world, became established as a direct consequence of the war. Instant coffee was introduced to us by the American GI and soon became established in its own right, first in a spray-dried form and more recently also as a freeze-dried product.

The other major innovation has been in frozen convenience foods, which have within 20 years become an entire new branch of the industry. The growth of frozen foods has run parallel to the acceptance of the refrigerator as a necessary piece of household equipment. Their success can be gauged by the fact that the fish finger is now one of the items included in the cost of living index.

Having sketched in the historical development of the industry it is necessary to go back again to look at technical developments.

Technical factors—Transport

The arrival of new technology has always been scrutinized by the food industry and rapidly adapted to its use. As has been said, the large scale transport of food into and within the UK became a necessity during the nineteenth century. The development of new technology in this field was therefore of great significance.

Improvements in shipbuilding techniques from 1800 onwards enabled bulk quantities of non-perishable foods to be imported from the newly developed agricultural lands of America and Australia and the ability to reach a large stable market in England in turn stimulated the rapid further growth of overseas agriculture. The limit in sailing ships was reached in the famous clippers of the 1870s, at the very moment at which steamships became available of a size and speed that had been unimaginable only a few years before. Speed was commercially important because a premium could be obtained for the first supplies of the new seasons' crops, whether the commodity was wheat or tea. Large quantities of North American bacon, cheese and lard were also reaching the English market 100 years ago. The availability of cheap overseas wheat compelled the UK farmer to concentrate more on the perishable products such as vegetables and meat animals, and here the network of railways as well as reliable coastal steamships ensured delivery to the city markets within a few days.

By 1920 a number of manufacturers had organized their own distribution systems based on horse vans or combinations of rail transport with horse vans and this was a cornerstone in the successful growth of their businesses. Reliable motor transport after the First World War made it possible for these private distribution systems to be extended and to become increasingly more specialized.

The importance to the independent retailer of direct distribution of branded goods from the manufacturer has already been discussed.

Preservation of foods

CHEMICAL PRESERVATIVES

Some means of preservation of foods is essential in the provisioning of large populations and it is an element of most food processing.

Various simple physical or chemical methods of preservation were developed empirically in ancient times, mainly by dehydration, salting and pickling. They were often uncertain in their effects because the procedures were not adequately controlled or the chemicals used were impure.

Today we have available a limited number of chemical preservatives whose use is subject to regulations framed after considering questions of need and safety. The quantity and type of preservative permitted in a specified food is laid down. For the manufacturer these preservatives are a valuable means of ensuring regular supplies of seasonal commodities like fruit and vegetables, and of preventing spoilage in a variety of food products. The criticisms sometimes made of the use of chemical preservatives do not adequately take into account the careful decisions taken on safety aspects or indeed of the risks of spoilage or food poisoning that would be incurred in their absence.

REFRIGERATION

The invention of refrigeration machines is one of the most important factors in the technical progress of the industry. The benefits of storing perishable foods at low temperatures were known for a very long time, and in the first half of the nineteenth century ice was being used successfully to transport salmon to the capital from Scotland. Nearer to home, a fishing fleet based at Barking made use of ice collected from flooded Essex fields in winter and stored in cellars.

The steamship made the supply of beef, chilled in ice obtained from the Great Lakes, a possibility from North America in the 1870s. This business was however difficult to manage, since the meat had to be sold quickly on arrival and therefore there was a risk of glut and low prices. Within a few years mechanical refrigeration systems became available in America, Australia and Europe, and imported frozen meat immediately became a major factor in the market. In consequence the price of English beef and mutton fell by 30 per cent between 1873 and 1893. It was observed in Parliament at this time that 'refrigeration was to meat what the spinning jenny had been to textiles'. It was also the key to progress in other branches of the food industry. For example in the 1920s ice cream was transported in insulated boxes chilled with salt and ice and later with solid carbon dioxide. The products were delivered into cold boxes which required daily replenishment with blocks of ice. For instance in 1926 Lyons, already one of the largest ice cream manufacturers, started to supply refrigerator cabinets to their retailers. The numbers grew from 1200 in 1931 to 12 000 in 1939 and latterly to 55 000 in 1971. The refrigerated lorry introduced in the early 1930s enabled distribution to be planned on an increasingly larger scale. This latter development between the Wars provided an essential link in the 'cold chain' of temperature controlled refrigeration that made possible the frozen food industry of the last 25 years.

More recently it has been found that the natural course of ripening and decay in fruits can be inhibited for months if refrigeration is combined with careful control of the gaseous composition of the atmosphere in the store. As a result fresh apples and pears of good quality are now available the year round.

CANNING

The foundations of canning technology were laid around 1800 by Nicholas Appert in France and in 1809 he won a prize of 12 000 francs for his method of preservation of foods by sealing them in glass jars or bottles and then subjected them to a heat treatment. The invention was very quickly taken up by Messrs. Donkin and Hall of Dartford and adapted to the use of tinned iron containers. Samples of tinned meats and soups were first submitted to the military authorities in 1812 and soon after naval ships on special expeditions were carrying them in their stores. In 1814 Sir Joseph Banks, then President of the Royal Society, commended 'the nutritious qualities of your embalmed provisions'. By 1820 50 000 lb of canned meat, soups and vegetables were being purchased by the navy in cans up to 3 lb in size. By 1814 Donkin, Hall and Gamble were submitting cans to a month's incubation at 90–110 deg F before despatch to ensure their good keeping properties. A further development at that time was the use of calcium chloride baths to raise the water temperature for processing.

These products were so valuable on naval and military expeditions that large orders were placed. Unfortunately it was decided to use larger containers without increasing the cooking time and, as a result, about 50 tons of underprocessed product was condemned in 1850. It was thought that the 'agent of putrification' was air and that the sole effect of the heat process was to displace the air. It was not until Pasteur's investigations of bacteria were extended to canned foods near the turn of the nineteenth ceutury that a sound scientific understanding of the process was obtained. Since then the expected developments of large scale mechanization and automation have occurred and very wide ranges of foods have been successfully canned.

Aseptic canning processes have in the last 20 years made possible a further improvement in quality, since the food can be heat treated and cooled before being sealed. The cooking process is therefore less severe and delicate flavours are retained better. Plastic or metal foil laminates are now available which can be subjected to sterilization after sealing and therefore some of the disadvantages of the rigid containers have been overcome.

OTHER FORMS OF PACKAGING

It is appropriate at this point to mention briefly other packaging developments. Packaging of many types is an important factor in the retention of good quality and appearance in processed foods. It is today designed specifically as a factor in the preservation of foods other than canned products. The modern use of packaging is subjected to criticism from time to time without sufficient consideration of its necessity and advantages. The fact that it represents a major factor in ingredient costs, but is not edible, means that in our highly competitive industry every manufacturer reviews the function and cost of his packaging carefully and continuously.

The positive functions of packaging are:

(i) To protect the food product from physical damage during transport. Many foods are attractive because of their delicate structure.

(ii) To prevent microbiological and other contamination.

(iii) To provide a controlled gaseous environment for the food within the pack. Plastic films can now be selected to retain a vacuum or to provide varying degrees of permeability to oxygen or moisture vapour or other gases depending on the specific requirements for the retention of good quality in the product.

(iv) To enable the manufacturer to give information to his customer about the product. This may include brand name, description, weight, composition, and instructions for domestic storage and preparation.

The development of packaging as an integral part of the food manufacturing process has had some other very important benefits. Compared with the situation of 100 years ago, when any wrapping and weighing or measuring of food was done by the retailer, it provides far greater security from contamination and far greater certainty of correct measure. It is also much less labour intensive, and has been an important factor in the development of efficient retailing methods in supermarkets.

The nineteenth-century pioneers already appreciated the importance of a distinctive package as a means of representing to the consumer the quality of the contents. A quotation from the *Times Food Number* of June 1914 shows the general trend:

'Within the past 20 years the amount of food of various kinds done up and placed on the market in packets and tins has increased enormously. The phenomenal expansion of advertisement in recent years has been the means of establishing the proprietary article as an important factor in the people's food supply.'

The foregoing section has indicated some important aspects of progress relating to the industry as a whole. It is now proposed to discuss some specialized branches of the industry and to highlight salient features of their development.

Sugar

Sugar refining was the only food manufacturing process already well established on a large scale in 1875. This is because the UK had developed the sugar cane industry in the West Indies during the previous 100 years and obtained nearly all its supplies from there and other tropical areas in the form of crude sugar. The processes of breaking the sugar cane on mechanized rollers, extracting it and concentrating the dilute syrup in vacuum concentrators were established on the colonial sugar estates. The crude sugar was then shipped to large refineries situated at the main ports, especially Glasgow, Liverpool and London. Here the final steps of purification, concentration and crystallization were carried out. In principle the processes established a century ago have changed little.

Whereas the European countries had developed a sugar beet industry from 1800 onwards, such a move was officially discouraged in the UK because cane sugar was a vital crop in the West Indies and an important source of revenue to the Government by way of taxes on the imports. Sugar from beet only became established in England from 1912 onwards and received Government support by means of subsidies from 1925. This change of policy came about because of the recognition during the First World War of the strategic need for some home supply. An incidental benefit of this late development was that our sugar beet factories were of a large size and high degree of technical efficiency from the outset.

A further development of special importance to all the branches of the food industry that use sugar is the development of starch hydrolysis processes by acid and enzyme to produce glucose syrups. This source of sugar is of importance strategically, because it broadens the base of raw materials to include any readily available source of starch.

The recent problems in sugar supplies are by no means unique. A century ago the British refining industry was nearly brought to its knees by subsidized imports from Europe. The position there was that both imported and indigenous raw sugar carried a tax calculated on a theoretical standard figure for the expected yield of refined product. Exported refined sugar was entitled to a drawback based on this theoretical standard. Therefore any manufacturer who was able to improve his yield above the standard could use the excess drawback to subsidize his exports. This possibility was quickly realized in a time of rapidly improving processing technology. Several decades of international discussions at Government level were required to reach a position of fair competition.

It is of interest to note the parallel growth of sugar and tea consumption in the nineteenth century as shown in Table 3 below.

The popularity of sweetened tea as a drink was undoubtedly a factor in developing the sweet tooth for which this nation is still well known, and thus in turn laid the foundation of the highly developed UK sugar confectionery and cake industries.

206

Table 3

Year	Per capita consumption (lbs)	
	Tea	*Sugar*
1850	1·9	25·3
1860	2·7	34·1
1870	3·8	47·1
1880	4·6	60·3
1890	5·2	71·1
1900	6·1	85·5

Milk

One hundred years ago the quality of fresh milk supplies was unbelievably bad. The milk was often sour, was contaminated by bacteria and dirt, and adulterated with water. In that situation it was perhaps a mixed blessing that supplies in large towns were scarce. In 1866 London received enough for a daily average of only one-fifth pint per head, and more than 20 per cent of this was still derived from cows kept in town dairies as close to the centre as Paddington and South Kensington. The insanitary condition of such places, often in basements, can be imagined. The last of them only disappeared around 1914. Supplies improved with the use of rail transport and effective chilling methods, so that dairy herds at a distance could provide for the cities. However, milk continued to be a major source of disease, until Pasteur's scientific discoveries had been used to devise practical heat treatment methods at the end of the century. The rapid introduction of this new technology was due in part to the ready availability of large scale equipment for processing liquids in the brewing industry.

Before 1870 fresh milk was already being augmented by supplies of sweetened condensed milk in cans. This milk was preserved mainly by virtue of its high sugar content and not by heat treatment. Roller drying procedures were developed around 1900 followed by spray-drying, and it then became possible to draw supplies from abroad.

Recent technical developments have led to ultra-high temperature sterilization and to liquid milk with long shelf life. The situation today is that the consumer can take for granted an abundance of pure milk, of guaranteed nutritional and bacteriological quality, delivered on his doorstep. In this respect this country is now better provided than any other in the world. This position owes much to Government policy, which recognized the vital nutritional importance of milk in the 1930s and has consistently encouraged the development of the industry to its present state.

Flour milling and bread

The well known preference of the consumer for white bread can be traced back to Roman times. Juvenal's phrase 'the tender loaf, snowy white, made from soft wheat' is as mellifluous as any used by a modern advertising copy writer. Other references can be found in Horace, Seneca and Suetonius. By the time of the Emperor Augustus, 63 BC, three distinct types are described:

(i) 'Panis Candidus', i.e., white bread, suitable for the wealthy guests.

(ii) 'Panis secundus' offered to impecunious guests and considered suitable for poets.

(iii) 'Panis plebeius' or sordidus, probably made from barley and given to the slaves.

The milling technology developed by the Romans remained virtually unchanged until the nineteenth century, except that their water-powered mechanisms were adapted to wind power in the late Middle Ages. For many centuries after the Romans wheat was not the most readily available grain in northern Europe, much of the bread being made from other cereals, mainly rye or barley. The superiority of wheaten bread was however recognized and it was valued by the rich. One of the features of wheat is that by careful sieving, even primitive milling processes can produce a grade of fine white flour. In a bread dough the special characteristics of the wheat protein gluten enable it to retain gas and hence to make a well-risen loaf better than the other cereals.

The technical means of producing white flour efficiently arrived in the UK around 1880 with the replacement of the millstone with roller mills. They made it possible to break down the wheat grain by steps, removing husk and germ in between the 'breaks'.

In the same period the development of the vast American and Australian wheatlands resulted in a concentration of milling into large, well-equipped mills in the ports. Bread baking became industrialized more slowly. The economic circumstances of the industry since the 1930s have led to the integration of a large proportion of the bread bakeries with flour milling concerns.

In 1942 the extraction rate of flour for bread was raised to 85 per cent to reduce the need for imports and ensure the retention of vitamins. This step resulted in a significantly darker loaf, and the consumer's preference for white bread was very clearly demonstrated when supplies became free again after 1948.

One significant technical step of the last 20 years has been the introduction of the Chorleywood Bread Process, which has led to the use of a higher proportion of the 'weaker' English wheats and to greater production efficiency. Significant improvements in the keeping qualities of bread have also been achieved, resulting from a scientific understanding of the staling process. It is however still very important to organize for efficient distribution to ensure that bread reaches the consumer in good condition.

Margarine

The centenary of the invention of margarine was celebrated in 1969. The pressures of population and industrialization led to such a shortage of butter that in 1866 the French Government offered a prize to anyone who could produce a nutritious substitute. This prize was won by Hyppolite Mège Mouriès, using an emulsion of beef fat.

Mège Mouriès was unable himself to develop his invention because of political changes after the Franco-Prussian War, but he sold his patent to Jan Jurgens, who initiated the rapid development of the new industry in Holland. In the following 20 years manufacture began in other western European countries and in the USA, the first UK factory being built by a Dane, Otto Monsted, in 1889. Acceptance by the consumer was good, but growth was inhibited by limited supplies of beef fat until the process of hardening of liquid vegetable oils by hydrogenation was developed in 1902. It was then possible to use as raw material the vegetable oils produced in tropical climates and gradually to control the processes so that the desirable properties of butter could be closely approached. The recent introduction of soft margarines that remain spreadable from the refrigerator can fairly claim to have led to an improvement over the natural product, butter, in this respect. Margarine is therefore a unique example of a manufactured food, deliberately invented as a result of consumer need and Government policy and eventually established as a major food product in its own right.

Nutrition

A review of the food industry would be incomplete without brief reference to nutrition. It is a commonplace that man's main criterion in selecting his food is his enjoyment within the limits of his purse. His health, however, does depend on the consumption of the right foods.

In the second half of the nineteenth century the significance to health of a sufficient caloric and protein content of foods was just being established. There was almost complete ignorance of vitamins, although the ability of fruit juices to cure scurvy and of cod liver oil to cure rickets had been found empirically. The discovery of vitamins in the early twentieth century was not much applied until towards the end of the First World War, when food rationing was introduced. Between the Wars very important steps were taken to provide cheap or free milk for mothers and children. Large scale application of modern nutritional knowledge had to wait for the Second World War, when the nation's diet was completely controlled by the Ministry of Food under the technical guidance of Professor Drummond. The food manufacturer was asked to fortify flour with calcium and margarine with Vitamins A and D, and this, in addition to the special milk provisions and welfare supplements, ensured an adequate diet despite the supply difficulties.

In general the nutritional problems of Britain today are not those of deficiency. There has, however, been a change of balance in the type of food eaten. There has been a highly significant increase in the proportion of fats and sugar consumed over the last 100 years and a decrease in the proportion of grain products and potatoes. These changes are the result of increased affluence and the exercise of choice by the consumer among a greater variety of food available. Whereas 100 years ago a large part of our population was undernourished and striving to get enough food, now the attitude is increasingly one of seeking positive enjoyment by choosing foods that attract and please, as well as providing nourishment.

The nutritional requirements of young children, mothers and old people are now satisfied by specially formulated products, as are the needs of the sufferers from diabetes and some other metabolic disorders.

The future

It is clear that throughout the period reviewed the progress in our industry has been closely linked to progress in the country as a whole, and increasingly also to circumstances in other countries and continents. This will certainly be the case in the future. Any definitive forecasts would therefore be no more than flights of fancy. Nevertheless it is possible to discuss some of the factors which will have an important influence, and their importance is seen more clearly in the context of the historical review.

The first question to consider is the probable number of people needing food. Recent forecasts for the UK have changed quite substantially from those being made a few years ago. This point is clearly illustrated by the population estimates shown in Table 4.

Table 4

Year of estimate	1965	1970	1972	1973
UK Population expected in AD 2000 (millions)	74	66	62	59

It may be that within the next few years the number of people to be fed will be static. The average age of the population is however increasing and this may well point to an increased demand for convenience foods.

The second question is that of the prosperity of the nation. On an optimistic view we are at present seeing a temporary halt in the improvement in living standards which has occurred year by year since the 1950s. We are unlikely to see a return to the low food prices of the past. We will therefore, as a nation and individually, have to decide whether to sacrifice some of the variety of foods available or to spend a larger proportion of our income on food.

Of equal importance is the supply of food commodities, which needs to be considered more and more on a worldwide basis. Some of the predictions made of the effect on our food supplies of our membership of the EEC have already had to be changed as a result of the supply situation in the rest of the world.

Because of our very large imports our food supplies will always be more vulnerable to world shortages than those of other developed nations. It is possible that we could reduce our needs for imports quite substantially with a policy calculated to develop our own agriculture. Professor K Mellanby has shown recently that even today acceptable levels of nutrition could still be obtained entirely from home produced foods, provided we were prepared to make sacrifices in terms of variety, and especially in the quantity of meat eaten. However in the long term perhaps the most important action that the developed nations could take to ensure their own future food supplies is to improve the standard of agriculture in under-developed countries.

Research has already made some important contributions; in producing high yielding varieties of cereals, roots etc., in pest and disease control, and in looking for new food sources. In this field the main search has been for proteins. Large scale experiments in the intensive farming of fish and crustaceae are having success, and texturized vegetable proteins are becoming established. The exciting possibility exists that the current systematic research will establish some new or as yet unused plant product as a major food source.

It is perhaps worth emphasizing that texturized vegetable proteins are not 'synthetic foods'. They are the result of new processing methods applied to a natural food source, so as to make it more palatable and attractive to the consumer. Similar achievements in the past have produced from food grains the variety of breakfast cereals to which we are all accustomed, and have succeeded in modifying to our use oils and fats from a variety of sources.

These are good examples of the way in which the food processing industry can deploy technology to make the best use of food supplies, sometimes of unconventional origin, and further advances can be expected with confidence.

It may be appropriate to quote here the words used by Professor Alistair Frazer at the 1960 Pure Food Centenary celebrations. 'Very few of the raw materials from which our daily food is derived can be regarded as acceptable to a normal individual in their natural state. Conversion of the raw materials into acceptable and usable food materials is necessary.'

A major contribution to food supplies is being made by the systematic reduction of waste. This requires the application of a wide range of disciplines. Protection against insect and other pests needs to be provided on the farm and at every subsequent stage. After harvest the problems of microbiological attack and of chemical or physical deterioration during storage and processing have to be assessed for each food commodity, so that the appropriate preventive measures can be taken. Finally the processes within factories need careful design and control. Food manufacturers have already made a major contribution in getting a higher proportion of primary products on to the dining-room table, but the reduction of waste and the allied field of pollution control will continue to be areas of future progress.

When considering the environment in which future developments have to be brought to fruition we can see many difficulties.

The real challenge is no other than that of survival—not because of galloping inflation but because of legislation which just does not allow all the costs, which industry must necessarily incur in its operation, to be passed on to the consumer. Over recent years:

   (i) margins have plummeted from $5\frac{1}{2}$ to $2\frac{1}{2}$ per cent,

   (ii) the return on capital employed has been consistently below the cost of borrowing money,

   (iii) from a positive cash flow the industry has been subjected to a negative cash flow. In three years there has been a cumulative difference or shortfall of some £700 million for the industry.

There can be no doubt that the food processing industry has suffered more than industry as a whole. Perhaps it is because the total amount of food consumed does not vary very greatly that there is no possibility of getting out of trouble through increased volume. Perhaps because the industry works on such very small margins that even a modest erosion is damaging and the drop of 3 per cent—more than half the margin—is catastrophic. Or could it be that because food is so politically emotive the legislation has been interpreted more severely and with more enthusiasm for this industry than for some other industries?

Superficially things may not look too bad to the layman. There is food in plenty in the shops, even though various low margin products have disappeared, and although there have been closures of factories, reductions in job numbers, there has been no major collapse nor is any anticipated. At industry level, however, the picture is not so good—there has been a major cut-back in investment which is more far-reaching and far more serious than current figures might lead us to believe. This is because major projects already in hand are being completed and are reflected in the figures, but not being replaced or brought up to date unless there is virtually no alternative, with the result that it is only a matter of time before efficiency will decline.

At a time of national economic crisis the industry would not expect to embark upon a major re-equipment, but it is of real importance, not only to us but to the consumer, that it should make the very best use of the existing assets and maintain a normal flow of replacement and of innovation.

Yet no new product can be launched without large investments in research and production facilities and in advertising.

Our fear is that when economic growth returns to the country as a whole, our industry will not be able to respond adequately to the rapid rise of consumer demand that will develop. This is because of the time lag inherent in the planning and implementation of new production facilities. The present cut-back in investment will therefore have serious effects on efficiency over a number of years.

We entered the 1970s with the most efficient and technologically advanced food manufacturing industry in Europe. If this lead is lost, the people of Britain will in the future spend a greater proportion of their income on food, and find that their choice is significantly reduced.

Introductory remarks by Mr. Lawrence

The greatest value in looking backwards is to assist in clarifying one's thoughts about future trends, and rather than repeat points already made in the paper I am proposing to examine more recent changes in the social scene and their impact on the industry.

The consumer now has a more than adequate diet, and looks for convenience, the elimination of unattractive hours in the kitchen, variety, excitement and an attractive presentation. The old saying that 'a little of what you fancy does you good' applies and these factors are every bit as important as proteins and vitamins. Mandatory standards, important as they are, do not always take this into account and can all too easily frustrate innovation and improvement and all too often escalate cost. They should be kept under constant review.

With over 55 million people concentrated in the urban areas, there is literally no other way of getting food to them satisfactorily and if an industry such as ours did not exist it would have to be invented. It is all very well for the extreme wing of consumerism to scream 'back to nature' and denigrate processed foods, but there has been a fundamental change in the world supply position resulting from the very necessary increases in the standards of living of the emerging nations. As a result we will in the future need to search for new sources of food and new types of food products and this will inevitably demand more and not less elaborate processes.

The attitude of the consumer towards the inevitably higher level of food prices has not perhaps been given enough attention.

We can hardly blame him for wanting cheap food to persist *ad infinitum* but I cannot help wondering whether such importance should be attached to this very natural reaction. Many efforts have been made by Government to placate the consumer—subsidizing certain basic foods, arranging for the display of price lists, organizing Consumer Centres, etc. Anyone in the industry will know that subsidies are the cause of serious distortion in the market place and are not in anyone's long term interests. The rest is damaging as it has the effect of misleading the consumer. It implies that there are ways of continuing cheap food, whilst the fact is there are none. I do not cast doubts upon the motives of the Governments which took these measures but I do question their interpretation of the consumer's attitude. He or she knows perfectly well that in one way or another he must pay the economic price.

Surely the time has come to recognize that the consumer—and in particular the housewife who buys most of the food—is a realist. She does not expect the impossible, rather she places value on security of food supplies—just remember how she voted at the Referendum when this was one of the major issues. She is too intelligent to be taken in by cosmetic measures—she would rather have a job for her man, for herself, reasonable wages and good working conditions. These things are only attainable if the critical decisions affecting industry are based on long term economic criteria and not upon short term political expediency, however 'convenient' they may appear in the short term. Industry, any industry, must 'earn its corn'. The failure to accept this simple fact of life is now eroding the very fabric of our food industry and will make it increasingly difficult for it to continue to meet the ever changing needs of the consumer.

Successive Governments have instead introduced and maintained legislation which prevents industry from passing on all its necessary costs to the consumer. This has caused margins on food to drop by half to the quite unrealistically low levels with the result that there has been a reduction in investment—in real terms—not only in respect of major innovation but also of replacements. This sad situation can be expected to continue just as long as the legislation does—in anything like its present form. The industry is not, of course, about to go bankrupt but this unnecessary and artificial pressure can

214

only result in swiftly declining confidence, deteriorating efficiency, reduction of choice and in employment. All this for very little benefit to the consumer, as the apparent saving to him of some 3 per cent has to a large extent been offset by the costs of dealing with the requirements of the legislation and by the many inefficiencies caused by it.

There is, however, a ray of sunshine—the White Paper produced by MAFF and entitled 'Food from our own Resources' was warmly welcomed by the industry. Although import savings may not have the glamour of export, it is none the less the more certain of the two. Furthermore, its impact is immediate whereas an export is all too frequently paid for long afterwards in a £ of reduced value—so a declared intention by the Ministry to develop agriculture and in turn the relevant processing sector of the industry, on a long term and purposeful basis, came like a breath of fresh air. We are looking forward to it being backed up by action and we are optimistic enough to hope for further constructive measures in the future.

Discussion

Professor P P Scott (Nutritional Physiologist, Royal Free Hospital School of Medicine): We have all had a most delightful account, beautifully illustrated, presenting the history of a most fascinating industry which, indeed, occupies the life of a very large section of our population coupled with those who work in agriculture. It is very interesting to see in general terms how the actual work done has improved from technological developments in equipment and methods of handling.

This was particularly shown by the old bakery pictures in which the handling was maximal as compared with, for example, the Chorleywood process nowadays, or even the making of the Swiss roll, where handling has been reduced to a minimum. How much better from the point of view of safety and general control, quite apart from the possibility of continuous output.

We must heed Mr. Lawrence's warning that, if we do not put more back into the industry, we are going to lose in the future the enormous benefits in improved nutrition such as those we are considering today. We must therefore enter a plea for improvements in the money available for new equipment, new machinery and, last of all, may I make a plea for something that Mr. Lawrence has not mentioned and that is basic research. I myself have received most of the grants for my work in academic circles from industry. Nowadays, however, money is getting shorter and, as many of us in academic circles are aware, for some reason nutritional research is not a favoured activity either for academics, or for the MRC or the ARC. We are heavily dependent for our support upon industry itself, but with such small margins, now only some 3·0 per cent, how can industry support basic research?

The question I should like to pose to Mr. Lawrence is, what does he feel about the importance or the necessity of basic research? Is there any way in which, for example, even by curtailing such expensive items as advertisements, he could put more into this basic research which, I am sure, feeds back into his industry tenfold what is put into it?

Mr. Lawrence: This is not an unusual question and we must first consider why companies do advertise. Clearly they do not like spending money on advertising just for the sake of doing so, but the fact is that without advertising existing products they could not maintain their volume, and new products would not see the light of day. So, of course, they have to advertise and the question then is, how much to spend? In difficult times every company has tried cutting back on advertising. That is all right as long as you do not do so to a greater extent than your competitor; but as soon as you do, you will lose volume, lose market share; and ultimately your overheads will be uncovered. It is mainly those highly advertised products, or the ingredients which are behind them, which call for research and call for technical development. So, far from transferring money to technology, I suspect that if we tried to cut advertising significantly we would, in fact, spend less and not more money on science, research and technology.

It is a prime responsibility of management to decide the relative levels of expenditure in the different spheres. Not just in advertising and research; but also on people—probably the most important of all—on distribution, on marketing, on discounts, the lot. On the whole, the judgments made over many years have proved to be about right, because the industry in this country compares well with those in Europe and in the other industrial countries. So on average the outcome has not been too bad.

Dr. Harold Fore (Agricultural Research Council): Strong arguments can be put forward in favour of further research to support production of food on the farm side of the farm gate and this, of course, must compete with the money available for research in relation to food processing. I should like to know whether Mr. Lawrence accepts these arguments and, if he does not, what he would suggest should be done in order to counter them.

Mr. Lawrence: I do not see the two as directly competitive. Much of the expenditure on the food processing side is provided by the companies themselves, as opposed to the Government. There should always be a sensible balance between research on agriculture and food processing—just as we have previously heard that there should be a sensible balance between marketing and R & D within a company. The food processing industry, particularly in recent years, has recognized the importance of the farming industry, because without their products we should be in a sorry state. Also I would respectfully suggest that the farming community would be in an equally sorry state if there were no processing industry to buy its wares! So I trust that a proper balance will, by trial and error, continue to be achieved.

Dr. J Green (H J Heinz Co Ltd): I should like, if I might, to put the scientist's point of view from industry, as opposed to that which has been put so ably by Mr. Lawrence which is, I suppose, a kind of marketing man's aspect.

We are celebrating today 100 years of legislation and yet, apart from the pictures we have seen here, we have forgotten the factor that is always forgotten, and that is time. Times have changed in these last 100 years and we have forgotten the existence of the scientist in industry where he is now an able man contributing as much, if not more, than those engaged by Government or those engaged in the enforcement authorities whether whole or part time. I should like to think that we are much more a team than the impression that has been given, particularly yesterday when we were talking about the regulatory authorities and the enforcement authorities with the poor food industry in the middle.

Now I am not worried about those things which I know that I am doing; the food industry today is doing a responsible job. It is not trying to pull the wool over anyone's eyes on the things that it knows it is doing. The food industry is rather worried about the things it might be doing without realizing their significance, and that is the problem. That is why we need more research. The money that is being spent now on forming legislation and enforcing it is, to some extent, being wasted, because we are all in the same boat trying to serve the consumer. What we want to be doing is spending our money on looking to the future and trying to find out what we are doing that might be wrong, if there is anything, and that will help to protect the consumer. The money that is available should be spent more wisely than it has been in the past.

Last year the taxpayers gave to a leading motor manufacturer a sum equivalent to the money it spends on food research in 150 years. We must get our perspective right. More public money should go to the food industry so that we do properly the job of looking after the consumer. Anyone can go into the market today, spend 15p on a can of convenience foodstuffs and be astonished to find something wrong with it, but he will go and buy a £2500 motor car and be astonished if there is not something wrong with it.

I would ask Mr. Lawrence if he agrees that the industry now is an integral part of our society, a responsible part, we are all together in it, and if we go forward from that base we shall all benefit, Government, the food producer and the regulatory authorities.

Mr. Lawrence: I would certainly agree with nearly every word that the questioner has said and, as he said them so very much better than I could, I will not attempt to cover again the points he has made.

The only point on which there might be some slight difference is that he perhaps laid over-much emphasis on public money. I am all for having any money we can get for expenditure on research, but I believe that if the food industry were left a reasonably free hand to sell its wares at prices the consumer could afford to pay it would not need to beg for public money; it could manage as well as it has in the past. I should hate to see the food industry, cap in hand, joining the queue of derelict industries for Government hand-outs.

No one can deny that the Government is by legislation preventing us from charging the economic price. Why they do so I have never been able to understand because the food industry has always been content with very modest margins on very high turnover. Our return on capital has never been more than is necessary to sustain the industry and, on average, it has been well below that of industry as a whole, so there cannot be any accusing finger pointed at us.

A Consumer's Approach to Food

Peter Goldman

Director, Consumers' Association

God made the wicked Grocer
For a mystery and a sign,
That men might shun the awful shops
And go to inns to dine.

He sells us sands of Araby
As sugar for cash down;
He sweeps his shop and sells the dust
The purest salt in town,
He crams with cans of poisoned meat
The subjects of the King,
And when they die by thousands
Why, he laughs like anything.

But now the sands are running out
From sugar of a sort,
The Grocer trembles; for his time,
Just like his weight, is short.
(G K Chesterton—*The Song against Grocers*)

The Japanese have traditionally played Russian roulette with fugu, a poisonous fish. Early man must have learnt the hard way how to make use of the cassava without succumbing fatally to hydrocyanic acid. He probably wasted little time on introspection. Today many of us in the over-developed West worry obsessively about our food. Will we become too fat? Will our liver, heart, guts suffer? A five-course meal, though it may taste good, is now in poor taste. Long gone are the days of dinners consisting of a roasted shoulder of mutton, and a plum pudding, veal cutlets, frilled potatoes, cold tongue, ham, beef, and eggs in their shells, followed by fruit washed down with Madeira and port, both white and red. Gone too kettle-broth (bread, water and a little fat) for the very poor. Differences in diet have divided the classes of society. Today it is the differences between nations rather than within nations that are most intolerable. Harvest failures in the Third World have caused whole populations to move or brought about political upheavals. In 1974 a few British housewives—in slightly absurd imitation—ran riot in a supermarket when deprived of sugar.

219

A hundred years ago Britain had all the problems of over-rapid urbanization so familiar now in the Third World. One of the symptoms was, and is, food adulteration. People no longer grew, baked and brewed for themselves or bought from a neighbour. In 1850 the Committee on Food Adulteration reported on 'the widespread evil'. The old Assize price controls had gone, and no quality controls had been put in their place. Bread was often sold below the cost of flour. There was heavy taxation on goods such as tea, beer and sugar. So alum was added to flour together with potato flour, pipe clay and chalk. Oatmeal was mixed with barley and exhausted tea leaves were resold. The worst adulteration was found in the poorer neighbourhoods. Traders argued that people preferred the adulterated food and there is some evidence that this was true. If the modern Briton likes technicolour peas, his early nineteenth-century counterpart preferred tea dyed green and anchovies bright red. This was not something, however, that the law would then bless. The current edition of *Words and Phrases, Legally Defined* still describes adulteration as 'When a simple article such as tea has foreign ingredients added to it, like gypsum and Prussian blue, which are not required for the process of preparing and drying it, but are added for the purpose of making it look green, that is adulteration. *Roberts* v *Egerton* (1874)'.

A strong Royal Commission, appointed in 1869, laid down a number of 'requirements necessary for a civilized life'. They included food inspection, and well they might. An Adulteration of Foods Act had been passed in 1860 but no one was given a duty to enforce it—a mistake made many times since. Some still hoped for voluntary reform—a mistake also made many times since. It took several more years, and committees, before the familiar words which can mean so much, 'not of the nature, substance or quality demanded by the purchaser', became part of our heritage. In the British Consumers' Association we have often tried to paraphrase these so as to sell the concept to our fellow consumers overseas, but never wholly successfully. It is not only in politics that the Westminster model has proved difficult to export.

In many ways 1875 was the beginning of a good time for food. In the years ahead the granaries of the North American continent were to overflow and cheap wheat was to be available. Prices would fall. There were already glimpses of the future. Work on refrigeration was under way and the first frozen mutton and beef was to arrive from Australia and the Argentine in the next decade. In 1888 J E Panton wrote, in *From Kitchen to Garret*, 'Dress and house rent are two items that have risen considerably during the last few years; otherwise, everything is much cheaper and nicer than it used to be before New Zealand meat came to the front, and sugar, tea, cheese, all the thousand and one items one requires in the house, became lower than ever they had been before . . .'. The us was soon to start exporting canned fruit and vegetables.

Another 70 years were to pass before the arrival of the supermarket but the changes were starting. Meantime food for some people was strictly a matter of bread, and inadequate bread too. Roller-milling, which enabled the wheat-germ to be removed, had arrived but not the nutritional knowledge of the value of the wheat-germ and fortification of food. A diet of unfortified white bread, margarine and jam and condensed skimmed milk produced a malnourished generation who disturbed the Army doctors recruiting for the Boer War. Sweet things are a comfort in trying conditions.

For the prosperous this was a great time of conspicuous consumption. Magnificent new hotels and restaurants were built and dining out became a fashionable way of spending leisure. Elaborate dinners at the Carlton or Savoy would cost £2 or £3 for two. But Colonel Newham-Davis, a turn of the century Raymond Postgate, wrote 'If you or I, in the absence of the maitre d'hotel and the head waiter, fall into the hands of an underling, heaven help us. He will lure you or me on to order the most expensive dinner that his limited imagination can conceive and thinks he is doing his duty to the patron'. In the decades which have passed more and more people have started to eat outside their own homes. No longer in grand hotels—now strictly for tourists and social anthropologists—but in a few select and expensive places and in many modest pubs, cafes, in Italian, Indian and Cypriot restaurants and in staff canteens.

The people who write to recommend restaurants for *The Good Food Guide*, started by Postgate and continued by Consumers' Association, are a mixed bunch with one common bond—an interest in restaurants where food is taken seriously and treated with respect. This does not necessarily mean places where a brigade of chefs produce elaborate, classic dishes. In the last 10 years or so in particular a new generation of restaurateurs has emerged—chef/proprietors doing things on a small scale, with an emphasis on much simpler dishes, probably using cheaper ingredients to advantage. In the same year that the Ritz Grill closed down, one of the *Guide's* food distinctions was awarded to an industrious young couple who, in a simple shop-front restaurant in a cathedral town in Wiltshire, cook the sort of food they would offer their friends at an informal dinner party. Making a profit from a restaurant is a challenge which is being met by many such young enthusiasts, who in their turn are helping to educate the eating-out public away from over-elaborate nonsenses towards what one of our correspondents described as 'real cooking in a plain, whitewashed room'.

A new 'old' problem appeared as eating out began to boom. In the late forties and early fifties the cause for concern was no longer food adulteration but food poisoning. During the debates in Parliament prior to the revision of the Food and Drugs Act in 1955, argument concentrated on the need for registration of restaurants, a debate which has still not been resolved. Meanwhile the Food Standards Committee was really getting down to work on food standards, additives and labelling. There was plenty for them to think about. People were now spending about as much on biscuits and cakes as on bread—Vive Marie Antoinette—on breakfast cereals as on flour, and convenience foods were beginning to be all the rage. Into this hive of activity was born the British Consumers' Association (CA) with its penchant for dissecting things and publishing, in *Which?*, what it found. CA had (and has) some of the spirit of the famous *Lancet* Analytical Sanitary Commission, which for four years in the 1850s conducted a weekly survey of every major article of food and drink and fearlessly published the names of hundreds of fraudulent traders. But in the 1950s we had had 80 years of the Food and Drugs Act, so a cooler approach was appropriate.

In the early days *Which?* examined a number of foods with a singular lack of emotion:

'Cake mixes: These mixes are good, they are convenient, and they are easy to make. But you pay for the time and trouble you save.' *Which?* No. 1, Autumn 1957.

'Orange drinks: The taste test we carried out also shows that mothers may be under considerable pressure from their children to buy the drinks which do not contain Vitamin C.' *Which?* No. 3, Spring 1958.

'Tinned stewed steak: Eight of the eleven brands of stewed steak analysed had a meat content higher than 95 per cent. . . . *Dorchester Casserole Steak* had the lowest meat content (55 per cent) of all the brands analysed.' *Which?* No. 6, Winter 1959.

CA's only comment on this 1959 variation in the quality of seemingly similar products was '. . . the Association of Public Analysts is making representation to the Ministry of Agriculture, Fisheries and Food, suggesting that statutory standards should be reintroduced for certain types of tinned meat'. Even in 1961, when we noted that the Food Standards Committee had made certain recommendations on processed cheese still not implemented after five years, this was stated as a fact rather than a matter of sorrow or rage. By 1962 we were hopefully saying of canned fruit salad 'It would certainly help shoppers to make a wiser choice if the minimum drained weight of fruit was also clearly stated on the label'. This cry we still make. But in 1975, when yet another legal battle has taken place between the Champagne district of France and the orchards of Somerset, it is pleasant to record that about 10 years earlier CA had said, in its Cider and Perry report (December 1964), 'We think the word "Champagne" is rather misleading, and like the Food Standards Committee we think it should be used only to describe wine coming from the Champagne district of France . . . these drinks should simply be called Sparkling Perry, which is what they are. And as with cider, we should like to see the ingredients and the alcohol stated on the label'.

The Cider and Perry report, as the suffering editors of the day still recall, marked my own advent at CA. I had come from the world of politics; and I saw and still see the consumer movement first and foremost in a political context, as a means of altering the balance of power in the market-place, of giving some substance to the airy concept of 'consumer sovereignty'. In 1966 our Management Meeting minutes contain a note which reads: 'A committee under the Director's chairmanship will be responsible for implementing "follow-up" action arising out of *Which?* reports. They will decide which subjects need to be brought to the attention of the authorities, and will pursue them until satisfaction is obtained.' I am not sure if all of us clearly understood then what a large and long-term commitment we were making and certainly none of us foresaw what patience we should need.

The British consumer movement has been strongly biased towards information for buyers. The consumer organizations themselves are great producers of information. They ask trade to do the same. Compelled by the frustrations of finding inadequate information available about the products they tested, CA began to knock at various doors to ask if anything could be done about it. With food we hardly had to knock to get a hearing. The door at the Ministry of Agriculture, Fisheries and Food was open; for they were almost certainly the first Ministry to realize that we qualified as interested parties and sent us draft regulations for comment. They were patient with our early efforts. We responded by biting their hand. In 1969 I wrote of the delay in implementing the new labelling regulations: 'The postponement . . . is totally unacceptable to us and the procrastination suggests a lack of genuine concern for the consumer interest.' The hurt but considered reply was the beginning of a good relationship for which we are grateful.

Keeping a cool head over food is not always easy. According to some schools of thought the right food will foster all the virtues, the wrong food all the sins. Unfortunately doctors, nutritionists, and plain devotees of various theories cannot always agree on the good food and the bad food. How much milk should we drink? Is our Government right to say cut down all fats, not just animal fats? Many of our overseas colleagues believe passionately that additives should not be used in foods. Are we sensible to trust the toxicologist? Are we right when we do not worry too much about additions to simple foods? Some of our overseas friends regard the addition of sugar to orange juice as adulteration. One of CA's senior staff lunching with a Swiss official was told forcibly that the British had been corrupted by their puddings and cakes into which everything is tipped, given a good stir, then cooked. We had no respect for pure food. She was tempted to tell him that a Scot might not think much of Muesli. Then she remembered Hardy's description of furmety: a 'mixture of corn in the grain flour, milk, raisins, currants and *what not*' to which rum was added. Each country and not least its consumers wants to defend traditional foods.

CA is a founder member of a world-wide community of consumer organizations, the International Organization of Consumers' Unions (IOCU), now a hundred strong. So we have not developed our ideas on food legislation in isolation. We have been stimulated by the thinking and practices of people in many other IOCU countries. Against this background we came to the conclusion that high mandatory compositional standards are necessary only when a food forms a significant part of the total diet. Normally standards should not be used to lay down too rigid compositional standards which will restrict consumer choice between the traditional products of various countries or limit consumer choice to a high-price high-composition product. We think that it should be possible to differentiate by names and other labelling. This does not mean that we think traditional foods should be adulterated. Nineteenth-century consumers might from habit be prepared to accept alum in bread. Twentieth-century consumers may accept water in chicken. But this type of acceptance does not mean that economic and nutritional interests are not being harmed.

We might have saved ourselves much mental effort if in the 'sixties we had read the report of the 1894 Select Committee on Food Products Adulteration. Certainly when it was read in CA this spring we strengthened our evidence to the Food Standards Committee on water in food. To our less mealy-mouthed ancestors water in milk and butter was adulteration. They were already regretting by the end of the century that the earlier Adulteration of Food and Drink Act—under which a spade could be called a spade—had become simply the Food and Drugs Act. We also learnt from the report that the modern consumerists, as the food trade like to call us, are often not saying anything very new. The spokesman for the Society of Public Analysts told the Select Committee that it is desirable that the ingredients of a mixture and their relative proportions be also plainly stated on the label. Nearly a century later we have reached the same conclusion. We have for some time advocated the declaration of the minimum percentage of the main characterizing ingredients in a product such as the fruit in jam, fruit drinks and squashes, canned meat products. We think this information is essential for purchasers to make realistic price comparisons. The information would also help a potential purchaser to judge absolute quality even when a direct price comparison is not being made. The main characterizing ingredient may be costly and a greater quantity increase the price of the product. Yet CA has found in discussion groups with members of the public that people do not appreciate distinctions in names, e.g., squashes and drinks, pastes and spreads. Further, there is always the easy way around protected names. Adopt a new one. Until recent years paté was a meat mixture cooked in a tureen without a crust. Before that it was just a meat or fish pie. Now it is a paste looking like a sausage or just in a can or jar crowding the supermarket shelves.

Plus ça change. . . . The witnesses before the 1894 Select Committee commented on the smallness of size of type on labels. They called for the registration of milkmen. One of them described 'Fine French Coffee, a blend of finest East India and other coffees carefully prepared by the new French process, whereby the aroma and properties of coffee are fully developed', which turned out to be 90 per cent chicory. A Treasury minute of 1851 had permitted the sale of mixtures of coffee and chicory provided the product was labelled as a 'mixture'—a good example of partial information which is misleading. The Public Analysts commented that 'In England about every perishable food substance is chemically preserved. In countries like France they absolutely prohibit their consumption', and the Committee concluded that 'it would be difficult to prove that some colouring agents and antiseptics are injurious to health, but the opinion has been expressed that some limits to their use should be imposed'. (They certainly had a point about France. The orders of the Préfet de Police of Paris on 10th December 1830 read: 'It is expressly forbidden to make use of any mineral substance for colouring liqueurs, bonbons, sugar plums, lozenges or any other kinds of sweetmeats or pastry. No other colouring matter than of a vegetable nature shall be employed for such purpose, except gamboge and archil. It is forbidden to wrap sweetmeats in paper glazed or coloured with mineral substances. It is ordered that all confectioners, grocers and dealers in liqueurs, bonbons, sweetmeats, lozenges, etc shall have their name, address and trade printed on the paper in which the above articles will be enveloped. All manufacturers and dealers are personally responsible for the accidents which shall be traced to the liqueurs, bonbons and other sweetmeats manufactured or sold by them.') We can but admire the perception of these *fin de siècle* MPs who lived before the great food technological revolution, and who would have been pleased to know that in Britain the acceptable colours are now declining in number preparatory, maybe, to a healthier acceptance of duller looking food.

Where should we go next? It is not a nice time for prophecy—this summer when the onset of hyperinflation may seem to give the 'requirements necessary for a civilized social life' a doomed and anachronistic ring. But if one cannot prophesy, one can still have faith. I have faith that CA will continue comparative testing. When we think people are being deceived because they are not given enough information or standards have fallen drastically and without warning, I believe we shall say so. I hope too that the local authorities and the analysts will increasingly test whole ranges of the same food products for all the important food characteristics—ingredients, nutritional values, additives, residues. This is costly. To ask for it now may seem unrealistic. I suggest, however, that if local authorities were to co-operate, establish priorities, design joint programmes and develop their own specializations, then enforcement and monitoring could be more efficient and effective. A certain amount is happening already. It should be encouraged nationally and adopted with enthusiasm locally. For there is no point in having admirable laws if they are not enforced. We are inevitably going to have increasing numbers of mandatory food standards as the international standards harmonization programme progresses. The cost of chemical analysis to ensure that standards are met is already becoming prohibitive. Some checks will have to move to the factory. This leaves imports. We consumers need to be reassured that government and local authorities are seriously thinking about ways of meeting these growing problems.

But our own problems should not claim our whole attention. Certainly they do not claim the whole attention of the British consumer movement, which has played a leading part in IOCU's work for consumers in developing countries. Food accounts for a large proportion of every family's budget, but the poorer the family the larger the proportion. When consumption patterns are distorted by inappropriate marketing techniques, it is the nutritional levels of the poor that are in gravest jeopardy. On this indictment the verdict of the Group of Eminent Persons, appointed by the UN Secretary-General under a resolution of the ECOSOC and reporting to him last summer, was as follows: 'Since products of multinational corporations are often geared to the consumption patterns of advanced countries, the needs of the majority of the population in poor countries may not be fulfilled.' This is pre-eminently true of food and drink. The 'new consumers' of the developing world, passing from agrarian subsistence into the market place, are frequently pressured into dietary tastes and habits whose high cost is related less to nutritive value than to the promotion, packaging and profits of foreign brand-owners. The evil lies not merely in the dissonance between this marketing system and the needs of the poor majority, but in the market dominance of multinationals which in some countries makes it less and less possible for alternative high nutrient foods to be produced and sold at accessible prices. IOCU, on whose behalf I testified before the Group of Eminent Persons in Geneva in November 1973, has endorsed that Group's assertion of the right of governments to discourage or even ban socially undesirable products.

In common with the export of brand-names, the export of food from some industrialized countries—whether by way of trade or aid—is a subject of disquiet among consumer organizations. Assisted by the UN Regional

226

Economic Commission and by UNESCO, 24 of these organizations drawn from countries throughout Asia and the Pacific participated in an IOCU seminar in Singapore in February 1974. Again and again their discussions and resolutions voiced anxiety that developing countries were becoming a litter bin for rejected produce. Even when food is safe and nutritious, but organoleptically or in some other way sub-standard, there is resentment. Far more serious is the possibility that developing countries without strong food controls or adequately staffed inspectorates will have hazardous foods dumped on them. The Codex Alimentarius Commission has been giving consideration to the feasibility of elaborating a Code of Ethics for international trade in food, and at its tenth session in July 1974 IOCU's accredited representative supported the lead given by a number of African countries. In a statement to the World Food Conference in Rome last year I urged on IOCU's behalf that such a code be developed in the general interest of all consumers, that its operations be monitored by FAO, and that an international warning system or 'Food Interpol' be established which would speedily disclose to the authorities concerned when unsatisfactory food is being hawked around the world.

The relative neglect of marketing systems and practices in socio-economic development shows up most clearly on the retail market. It is here to an ever-increasing extent that the abstract statistical concept 'standard of living' is translated into the solid economic realities of quantity, quality and price. Yet it is here that families in poorer countries commonly find the whole gamut of consumer ills from which industrialized countries are, though all too slowly and unevenly, freeing themselves—adulteration of food and drink, short weight and measure, absence of price-posting and labelling, fraudulent advertising and sales practices. Even where an armoury of legislation exists to protect the consumer of food and similar necessities, the administrative machinery to implement and enforce it may be lacking. Many affiliates of IOCU in developing as well as developed countries are now playing, within the limits of their resources, an innovative role to achieve market protection— through direct participation in the regulatory process, and through consumer education, information, mobilization and even boycott. IOCU, which gives them constructive help internationally and on a regional basis, drew the attention of national governments represented at the World Food Conference to a need for further support. As the Group of Eminent Persons said in its report to the UN Secretary-General, 'We believe that national consumer organizations in both developed and developing countries should be encouraged and given the necessary facilities towards achieving their goals'.

Introductory remarks by Mr. Goldman

I am pleased that in celebrating this century of progress you did not forget to invite an official representative of its presumed beneficiaries. And I am sure you will expect me, in drawing together the threads of my paper, to list succinctly those additional benefits for which *we* are now looking.

1 The hygienic quality of food should be established by the wide use of statutory and mandatory microbiological standards.

2 The modification of food by the addition of non-nutritive substances should never be allowed unless what has been done is clearly and unequivocally declared.

3 The work of ensuring that permitted food additives have received adequate toxicological clearance and been proved technologically necessary should be speeded up.

4 The authorities should maintain and in some areas increase their programmes of monitoring for the levels of contaminants and additives in the diet of the population.

5 A concerted effort should be made by all of us to find ways of describing foods so that people really do know the true nature of what they are buying, and we avoid over-detailed compositional requirements for each and every food.

6 All foods packed in a liquid medium, whether or not this is normally discarded, should carry a declaration of the drained weight of the food.

7 All pre-packed food should be obligatorily marked with a date—either expiry date or production date plus shelf life—after which it is likely to have deteriorated either microbiologically or in nutritional quality or in flavour.

8 National codes of hygienic practice should be applied not only to production but also to distribution, within national borders and for export, and at the point of sale.

9 The power at present provided by private Acts in only a handful of cities, under which magistrates' courts may close food premises until their hygienically unsatisfactory state has been remedied, should become nationwide.

10 Above all, there must be a numerically adequate and sensibly remunerated inspectorate, backed up by analytical staff and equipment, to enforce the country's food laws effectively and fearlessly.

To make that amount of progress, it really shouldn't take another century.

Discussion

Mr. H W Symons (Birds Eye Foods Ltd): I never realized that I lived in an Augean stable. I am quite sure, also, that not one other person in this room would agree with all the 10 points which Mr. Goldman so clearly enjoyed enunciating, but we did enjoy very much indeed his Good Food Guide, 1875–1975.

I should like to pick up one rhetorical question which Mr. Goldman asked in his paper, 'Are we sensible to trust the toxicologist?' The straight answer is, 'Yes', but there has also been another point made during this Symposium which is, of course, about food law and not gourmet feeding, and that is that we have been accused of complacency.

I must admit that I find it surprising that nobody has mentioned, in conjunction with that accusation, the name Neuberger, which was an astonishing report recently produced. I would suggest that we have, to go back to Mr. Goldman's paper, to trust the toxicologists because we have a long way to go still.

In 1875 we cleared up the alum, the copper, the sand and the Prussian blue, and Hassall and Accum were probably the first food consumerists, although they would not have understood that. Now most of us here would agree that we seem to have arrived at straining at gnats, at the parts per billion of additives or contaminants that may or may not be present, depending on how well your computer is working, at defining zero, whereas if you read Neuberger he says that many of the killers around today, particularly in an affluent society, are diet based. The sort of killers he has in mind are IHD, cancer, diabetes, appendicitis, atherosclerosis, just to mention a few.

I would therefore suggest that we have a long way to go, and my first question to Mr. Goldman concerns the part the consumer movement is going to play in the progress we have to make. I think that we are probably now rejecting the idea that there is any single cause of our ills in food; not all of us are convinced that saturated fats or the empty calories really are a single answer to one or other of our problems. It is probably a very complex relationship. Therefore we have in the future to keep cool. My concern is that the food consumerists, allied with the media, intend to do precisely the opposite. That worries me a lot, because the media and the consumerists have a part to play, but I frankly do not like the way that either of them is playing it at the moment.

We have more to do. The food industry, the legislators, the food scientists are not satisfied that they have solved all the problems. There are going to be false starts, there are going to be scares, there are going to be all sorts of things going on. My first question to Mr. Goldman is, therefore, is the consumerist really going to set out to explain what the real problems are? With the greatest respect, I do not think that his 10 points covered one. There are some nice definitions around—the customer is somebody who pays; the consumer is somebody who eats it and either likes it or, perhaps, dies; the consumerist merely creates a fuss about it.

There is another name that has not been mentioned in these last two days; Ralph Nader was the first name I looked for on our list of delegates, but when he was absent I remembered that the Ministry were putting on this excellent Symposium at a very small cost and, knowing how very careful they are about expenditure, I guessed that they had probably turned down Ralph Nader because he could command $3000 a throw and they probably could not afford it. I also wonder why we do not hear so much about him. Is it because the purchaser of the automobile in America has decided that, on the whole, he would prefer to take that one chance in a few thousand million, that mouldy peanut that was worrying Dr. Pereira yesterday, or that one person in the whole of Europe that Bob Giles was a bit concerned about, rather than having to pay for additional safeguards which, on the whole, he did not want?

So my second question to Mr. Goldman, allied to the first, is does he not see a greater need for the consumerist movement to do more positive education and a little less shouting?

Finally, would Mr. Goldman agree that, broadly speaking, industry gets the consumerists it deserves? Is this, therefore, why food consumerists on the whole are so comparatively ineffective? To put it another way, would he agree with the article some time ago in *The Times* that did a 'Which on Which' and concluded that, on the whole, it was not a very good buy?

Mr. Goldman: First of all, I should like to make a correction. I am not a consumerist; the word does not exist except in the realms in which the last speaker lives his life. It is a sort of new word by which consumers, or those who are protagonists on behalf of the consumer, are given a name which does not differ too much from 'Communist'. I was, in fact, in charge of the education movement of the Conservative Party for more than 10 years, so I must say that I find it rather amusing to have been given this particular label at this particular period of my career.

It is not a question of whether I think *Which?* is or is not a good buy or a best buy; it is a question of what consumers think about *Which?* and, as long as three-quarters of a million of them are prepared to subscribe to it, that is the test that I would use, just as it is the test of whether your corn-flakes or your technicolour peas are or are not a good idea.

Yes, of course the evaluation of the toxicological evidence is for experts, and we are not opposed to the use of food additives, if the additive being used has received toxicological clearance by national regulating agencies; *and* is necessary for the preservation of food; *and* facilitates lower cost production; *or* secures consumer acceptance of a nutritionally satisfying food which would otherwise be rejected.

On the other hand, I am against the use of additives to deceive the consumer and that, of course, happens a great deal.

What am I going to do about education? In the modern world it is very necessary to shout, otherwise you do not get heard. Even when you do shout, and even when you do educate, you still do not get heard.

Diet: take just one example. What kind of hypocritical society are we living in in which smoking is recognized as a killer and yet we spend £70 million a year on promoting it?

Professor A E Bender (Queen Elizabeth College, London): May I ask Mr. Goldman a simple question, and I am sure that here everyone would be on the same side? What are we going to do about the media? I am sure that everyone in the audience has, at some time or other, written, or been quoted, or been seen on television, radio or Press and so forth. I am sure that we all do our best to produce facts and figures, but we know that the Press and radio—radio to a lesser extent, but the Press certainly—and television certainly, select the facts that they want. They select those that are sensational and they will often deliberately distort. Only Sunday morning at 11 o'clock I was telephoned by Granada asking if it was true—and it was not—that I had published something saying that fish and chips were better than school meals, and could I give them facts and figures—which chips, which fish, which meals. Certainly some of our publicized programmes are done with the best intentions, but I remember one where, after three hours of intensive scientific fact-giving, they said that they now intended to tell everyone in the country the causes of heart disease, and the cures as well. That was done with the best of intentions, but I have had many others who have deliberately said, 'If it's not going to be sensational then we don't want to do it'. I think that many members of the audience suffered recently in a programme about food and food manufacturers where speakers were cut off, facts were changed, and the producers had deliberately set out to say, 'Let's have a sensational programme. Let's do some sneering and smearing, and we don't really care very much if the facts are correct'. I am not overstating the case because I can give you references; you probably know them as well as I do. But what can we do about all this?

Mr. Goldman: Some of the most responsible people working in the media would accept that. There are extremely responsible producers and performers in all the media today, both in the Press and in radio and television, who recognize the public responsibilities of the media, and the growth of informative and educative material in the media over the last decade seems to me to have been one of the more encouraging aspects of the life we lead. The door is open; we have to walk through it with a certain amount of dignity. But I do not take as tragic a view of free speech as you do.

Mr. T McLachlan (Thomas McLachlan and Partners): I accept all of Mr. Goldman's 10 points, but I would ask him whether he would not like to qualify one, and that is the question of drained weight in a canned product. For most of them I would accept drained weight but, particularly with soft fruits, enzymic action may play Hamlet with the drained weight of the original fruit put into the can.

Mr. Goldman: I certainly think that, in the case of soft fruits, there are serious problems with inconsistent changes taking place after packaging and I accept, therefore, what you say about this. However, I think that ways of overcoming the consequent enforcement problems are administratively possible and would enable a drained weight declaration to become a general requirement if that were taken into account.

Food Quality and Safety Symposium: Summing-Up

Lord Zuckerman, OM, KCB
Symposium Chairman

Ladies and Gentlemen, this Symposium has clearly been a success, and reflects great credit on those who have spent months in organizing it and bringing together the people who have contributed to a very balanced programme. We have been presented with a clear picture of the history of food legislation. The problems which now beset us have been reviewed, and we have been encouraged to peer into the future.

I am down on the programme to give 'a summary', but obviously I cannot do that. I clearly have to be selective. That is a chairman's privilege, though not one without its pitfalls; it does sometimes also disclose a chairman's prejudices.

Food legislation has obviously achieved much that it set out to do, and there have been real gains over the past 100 years. References have been made to improvements in public health, and we have been told that we no longer suffer from the kind of abuses in trading which were prevalent when the 1875 Act was introduced. However, we all know that culture does not move evenly across the globe; it never has. Three weeks ago I was in South Africa, in a part of the country where witchcraft is still prevalent. On one side of the counter of a shop into which I had gone beads were being sold to tourists such as myself; at the other, natives were being given concoctions of lizard tails, and other strange remedies. The world is not a uniform place, and what we in the West have achieved over the past 100 years is what the greater part of the world's population has to try to do over the next 100.

Mr. Kermode dealt with some of these problems. His paper gave a very fair picture of the present world situation. But we should always remember that change is not uniform, and that even this audience represents different phases of world culture. We have certainly not—and I think it would be unfair if I did not make this point now—achieved all that we might have done. Yesterday Dr. Hugh Sinclair challenged the proposition that our food legislation had helped to improve health to the extent which is generally claimed, and he quoted figures—unfortunately I did not make an accurate note, but he can correct me if I am wrong—which implied that men who were

233

in their forties some 150 years ago enjoyed the same expectation of life as men in their forties do today. In other words, if you managed to survive into your forties in the mid-Victorian era, if you managed to overcome all ailments of childhood, you were as well off then as you are today. You were possibly better off, since according to Dr. Sinclair there are more degenerative diseases of old age to contend with today.

Dr. Schmidt made a related point when talking about microbiologically-transmitted disease. He referred to published figures about the prevalence of such diseases in this country, and suggested that they were far too low. He reminded us that practically all of us in this room have, at one time or another, or on many occasions, suffered from the contamination of food by bacteria. If one takes into account both Dr. Sinclair's and Dr. Schmidt's statement, what then are the yardsticks of progress on which we have been relying these past 100 years? In so far as western civilization is concerned, are we dealing with mortality statistics, morbidity statistics, average expectation of life in different age groups? I do not know. What should be the yardstick of progress in this field of social endeavour? It is because I do not know the answer to this question that, after his opening paper, I asked Mr. Giles whether we would not reach a point when further legislation in this field would yield only diminishing returns—legislation which is always very expensive and frequently impossible to implement. I gained the impression that he thought not. I myself am not convinced that we do not get diminishing returns—whether we are not straining at gnats, as was said by one speaker this afternoon—in the effort to ensure that we do not poison or cheat each other!

On the other hand, in the light of what was said—particularly in the earlier part of this Symposium—I am confident that it is better to introduce new legislation, where essential, than try to enforce food regulations through codes of practice. But we need to be very circumspect about the kinds of new legislation which we might wish to encourage.

A question which was put several times but never really answered is whether more regulations, more legislation, will inhibit technological innovation. We have been assured that this is not the intention of the people who are concerned in this country with the introduction of new legislation, or of those who negotiate the directives that emerge from Brussels. But the question remains open.

We were given an interesting survey of the past and were encouraged to peer into the future. We all know, and the point has been forcibly made by Mr. Lawrence, that we, in the western world, are boxed into the urban civilization which we have evolved. Urbanization, even though it changes in quality, even though it changes in quantity, is the kind of world to which we are committed as we try to improve our standards of living—whatever contrary views may be expressed by those who feel that mankind has been over-materialistic in his endeavours. The belief that any human beings, other than perhaps a few primitive tribes, would deliberately reject the advances of civilization in favour of the simple life is something which, in the light of experience, we can reject straightaway.

While we in the West are already boxed in, we have to realize that the developing world about which Mr. Kermode was talking wants precisely the same things that we enjoy; they want the benefits which an industrial civilization has brought us; they want an urban civilization, and they are moving towards it rapidly, without speculating about any secondary adverse consequences it might bring in its train. The Industrial Revolution about which we speak so freely was associated—and this we often forget—with an agricultural revolution. Without the latter it would never have proved possible to feed the people who flocked from the countryside into the new industrial towns.

The world of tomorrow, a world of bigger population and greater demand, is going to require the kind of 'food revolution' about which we have been hearing during the course of this meeting. There is little point in saying that not enough resources have been provided to the food industries for food research. Without question there has been too little research and development on food processing and food technology generally. The R & D resources that have been available to an industry on which the whole world is going to depend tomorrow have already been too limited. But one reason why there has not been enough research and development in the food industry—compared, say, to what has gone into metallurgy—is that it has never seemed essential. It was always possible to grow another ton of beans, or whatever else was wanted, off another man's acre. We cannot rely on that any longer. Very early on in our proceedings Dr. Elton revealed for us the trends with which we all have to align our futures.

We differ from some of our Common Market partners in this respect. The United Kingdom has been a big food importer for a very long time. As Dr. Elton reminded us, we in the United Kingdom may have to look to new and possibly unconventional sources of food. Given one takes into account our future balance of trade problem, he has suggested that the net product of British agriculture will have to grow at a rate—which Dr. Pereira was not prepared to deny—of possibly $2\frac{1}{2}$ per cent per annum. He also pointed to the fact that we are now importing annually far more from our Common Market partners than from the distant parts of the world on which we previously depended.

Mr. Barthelemy spoke about the enormous problems which are entailed in the harmonization, not only of legislation and legislative procedures in the different Common Market countries, but also of the different tastes and habits of our partners. This is an enormously difficult problem. The only comment I can make here is that if you were left with the impression that the process of getting a draft EEC Directive adopted is a very slow one—in some cases it takes years—NATO, which is an even older institution, has not yet even standardized its weapons. We can take whatever comfort we can from the fact that agreements within international bodies are reached very slowly. People do not leap at the opportunity of changing their national habits, tastes and attitudes.

There are language barriers too. Dr. Schmidt has had to return to Washington, but he might perhaps have endorsed the old quip that the Americans and English are separated from each other by the Atlantic Ocean, and divided by a common language. If that was once an apt comment on our relations with the United States, how much more of a problem exists between the Common Market countries, with all their differing languages?

Mr. Kermode pointed out that the future is very different for the different parts of the world. In many there is scarcity, there is hunger, there is impatience, there is maldistribution, not only of goods, but also of knowledge. He was emphasizing the need for the developing countries of the Third World to develop an infrastructure with which to sustain a modern food industry. I think that this is a problem which is almost more difficult than the problem of, let us say, devising a system whereby we could rid the whole of Africa of helminthic diseases.

Our discussions have therefore made me feel that the future trends in food laws are likely to differ widely as between the Common Market countries on the one hand and the rest of the world on the other. And I should therefore return to an issue which cropped up early in our deliberations. Will the principles which underlie the legislation with which we are now concerned be the significant ones of tomorrow? As I understand it, legislation in this field was first called for because of the need to protect the purchaser from adulterated food—but we have been assured that this problem ceased to be a worry a long time ago. Then came the need to protect the individual's health as a matter of public health. Should these two issues now be separated? Can they be? Are we really clear about their nature in a modern context? The issue is not as obvious to me now as it seemed when it was first referred to yesterday morning, particularly in the light of what has also been said about the likelihood that more and more chemical compounds will be detected in foods as more and more sensitive methods of detection and measurement are developed.

It is conceivable that today the issue of protecting the purchaser or consumer, the man or woman who buys the food, from fraud, is more or less the same as protecting his health. But it may not be, and, if they are separate considerations, what principles should guide the legislator of tomorrow? I do not think we have faced that question squarely, particularly in the light of the changes which are likely to occur in the supply and demand picture in the world as a whole, and then in our own country, where we are so dependent on food imports. The problems of the developing world—including the question of malnutrition affecting 600 million people—are enormous. Can the principles which should underlie an updated legislative system about food quality really be the same as those which animated the people who introduced the 1875 law? Are we not going to be more concerned tomorrow with scarcity, with malnutrition, and ultimately with the maintenance of an urban civilization rather than protection from fraud and from additives which could conceivably constitute some remote risk to health?

The spectrum of our problems is wide. We have the problems of today. We have to promote trade. As Mr. Berthelemy explained this morning, many of the problems with which officials in Brussels have to deal fall into this domain. Similarly, when Mr. Kermode was talking about the Third World, he was also explaining the need for an infrastructure which could deal with the quality of the food which the developing countries export.

I therefore find myself asking whether the six priorities which Dr. Schmidt tells us apply to the future of the United States are relevant to the world as a whole. In the order in which he gave them they were: food-borne infection, malnutrition, industrial environmental contaminants, manufacturing processes, pesticide residues, and lastly—this must have given Professor Weedon a feeling of confidence—the control of food additives, to Dr. Schmidt a relatively simple problem. Are these the priorities for the world as a whole? Is there not a danger of the United States urging its order of priorities to the detriment of the interests of some other parts of the world? He spoke about risk/benefit. Others have spoken about risk/benefit. But the risks and benefits which apply to the United States are not necessarily those which are relevant to the UK or, say, India. He told us about his very empirical approach to the problem of dealing with the Delaney Amendment, an amendment which, as he said, cannot be expected to disappear by the wave of a wand. No member of Congress or the Senate could declare that he was opposed to the Delaney Amendment; he might as well announce that he was in favour of sin and against motherhood. The world is not going to be easily rid of the Delaney Amendment. Encouraging the public to understand a different, a more empirical, concept of 'non-risk' rather than the arbitrary one implicit in that piece of American legislation, seems to be very wise as far as the United States is concerned. One set of risks has to be judged against another. I have always felt that this is something we also should do in this country. We should measure the risk of being poisoned by food additives against the risk of being killed in a traffic accident or in an aeroplane crash.

One reason why I am uncertain about the wisdom of exporting the new list of American priorities derives from an answer Dr. Schmidt gave me about the amount FDA spends on its own operations. It turns out to be $250 million a year. I asked Mr. Giles whether he could get me figures of how much we spend in this country, both centrally and in local government, in the enforcement of food legislation. If we take into account research as well, our figure is a little above £5 million. Dr. Schmidt, as head of the FDA, is not responsible for the activities of all the people in the United States who are concerned in this field. He told us that there were as many as 30 000 people employed in the United States on food legislation enforcement. On the basis of his figures, and taking into account the differences in the sizes of our populations, I calculate that in order to protect themselves from remote and often illusory risks, the American public is prepared to spend each year 30 to 50 times what we do per head of population in this country. I believe that we do just as well as does the United States without approaching its level of expenditure.

Somehow or other I do not feel that either the British public or the public of the Continent is going to fall over itself in order to follow the American example. I also wonder whether this great social expenditure is justified. So I return once again to my question, how should a public judge whether it is getting value for money in its pure food laws?

I am at one with Dr. Schmidt in believing that it is easy to legislate so as to eliminate all scientific judgment. But then I ask, without scientific judgment, how is one to arrive at any reasonable assessment about what the world in general can afford in the way of food protection? Just let me remind you of a story which I did not believe when I first heard it. But it happens to be true, although little of it appeared in the Press. It is the story of what occurred in Ceylon, now Sri Lanka, when the DDT spraying campaign was stopped in 1960, partly for economic reasons, partly because DDT had come under suspicion as an environmental poison. This programme had been carried out under the auspices of WHO, and when it stopped, malaria had virtually been suppressed. In 1964 the disease reappeared. Within a couple of years there were a million cases. It took an immense effort to get the new epidemic under control, and the task is not yet completed. The explanation of this sad story is at least partly that a Western priority was exported to a country like Sri Lanka—by which I mean that whether or not DDT was a deleterious substance in the USA, it was not that in Ceylon.

238

This brings me to the question of education, a point which several speakers have raised. There are obviously many meanings to the term 'education'. There is the question of labelling. There is the question of the advisory bodies on whom the authorities have to depend—and how many overlapping advisory bodies can we afford? There is the question of joint consultation with industry—a very important point to which attention has been drawn. There is the responsibility of the media. My information, however, is that we have been talking only about a narrow part of this business of education. Early on in our discussion the point was made that the public is encouraged to be fearful of new technological developments in the food industry. This is merely one aspect of the fears that the public now entertains about almost any scientific or technological development.

It comes up from every quarter in the environmental field. We know of it, too, in the field of energy. Who has not heard of those two American 'authorities' who are quite certain that the American Government's standards for plutonium are 100 000 times too lax—as though any government could risk being out by a factor of 100 000 in such a toxic field! We depend on the media, and they have a very responsible part to play in educating the public about food legislation. But only too often they generate unnecessary fears.

A responsibility also rests upon environmental groups. When they condemn what governments do, let them, in good faith, put forward alternatives of action, alternative plans which can be used by governments to bring about the changes which all may deem necessary. When critics say that this or that should not be done by these or those means, let them tell us which way to do what is necessary.

I believe that one of the highly unfortunate consequences of the propaganda of, no doubt, well-intentioned enthusiasts for 'the good, the true and the beautiful' has been the denigration of national academies and authorities. Dr. Schmidt referred to this point. In the United States, the National Academy of Sciences, which is a court of appeal for the FDA, is suspect because the media have made it suspect. The media, encouraged by Mr. Ralph Nader and by others, have encouraged people to think that the Academy's members are, one and all, men with vested interests. That is why I was pleased when Professor Ward, in his opening address, stressed the independence of the people who serve on the advisory bodies on which the British Government depends. The denigration of national academies relates particularly to the Western world. I do not believe that it is occurring in the USSR or in China. If national academies become suspect, if expert bodies are suspect because they are prepared to offer advice to governments on matters such as those which we have been discussing, to whom else will governments turn? To Ralph Nader and his organization? I do not think so.

One further thing which worries me about education is that new dangers will no doubt be conjured up as new techniques for measuring food contaminants and additives are developed. But I was delighted to learn from Professor Weedon yesterday that the chemicals responsible for the yellow colour of mussels have not yet been properly identified, and that we do not yet know how much of them we could safely absorb. Those like me, who enjoy eating mussels, will no doubt go on doing so however many new chemical substances are identified in the flesh of shellfish.

New techniques reveal new facts. When presented in a dramatic way by the media, new facts become new fears in a public which has become highly sensitive to statements about the dangers of our technological age. Someone at this meeting has reminded me of a remark, a statement of belief that I have made before, namely that if technology has got us into a mess, only better technology is going to get us out of it. May I repeat it now?

I agree with Mr. Goldman that the United Kingdom is not going to commit national suicide. I believe that 100 years from now there will be a bicentenary Symposium to celebrate the 200th anniversary of the 1875 Act. I believe that 100 years from now our species will still be extant and that men will still be mortal. There are going to be many more of us. And here I associate myself fully with what Dr. Schmidt said at the end of his address. I think that man's condition will go on improving.

As we review the legislation which we have been discussing, as we go on reviewing the advice which is tendered to governments, I very much hope that nations will exchange reliable information and that there will be some interdependence of advice. Food is an international commodity. It will remain so not only in its present three-dimensional form, but, more particularly, because we must all share the knowledge which will be used to increase the raw material base from which we derive our nutrients.

May I conclude by repeating that what I have said is not so much a summary as the main impressions I have gained from a seminar which has taught me a great deal I did not know before. We all owe an enormous debt to the speakers, both those who gave the papers, and those who discussed them.

Closing Address

Michael Meacher, MP
Parliamentary Under-Secretary of State (Health and Social Security)

MY LORD CHAIRMAN, LADIES AND GENTLEMEN,

First of all, Mrs. Castle is indeed very sorry that she is unable to be here this afternoon to speak to you but, if her statement goes right, she should be speaking in the House of Commons at this very moment.

I am very glad myself to have the opportunity just to say a few words at the end of this important Symposium. It is, I think, appropriate in view of our joint responsibility for the administration of the English Food and Drugs Act that your proceedings were opened by Fred Peart, for the Ministry of Agriculture, and that I am representing the Department of Health in closing them. However, we both join with the various other Departments concerned— and I do know how close that collaboration is—in making sure that we secure a sensible uniformity in food law for the United Kingdom as a whole.

I will not attempt to add, my Lord Chairman, to your excellent summing up of the proceedings, except to say that I obviously missed a great deal by not being able to be present for the whole of the Symposium. The speakers have, of course, all been expert in one aspect or another of food quality or safety and, obviously, everyone here has a very close interest in this important subject.

It has been said that the quickest way to a man's heart is through his stomach, and it is certainly true that eating good food in good company is one of life's minor—perhaps some would say major—pleasures. Unfortunately, however, as we all know, food can also be a serious hazard if it is not cooked or processed properly. I think it is reassuring that so many of you, not least our visitors from overseas, have been taking part in this gathering devoted to ways in which we can best protect ourselves from bad food.

I would, therefore, like to thank you all for attending and I hope that this last couple of days has been both interesting and profitable.

You have heard the speakers talking about the history of food quality and safety legislation in this country, how it was set up in the last century, how it has developed over the years and how it stands at the present time. You have heard, too, of the part played by independent advisory committees, by the Government Chemist and the Public Health Laboratory Service. Food legislation in the United Kingdom is the result of a continuing process of close collaboration between Government and the bodies I have mentioned—the food industry, consumer representatives, research organizations and the academic world—in a way which I think is probably peculiar to this country.

Perhaps equally noteworthy, though, is the way in which our food laws are enforced by our local authorities, who know their own local communities well and are perhaps the people in the best position to know if anything goes wrong on the food front and do something about it.

I do not say that our own particular methods of ensuring food safety are the only possible ones, of course they are not, but I do think that they work and that they succeed in protecting the British public, a public which, I suspect, is largely ignorant of the very considerable effort that goes into providing this protection. It may be that the greatest compliment to our system of food hygiene and quality control in this country is that any outbreak of food poisoning is news.

Now modern analytical methods are capable of revealing toxic substances in food in amounts which, only a little while ago, were not detectable, and modern research is not slow to find links between disease and food components which we once thought were perfectly safe. However, in an industrial society we have to find the right balance, doing all we can to protect ourselves from bad food but, at the same time, recognizing that the food producer needs all the technological help he can get in order to provide us with food which is not only convenient but also at a price which we can afford.

Nevertheless, this is not to say that we can afford to be in any way complacent. We must always keep in touch with changes in technology and ensure that the law is relevant to practice in the food industry of today. It is particularly important that the local authority officers who have to enforce the law are aware of how particular processes fit into the framework of statutory requirements on the one hand and good trade practice on the other. This puts a particular burden on the enforcement officers and local authorities since they need, obviously, to have a close understanding and knowledge of the different trades and processes.

I think we must always be ready to learn from others, and I am very glad to see that you have had the benefit of hearing about the ways in which the United States deals with food safety and quality. You have also heard much about the vital work being done on the international front by the Codex Alimentarius Commission to ensure that standards of food safety are raised to the same high level throughout the world. I should like to think that, as a nation with a great deal of experience and technical know-how in this field at our disposal, we also have a good deal to contribute here. Clearly, Great Britain's decision to remain within the European Economic Community has a deep significance for the way in which the United Kingdom's methods of food control can be expected to develop over the next few years, and you have been given an account of the EEC's programme for the harmonization of food laws. Of course, members of the Community, including ourselves, have developed over the years systems of food control which suit each particular country, but, for the sake of increased trade and also a great diversity of trade between Member States, we are now engaged in harmonizing the food laws. We must seek to ensure that this will bring together all that is best in the national laws of the Member States and that a common European law will be evolved which will serve us well in the future.

It remains for me therefore, Ladies and Gentlemen, to thank you once again for attending and for contributing to this very important Symposium, and to hope that it has helped to forward the cause of food which is both good and safe to eat.

On your behalf, I am sure you would also wish me to thank your Chairman, Lord Zuckerman, for presiding over your proceedings. I hope, Sir, that you have found it an interesting and worthwhile experience.

Printed in England for Her Majesty's Stationery Office
by The Campfield Press, St. Albans

Dd. 497376.   K.12   1/77   Gp. 3319